Islam and Modernity

In memory of John Cooper,
dear friend and colleague.
With gratitude for all he has
given and taught us.

ISLAM and MODERNITY

Muslim Intellectuals Respond

Edited by

John Cooper, Ronald L. Nettler and Mohamed Mahmoud

I.B. Tauris *Publishers*

LONDON • NEW YORK

Paperback edition published in 2000 by
I.B.Tauris & Co Ltd
Victoria House
Bloomsbury Square
London WC1B 4DZ
175 Fifth Avenue
New York NY 10010
Website: http://www.ibtauris.com

In the United States of America
and in Canada distributed by
St Martin's Press
175 Fifth AVenue
New York 10010

First Published in 1998 by I.B.Tauris & Co Ltd

Copyright © 1998 John Cooper, Ronald L. Nettler and Mohamed Mahmoud

A full CIP record for this book is available from the Bristish Library
A full CIP record for this book is available from the Library of Congress

ISBN 1 86064 531 3

Printed by SRM Production Services Sdn Bhd, Malaysia.

Contents

Notes on the Contributors

Nadia Abu-Zahra is an anthropologist. She received her PhD from Oxford University and has since done fieldwork in The Sahel of Tunisia and in Cairo. Her articles and books cover various areas of the Middle East; currently she writes on Muslim society. Her most recent book is *The Pure and Powerful* (Reading: Ithaca Press, 1997).

Nasr Hamid Rizk Abu-Zaid received his university education in the Faculty of Arts at the University of Cairo, where he received his PhD in Arabic and Islamic studies in 1981. Since then he has been teaching in the same department, reaching the level of full professor in 1995. From 1985–9 he was Visiting Professor at the Osaka University of Foreign Studies, and from 1995 he has been Visiting Professor at the University of Leiden. In May 1993 he was awarded the Republican Order of Merit for his services to Arab culture by the President of Tunisia. He has published extensively in Arabic on Qur'anic exegesis and Islamic law, as well as on the critical study of Muslim religious discourse; one of his works, *Naqd al-khitab al-dini*, has been translated into German by Cherifa Magdi as *Kritik der religiosen Diskurses* (Frankfurt-am-Main: Dipa Verlag, 1996).

Mohammed Arkoun was born in Taourirt-Mimoun (Algeria). He studied at the University of Algiers before taking up the post of assistant professor at the Sorbonne (1961–9). He received his doctorat at the Sorbonne in 1969, and went on to occupy the post of professor there from 1970–92. He is presently Emeritus professor at the Sorbonne, Paris III, and Visiting Professor at the Institute of Ismaili Studies in London. He is also the director of the scholarly journal *Arabica*, and a jury member of the Aga Khan Award for Achitecture. He has published many articles and books in Arabic, French and English; his books include: *L'humanisme arabe au IVe/Xe siècle* (2nd ed., Paris: J. Vrin, 1982), *Critique de la raison islamique* (Paris, 1984), *Lectures du Coran* (2nd ed.,

Tunis, 1991), *Rethinking Islam: common questions, uncommon answers* (Boulder, Colorado, 1993), *La pensée arabe* (Paris: PUF, 1996).

Andreas Christmann is a graduate student of the University of Leipzig where he is completing his PhD dissertation in the Department of Religious Studies. In 1995-7 he was the Volkswagen Visiting Fellow at St Antony's College, Oxford. He did fieldwork in Syria in 1995 and 1996 on the observance of Ramadan and the use made of various media for the dissemination of Islamic teachings during that month. His main interest is the analysis of Islamic discourse and its impact on religious practice. He has published articles on contemporary Islamic rituals and the Muslim media in German and English.

John Cooper studied at the University of Oxford and the traditional religious schools in Qum and Tehran. For the last seven years he has been the E. G. Browne Lecturer in Persian Studies at the Faculty of Oriental Studies at the University of Cambridge. His research interests include Islamic jurisprudence, philosophy, and mysticism, and he has published numerous translations of classical and modern texts from Arabic and Persian, including the first volume of al-Tabari's *Commentary on the Qur'an* (Oxford: OUP, 1986), as well as articles on aspects of the history of the Islamic religious sciences.

Abdou Filali-Ansari was born in Morocco in 1946. He obtained his doctorate from the University of Dijon with a dissertation on the philosophy of Spinoza and Bergson. He has taught philosophy at the Faculté des Lettres in Rabat (1970-3), and has held posts in the Moroccan administration. In 1985 he was appointed Director of the King 'Abd al-Aziz Foundation for Islamic Studies and the Human Sciences in Casablanca. Since 1994 he has been the editor of *Prologues: Revue maghrébine du livre*. Among his works are articles and books on contemporary Islamic thought, and a French translation of 'Ali 'Abd al-Raziq's *Islam and the Foundation of Political Power* (Paris: La Découverte/Casablance: Le Fennec, 1995).

Derek Hopwood is Reader in Middle Eastern Studies at the University of Oxford, Fellow of St Antony's College, and Director of the Middle East Centre. He is also President of the European Association of Middle East Studies. Among his books are: *Egypt: Politics and society 1945–90* (1991), *Syria 1945–1986: Politics and society* (1988), *Habib Bourguiba of Tunisia: the tragedy of longevity* (1992), and *The Russian Presence in Syria and Palestine 1843–1914: Church and Politics in the Near East* (1969).

Mohamed Mahmoud has taught at the Faculty of Arts at the University of Khartoum and at the Oriental Institute at the University of Oxford. At present he teaches at the Department of Religion at Tufts University. His research interests include the Qur'an and modern Islam.

Javed Majeed is currently lecturer in the Department of South Asia at SOAS, University of London. He graduated from Magdalen College, Oxford, where he also did his DPhil. He is the author of *Ungoverned Imaginings: James Mill's The History of British India and Orientalism* (Oxford: Clarendon Press, 1992), and also of a number of articles in scholarly journals and chapters in edited books. He is the co-author with Christopher Shackle of *Hali's Musaddas: the flow and ebb of Islam* (Delhi: OUP, 1997).

Ronald L. Nettler is Fellow in Muslim-Jewish Relations at the Oxford Centre for Hebrew and Jewish Studies, Hebrew Centre Lecturer in Oriental Studies at the University of Oxford, and Fellow and Tutor in Oriental Studies at Mansfield College, Oxford. He does research and has published widely on modern and medieval Islamic religious thought, as well as on the history of Muslim-Jewish relations.

Preface

This book had its origins in a workshop held at the Middle East Centre, St Antony's College, Oxford, in April 1996. The purpose of the workshop was to discuss the ideas of some important Muslim intellectuals of the twentieth century who have attempted to develop an Islamic outlook consonant with modern thought and institutions, yet rooted in religious tradition and its sources. For the most part, these thinkers post-date the early wave of influential 'modernists' such as Muhammad 'Abduh and Rashid Rida. They also go beyond and sometimes diverge from these early figures in their thinking, particularly in approaches to the Qur'an, the evaluation of Islamic law, ideas on the connection between Islam and politics, and views on inter-religious relations, to cite but some prominent examples.

The provenance of these thinkers is diverse, ranging from North Africa through Egypt and Syria to Iran and India. Their particular angles on Islamic thought are correspondingly varied, though the issues of special interest mentioned above do provide a strong connecting link among them. The positions they take, though again derived from a variety of perspectives and (sometimes even local) concerns, also connect them in some sort of consensus. For example, most would emphasize the centrality of the historical context in understanding the Qur'an and later Islamic thought and institutions, arguing thereby for a modern tradition unfettered by the felt need for 'imposing the detail of the past on the present'; the present here could (and ought to) be imbued with the spirit and certain values and traditions of the past, but it must be moulded according to its own religious, historical, and intellectual lights. Or again, their notions of the 'proper' relationship between religion and politics in Islam would seem, at least loosely, to agree on the need to maintain some sort of separation between the two and to reject the total political control or domination of religion. In these senses, and others, they share a discernable worldview and constitute a true intellectual trend.

This book represents the fulfilment of the 1996 workshop, after a process of reconsideration of thinkers and ideas, and with the addition of new and important subjects. We make no claim to comprehensiveness for the book—rather we believe it provides a number of analytical studies of some important Muslim intellectuals who represent this significant trend in twentieth-century Islamic thought throughout the Muslim world. Though much larger and more diverse than the contents of any one book can comprise, this modernist trend is, we hope, successfully 'captured' and 'exposed' in microcosm in the articles that follow.

Finally, we should like to thank the following bodies and persons for their help and support in making possible both the original workshop and the present book: The Programme for Near Eastern Studies at the Faculty of Oriental Studies, Oxford University; The Faculty of Oriental Studies, Oxford University; The Committee for Modern Middle Eastern Studies, Oxford University; Derek Hopwood, the Director of the Middle East Centre, St. Antony's College, Oxford; Anna Enayat our editor; Julian Murphy who copy-edited and indexed the book, and Caroline Hoffmann.

Introduction
The Culture of Modernity in Islam and the Middle East

DEREK HOPWOOD

The twentieth century has brought change to the world at a rapid and unprecedented rate. No area has remained unaffected. The Middle East—the Arab Islamic World—has had to face change no less than anywhere else. The problem, for many of us largely unresolved, is how to integrate change into society and into our lives. There are various responses to this problem, depending on our point of view. An economist has one kind of answer, a sociologist perhaps another. A secularist responds in one way, a Muslim fundamentalist in another. It is clear that for all of us there is no longer one clear line of change and development from, say, traditional to modern, but a series of ruptures, of transformations which may form new foundations. The former belief of the nineteenth century in steady progress to some duly perceived millennium is outdated. To such believers in Victorian England what they lived was good and getting better; to them traditional was backward and non–European, modern was progressive and European (Western). According to this belief the more that traditional (Eastern) backward peoples became Europeanized the better.

If change is not integrated smoothly (and it rarely is) it can disrupt societies and dislocate values. Individuals may become alienated, divided against their societies and each other, in situations where previously held values have not yet been replaced by other generally accepted norms. Such divisions may lead to political instability, social and religious tensions, psychological disturbance, and economic imbalances. We can all recognize societies suffering from one or other of these problems.

Change is brought about by many factors, but tension is usually caused when a traditional society is faced with challenges posed either by the outside world or by decisions to modernize from within. In the Middle East change was initiated, at least in the first place, under European influence and colonization (in its widest sense). Long held ideas and traditional methods of life were challenged, and some kind of response had to be made. The challenge had come in the name of the modern outside world, and this raised the question in the minds of Middle East intellectuals of what it is to be modern. There was no general agreement; but here the distinction should be made between modernization and modernity. Modernization is the introduction into society of the artefacts of contemporary life—railways, communications, industry (less often nowadays), technology, household equipment. Modernity (modernism) is a general term for the political and cultural processes set in notion by integrating new ideas, an economic system, or education into society. It is a way of thought, of living in the contemporary world and of accepting change.

Modernization began in Europe with industrialization and commercialization or commodification, basically economic processes whereby society had to accept new methods of production and distribution and abandon traditional modes of economic relations. Accumulation of capital became the overriding principle. People, instead of being tied to the land and to the seasonal patterns, began now to make individual economic choices and decisions. Making such choices takes people away from traditional society and broadens their expectations. Industrialization occurred in the West in specific circumstances, and led to innovations which changed men and women and society. People had to become more mobile, and capable of conceiving and absorbing change. Modernization then moved on, and, in the so-called post-modern age, industrialization is no longer a prerequisite. Technologies are now imported wholesale and large scale industries are declining.

Modernization is the process normally leading to modernity, which begins when a society assumes an attitude of enquiry into how people make choices, be they moral, personal, economic, or political. The problem of rational choice is central to modern men and women. Choice implies weighing alternatives in the balance, the freedom to doubt the efficacy of solutions available traditionally or offered by politicians.

Modernity has rightly been called the institutionalization of doubt. Choice and doubt imply rationality, debate and discussion, which lead to conclusions over which rational men and women may disagree.

One of the main beliefs of modernism has been in the capacity of man to control and change social and natural phenomena. In the nineteenth century there was widespread belief (in the West) in the inevitability of progress and the power of human reason. In the contemporary world, while modernization inevitably exists, belief in total solutions has all but disappeared and progress, if made at all, is perceived as merely partial and discontinuous.

Opponents of modernity, who defend what they see as traditional ways of thought, perceive unsought change in the modern world. They observe something merely new and present. Modernity is to them ways of doing things which have replaced other ways, and which are no improvement. They claim there is no necessity for these new ways to enter people's hearts and minds.

In the Arab world a debate has raged over the relative values of modernity and authenticity (*asala*), meaning remaining true to oneself. Proponents of the latter claim that it is essential that integrity be maintained in face of change of a rapid and profound nature. They see change as the corruption of original cultural values, and as something which can be reversed by new beginnings. The present to them is but an interval between perfect origins and their re-establishment. They lead a fight against the modern world. The outside world may change, but Arab man's authentic, original, eternal soul must be saved—that soul as expressed in language, culture, history, or—in one word—Islam.

The modern Muslim has had to define his relationship to the Islamic past, for at the heart of modernity is a principle of development which itself rejects the past. He lives in a sharp discontinuity with his pre-modern history and his transition to contemporary conditions has been distorted both by its speed and, often, by a sense of radical dislocation, caused by a feeling of political and spiritual defeat at a time when the West appeared to be invincible and omnipresent. The break with the past was too sudden and abrupt. As a result of this, many Muslims have now to try to regain that past, which includes all beliefs and attitudes, and to reintegrate it into the modern world—which raises the obvious question of how it is possible to revive the past in totally changed conditions. As a contemporary Moroccan intellectual, Abdu Filali-Ansari, puts it:

> How can one be a Muslim today? There is no simple answer. On the one hand, Islam seems to be a compendium of beliefs unchanged over the centuries, on the other, modern life offers us a collection of more up-to-date concepts, more in conformity with contemporary scientific theories and ideas developed by modern man which are in general more satisfying from an intellectual point of view. There is often no compatibility between the two aspects; not just with Islam as a faith but also with Islam as a form in which it is lived in the consciences of millions. Most Muslims live an ambiguous life in which they maintain an attachment to the Muslim community without adhering totally to all the beliefs which flow from it. Therefore, everyday life and belief can be in sharp opposition.

This succinctly states the problem with which Muslims have been living for over one and a half centuries, how to be modern and Muslim. Responses to this problem have been numerous. Some have said it is impossible, and have accepted a secular world or rejected their faith. Responses within the faith have been categorized as renewal (*tajdid*), reformism (*salafiyya*) and fundamentalism. *Tajdid* was preached as early as the eighteenth century in Arabia by Ibn 'Abd al-Wahhab, and in the nineteenth by Muhammad b. Ahmad, the Mahdi, in Sudan. They saw Islam as a complete and perfect religion which had been corrupted by man-made innovations (*bid'a*). They took on the role of renewer (*mujaddid*) and called for the replacement of existing regimes by ones under their leadership, for the cleansing of Islam and the observance of the law (*shari'a*)—by force if necessary. They quoted the Qur'an to stress the necessity of renewal.

Reformism was more of a reaction to the challenge posed by the modern world and its ideas. The Middle East had been opened up to Europe by Napoleon's invasion of Egypt in 1798, a short occupation but decisive in that it led to the seizure of power by Muhammad 'Ali and his reforming Westernizing dynasty. He tied the Egyptian economy to Europe. He and his heirs were not overly concerned with Islam, they wanted no opposition from al-Azhar to their policies, and sent Egyptian students to the West to acquire practical modern knowledge. Some of these students saw that the secret of European development lay in people's minds being freed to think critically, to change policies, and to apply modern science and technology to the solution of problems. This entire situation began to concern Muslim thinkers and activists.

Jamal al-Din al-Afghani, not an Egyptian himself but living if Cairo, was one of the earliest. He began to formulate ideas on how Islamic society should react to what he saw as the threat from Europe. He did not reject all Western ideas, and was in fact influenced by some of them. He believed in man's ability to act to change his condition and make progress in social and individual development. Progress made would, however, depend on his moral state. He also underlined the necessity of acting rationally and accepting ideas produced by reason. Islamic society would progress again if it accepted these ideas and became unified; he was a strong proponent of Pan-Islam . Society could reform itself if it returned to the truth of Islam—thereby coming up against the perennial question of what is 'true' Islam, and who should define or redefine it.

Islam, to al-Afghani, was foremost a belief in the transcendence of God and in reason. *Ijtihad* (independent judgement, interpretation) was a necessity, and the duty of man was to apply the principles of the Qur'an afresh to the problems of the time. If society does not do this it will stagnate or merely imitate. Imitation corrupts society. According to al-Afghani 'If Muslims imitate Europeans they do not become Europeans, for the words and the actions of the Europeans spring from certain principles which are generally understood and accepted within Western society.'

Islam must be active and energetic. Al-Afghani quoted the Qur'an in support of these principles: 'God changes not what is in a people until they change what is in themselves.' Europeans had integrated change; Muslims must do it in their way by becoming better Muslims. He thought that Europeans had modernized because they were no longer really Christian, and that Muslims, conversely, were weak because they were not really Muslims.

Al-Afghani was foreign to Egypt and an activist. His follower, Muhammad 'Abduh, was Egyptian, less activist and probably more influential—an influence he retains today in some quarters. In general he approved the changes made by Muhammad 'Ali and others, but he was also witness to the British occupation of his country. He saw the dangers of this, the dangers of increased secularization, of following principles derived by human reason for worldly gain. He was also aware

6 DEREK HOPWOOD

of how fragile the European culture was amongst those who adopted superficial French manners. He claimed that 'although Orientals imitate Europe, there is no profit in that unless they perfect their knowledge of its sources'.

He asked how the gap between Islam and modernity could be bridged, and answered that Muslims had to accept the need for change based on the principles of Islam. Islam demanded change, but only if this change were rightly understood in the light of the original and pure sources of the faith. An earlier thinker, Khair al-Din al-Tunisi, had asked (in 1830) whether devout Muslims should accept the institutions and ideas of the modern world. 'Abduh turned the question round and asked whether someone who lived in the modern world could still be a devout Muslim (the question still posed by Filali-Ansari). He replied that Islam should be the moral basis of a modern and progressive society, but that it could not approve everything done in the name of modernization. Islam should act as a restraining principle. Islamic society should live according to God's commands and, by reasoning, affirm what is relevant to contemporary society. A Muslim society could adopt European ideas and sciences without abandoning Islam itself.

'Abduh still left many problems unsolved—which commands of Islam should society live by, which ideas from Europe were acceptable. Some later Muslim thinkers claimed that he had made such concessions to modern ideas as would eventually lead to secularization. Some still follow him today, some have reacted sharply by turning to more radical and oppositional forms of fundamentalism. The Ikhwan al-Muslimun, founded by Hasan al-Banna, were an example of this latter form of reaction. To al-Banna, Islam was a faith and an ideology which encompassed and regulated all human affairs, and which did not shrink from facing new problems and necessary reforms. He saw the West in negative terms as a threat, an invasion of Muslim life and a challenge 'which is armed and equipped with all the destructive and degenerative influences of money, wealth, prestige, ostentation, material enjoyment, power, and means of propaganda'. The Ikhwan was a product of the twentieth century, of local conditions in Egypt, and was more concerned with obtaining freedom from British occupation than with less immediate and political questions, such as how to reconcile modernization and Islamic renewal. The movement believed that modernism had already gone too far, and blamed the West. In particular, al-Banna criticized the effect of modern Western education systems which sowed *doubt* and heresy in the minds of Muslims.

The solution of al-Banna and the Ikhwan was seen in political terms. An Islamic state would halt the moral decline of the country and reintroduce the *shari'a*. Reinterpreted, Islamic culture and tradition would be able to resist and eradicate Western encroachment.

The Ikhwan were actively politically—forming a party—and militarily—fighting in Palestine against the Zionists and in Egypt against the British. Al-Banna himself was assassinated in 1949 (probably by agents of the government) but his message continued, and is followed even until today. Sayyid Qutb hardened al-Banna's message. He had a very gloomy view of Western civilization. To him Islam and the West were incompatible, two camps between which coexistence was impossible. There could only be a struggle between believers and non-believers, between secularism, capitalism, and Islam. Modernization to him was the triumph of the West and the defeat of Islam. Perhaps strangely, he believed that the West was attempting to destroy the individual, largely though the imposition of mass ideologies. Modern man was in a state of spiritual and mental chaos, and had no firm notion of what the future held. He thought that the West, with its emphasis on science and technology, was obliterating the validity of religion. People were being forced to abandon the spiritual for the material. The West had failed to provide for the dignity and welfare of humanity. All this he termed *jahiliyya* (the state of ignorance before Islam) in which he included much of the contemporary observance of Islam itself.

What were Qutb's solutions to the problems of the modern world? For him Islam was a 'complete social system which caters for all people's needs and which differs fundamentally from all other systems. The past of Islam must be summoned up to combat the West and modernization and all ideas of *jahiliyya* should be destroyed.' He predicted the death of capitalism, and criticized all attempts to reconcile Islam with contemporary society, demanding instead that contemporary society should comply with the values of Islam. Modernity should be dismantled—although he did accept as useful some of the scientific advances achieved in the world. The key to an Islamic renaissance was, for him, the education of young people into the Islamic spirit.

Qutb argued that Muslims would have to fight against the state in order to recreate their ideal society. He condemned democracy, political parties, and a sovereign electorate which he saw as *shirk* (polytheism). He would lead the struggle against the ruling state, and a new generation would recover Islam. No victory would be possible unless Muslims dissociated themselves completely from the state and actively opposed it. Because of his clear stand against the state Qutb was arrested on charges of terrorism, and was executed in 1966.

Small groups, mainly of young men, formed themselves in Egypt under Qutb's influence and have carried out his principles by assassinating President Sadat and others. The leader of one group, al-Takfir wa-'l-Hijra, cried out: 'I reject the Egyptian regime and Egyptian reality in all its aspects because everything is in contradiction to the *shari'a* and is heresy. We reject everything that has to do with so-called modern progress. Mechanised society has made people forget the essence of their being, their reality and their religious duty'.

This extreme rejection of modernism stems from despair in the existing situation, to which the only answer is the reinstatement of Islam—'Islam is the solution'. Other Islamic leaders and thinkers are less extreme in their views. Hasan al-Turabi, the Sudanese leader is, for the moment at least, prepared to work with the government to change society as a whole. He has said that he and his followers are not a 'political movement exclusively. We are a religious movement for the education and spiritual development of the individual, and we have much more substantial achievements in the field of reforming society, in *changing* (italics added) individuals and in modern education than in politics.' He repeats that changing people is important—'changing society, that is changing *sufis*, tribal leaders, students, women, and so on is very important.' By changing, he means making people better Muslims who are able to live successfully in the modern world. In a sense he is trying to Islamize modernity, rather than modernize Islam. This kind of programme is an Islamic 'post-modern' reaction, stimulated by the collapse of communism, to the kind of modernism experienced by the developing world.

Muhammad al-Ghazali, a former member of the Ikhwan, feels that he can accept certain elements of the modern West, but very selectively. 'There is the scientific element. We support scientific progress and are willing partners in that. But there are philosophical standpoints which are unacceptable to us, such as atheism and communism. The third element is to do with stimulating desires, which we consider to be socially damaging and which we wish to contain.'

Other, more moderate, Muslim thinkers still struggle with the concept of modernity and the need to integrate the Muslim world. To them a Muslim has to coexist with modernity—and, nowadays, with the more problematic set of concepts grouped under the umbrella of 'post-modernism'. The problems of the world are the problems of every Muslim. To these thinkers the emphasis on *asala* is only an attempt to ignore the conditions created by the modern world. Some would say that modernity has existed in Arab society for the past 150 years, and is not something to be rejected or accepted. They want a more open society, in fact they are looking for a political solution which pays heed to democracy, human rights, women's rights, and minorities. They believe in an education which will open minds rather than close them, which encourages doubt, criticism, and questioning.

Perhaps the most satisfying statement comes from an Islamic modernist in Tunisia, Muhammad Talbi. There is no ambiguity for him. His faith is absolute, and his attachment to coherent and satisfying views for modern man is also total and firm. He is one of those rare intellectuals who has worked openly to gain a satisfactory balance between a living faith and an uncompromisingly modern vision. For him faith is the free choice of the individual which does not conflict with, or constrain, reason. God has given man entire freedom in this. As he says: 'There is no meaning to faith if there is no freedom or choice. The renewal of Islam is more to do with questions of the social and political order than with questions of theology which remain entirely sound. Muslims have suffered because they have used Islam politically.'

Talbi and others are trying to harmonize their faith with the world in which they live. They are working to renew religious concepts and to keep them alive as valid responses to the problems of 'post-modern' man. He advances a positive Islamic vision of people with freedom of choice, able to interpret the contemporary world and to fix their position in it for themselves.

The following chapters treat the thought of prominent Muslim intellectuals engaged with these issues from a particular perspective and in a variety of ways.

I

Nature, Hyperbole and the Colonial State
Some Muslim Appropriations of European Modernity in Late Nineteenth-Century Urdu Literature

JAVED MAJEED

Introduction

This essay explores some appropriations of modernity in Urdu literature in late nineteenth-century India. The starting points for this
exploration will be notions of hyperbole, nature, and reason in the work
of two of the main proponents of the Aligarh movement, Sir Sayyid
Ahmad Khan (1817–98) and Altaf Husain Hali (1837–1914).

Broadly speaking, the Aligarh movement represented the interests
of an Urdu-speaking elite and of the Muslim service gentry in late nineteenth-century India. Its aim was to enable these groups to adjust to
the new realities of British power after the traumatic suppression of
the Indian rebellion of 1857. The rhetoric of the movement focused
on education reform, and this saw fruition with the establishment of
the Muhammadan Anglo–Oriental College in 1875 at Aligarh.[1]

The prime mover behind the Aligarh movement was Sayyid Ahmad
Khan. He was instrumental in establishing the college, and his influence on the milieu of the college thereafter has been described as
'pervasive' (Lelyveld 1978: 202). Sayyid Ahmad Khan was also a key
figure in defining what has been called 'Islamic modernism' in India,[2]
and in this connection there have been a number of scholarly treat-
ments in English of his main works, such as his *Tabyin al-Kalam*, the
Mohammedan Commentary on the Bible (1862–5), and *Tafsir al-Qur'an*
(Ahmad 1967: 31–56).[3] This paper will pay more attention to exploring links between Sayyid Ahmad Khan's essays on topics such as

progress, magic, nature, and science, and his central ideas on a modernist Islam.

In many ways, Altaf Husain Hali could be described as the poet of the Aligarh movement. His biography of Sir Sayyid Ahmad Khan, *Hayat-e javaid* (1910), has been described as 'the most important single book that has been written on the Aligarh movement' (Lelyveld 1978: xiii). His major poetic work is his *Musaddas madd o jazr-e Islam* (*The Flow and Ebb of Islam*, 1879).[4] As the title suggests, the Musaddas is a meditation on the rise and fall of Islamic civilization on a global scale. It also reflects upon the condition of the Indian Muslim community and the rise of the European powers. As such, it could be described as a meditation on European modernity and its consequences for the Muslim community—especially the Indian Muslim community—and so it provides an interesting instance of a response to, as well as an appropriation of, that modernity. It is important to stress that both Sayyid Ahmad Khan and Hali spoke of the Muslim community as a homogeneous whole in British India; this is, of course, a fiction—as are its corollaries such as 'the Hindu community'.[5] As one scholar has argued, even in the 1920s there was no single 'Hindu' or 'Muslim' community in India. Rather, there were 'a multiplicity of identities which could be used and re-worked and reconstructed' (Brown 1994: 238). There were a variety of factors which gave rise to these communal categories.[6] However, I am less concerned with these constructs (and the rhetoric behind them) here, and will focus instead on other categories defined by Hali and Sayyid Ahmad Khan in their attempts to grapple with modernity in the late nineteenth century.

Another important text in this regard is Hali's *Muqaddama shi'r o sha'iri* (*Introduction to Verse and Poetry*, 1893) which is often cited as one of the first modern works of Urdu criticism (Schimmel 1975: 226, Steele 1981: 22, and Minault 1986: 13). The *Muqaddama* makes interesting reading alongside the *Musaddas*, as it reflects upon the decline of Urdu literary culture, and sketches out a programme of reform for the purpose of establishing a modern poetics in Urdu. In some ways, the *Musaddas*, although published before the *Muqaddama*, exemplifies the concerns of the latter. In Hali's case, then, the question of modernity was inextricably involved with the question of defining a modern poetics for Urdu poetry. Indeed, the texts of Hali and Sayyid Ahmad Khan as a whole are often taken to be the first examples of a modernistic

Urdu literature, and they themselves saw their texts as exemplifying
the innovations they wished to bring about in Urdu literary culture.[7]

It is important to note here that both Hali and Sayyid Ahmad Khan
worked closely with the British state in India at different points in
their lives. Hali was employed at the Government Book Depot in Lahore from 1870 to 1874 as a translator, whilst the Muhmammadan
Anglo–Oriental college was founded with a large measure of patronage from the British state, and was itself based on British models of
education.[8] Sayyid Ahmad Khan's stance has been described as
'loyalism in politics and modernism in institutions' (Ahmad 1967: 31).[9]
It was perhaps because of this loyalism that Jamal al-Din al-Afghani
opposed Sayyid Ahmad Khan—since their modernist views are otherwise broadly similar (Hourani 1983: 124–6). However, this closeness
to the British state cannot conceal their ambivalence towards it, an
ambivalence which was perhaps all the more powerful because of that
very proximity.

The argument

This essay explores the nature of this ambivalence by showing how
Hali and Sayyid Ahmad Khan tried to appropriate (rather than simply imitate) aspects of European modernity in their work. More
importantly, in their attempts to do so, they drew out the problematic
character of some of the defining categories of European modernity
itself. Hitherto most commentators have concentrated on how Islamic
modernism absorbed or imitated European modernity.[10] The focus
here is different. The aim is to show how, despite Hali's and Sayyid
Ahmad Khan's attempts to Islamicize the narrative of European modernity—whether in the creation of a modern poetic, or in the defining
of a new style of Qur'anic exegesis, this narrative unravels itself in the
translation from a European to an Indian Muslim context. In Hali's
and Sayyid Ahmad Khan's work, Islamic modernism becomes a mirror of modernity, both reflecting its major aims and purposes, but at
the same time teasing out and exposing its contradictions. Indeed, both
the outline of and contradictions within the categories of European
modernity are perhaps seen at their clearest against the background of
those societies and cultures which became part of European empires
during the nineteenth and early twentieth centuries.

Throughout this argument, I have used Anthony Giddens' *The Consequences of Modernity* as the definitive work on the subject of modernity, but I have also used parts of other works, most notably Michel Foucault's *Madness and Civilization*, and Theodor Adorno's and Max Horkheimer's *The Dialectic of Enlightenment*. I am aware that these authors do not always share the same perspective on modernity, but my purpose here is not to reiterate their arguments, nor to adjudicate between them (a task beyond my competence anyway), but rather to show how their characterizations of modernity are relevant to the subject in hand. For those readers who wish for definitions of modernity itself, I refer them to these texts and their bibliographies.

Natural realism and hyperbole

Antitheses are a characteristic feature of Hali's and Sayyid Ahmad Khan's work. This is especially evident in the latter's essay on old and new religious thinking, which consists of a simple list of contrasting statements ('Madhhabi khayal zamana-e qadim aur zamana-e jadid ka'—'Religious thinking of ancient and modern times', in Khan 1984: vol. 3, pp. 60–2). Antitheses also shape the rhetoric of Hali's *Musaddas*, which in some ways is governed by the oppositions between chaos and order, progress and decline. However, the founding antithesis in both Hali's and Sayyid Ahmad Khan's work is that between nature or reason (the two are often conflated) and its various opposites. This is significant because commentators on modernity have tended to see the category of reason as central to it. Thus, Foucault has argued that 'the Reason-Madness nexus constitutes for western culture one of the dimensions of its originality' (Foucault 1989: xiii), whilst Giddens has linked the emergence of modernity to the self-reflexivity of reason (Giddens 1991: 36–45). It is therefore fruitful to see how Hali and Sayyid Ahmad Khan construct a category of reason/nature in their work, and in so doing engage with its opposites. This engagement with the opposites of a reason/nature construct is central to Hali's attempt to lay the foundations of a modern poetics in Urdu literature.

Broadly speaking, the chief aim of Hali in the *Muqadamma* is to link reason with nature, and to expel hyperbole (*mubalagha*) from the rhetorical tropes of Urdu poetry. His aim here is to replace the prevailing genres of the *ghazal* and *qasida* with what he calls 'natural' poetry—it is

perhaps significant that the term 'natural' is often phonetically transcribed from English (for which, see below).

Hali gives a number of definitions for natural poetry, but by and
large he argues that there are three components to natural poetry. The
first and most important is *asliyat*. The standard Urdu–English dictionary defines this term as originality, reality, and genuineness (Platts
1983: 59), and the word as used by Hali does bear these connotations.
However, in the context of Hali's use of the word as a *literary* term in
the *Muqaddama*, 'realism' or 'natural realism' might be an appropriate
general translation (although the word would have to be rendered in a
variety of ways depending on the context). None the less, 'natural realism' captures the generally consistent way in which Hali uses the word
to refer both to a laudable literary quality as well as a general overall
attitude. His usage evokes a disciplined habit of observation, with a
continual reference to an observable nature as material for one's poetry as well as a measure for one's own work. Thus, recommending Sir
Walter Scott's poetry as a model, Hali refers first to Scott's verse as
never transgressing realism (*asliyat*); the poet never relied on imagination to such an extent that he departs from naturalism (*asliyat*). It is for
this reason that the scenes depicted in his verse pass before our eyes as
though they are those very scenes which the poet apprehended in the
first instance (Hali 1953: 139–40). Similarly, when discussing Milton's
three conditions for good poetry, Hali describes the second condition
as *asliyat*, and goes on to say that a poetic conceit (*khayal*) should have
as its basis an entity which exists, rather than a dream-like world which
cannot withstand the glare of daylight (Hali 1953: 151). This is reiter-
ated later in the book, when Hali states that the most crucial part of
poetry is that the poetic thoughts which are composed should be based
on what is natural (Hali 1953: 216).

As is evident from even this brief exposition, the term *asliyat* is far
from simple, and begs more questions than it answers. This is clear
from Hali's own attempt to tackle the term head on in the section
entitled 'What is meant by *asliyat*', in which he breaks it down into
three components. He says that the raw material of verse should be
reality (*nafs al-amr*), or the beliefs of people, or the opinion of the poet
himself (Hali 1953: 154). This extends the meaning of existing entities to include beliefs as entities in their own right, but, none the less,
the general sense of Hali's use of the word as a literary term is retained.

What is being recommended is poetry whose scope is circumscribed by realism, that is, by references to 'nature'. There is a great deal more that can be said about this, but for our purposes here we can conclude that, in general terms, Hali is advocating literature written in a mimetic realist mode.

According to Hali, the other two ingredients of natural poetry are *sadagi* (simplicity of style) and *josh* (passion or ardour). Once again, Hali's use of these terms is complex. For example, he defines *josh* as the expressing of a poetic conceit (*madmun*) in such an effective way that it is almost as if the poet has not composed the conceit, rather the conceit has taken hold of the poet and arisen by itself (Hali 1953: 158).[11] In other words, the quality of *josh* refers to creating the illusion that the poem arose spontaneously.

There are a number of other references to natural poetry, such as when Hali defines natural poetry as verse whose diction is consonant with the everyday language (*rozmarra*) of a community, and whose meaning is consonant either with regular occurrences in the world, or with those occurrences that ought to happen (Hali 1953: 184–5).[12] Leaving aside the confusion between is and ought that occurs in this definition, we can infer that in general (for Hali) the term nature described something that was real, simple, and open to view. What violates the representation of this simple reality is the trope of hyperbole (*mubalagha*), which is equated with lying, as is clear from the heading of the section entitled 'One should abstain from lies and hyperbole' (Hali 1953: 182–4). To simplify Hali's argument here, it is hyperbole which has corrupted Urdu poetry.[13] Evidence for this is to be found in the *ghazal* and especially in the *qasida*, which far from being simple expressions of genuine passion, have become insincere and convoluted artifices. Thus, he reduces the *qasida* to a species of flattery used to gain access to a court, and to receive rewards from patrons, and he links this to the restrictions placed on poets by despotic governments (Hali 1953: 115, 117–19).[14] He contrasts this degeneration of the *qasida* to its ideal function, namely a vehicle of social approbation and disapprobation, in which the figure praised (*mamduh*) genuinely possesses the qualities attributed to him or her by the poet (Hali 1953: 105, 260–4). In these cases, the *qasida* is founded on *asliyat*, and there is no scope for the use of hyperbole (Hali 1953: 157, 169–74).[15]

It is important to note that nowhere does Hali actually give a positive (as opposed to a negative) definition of hyperbole. Rather, he simply argues that 'truthful verse' (*sacha shi'r*) is much more effective than its opposite, and that the progress of science and knowledge in his time undermines 'false verse' (*jhuti shi'r*). The implication is that hyperbole is no longer viable in a modern poetics; not only should it not be used, the scope for its employment is necessarily restricted with the progress of science and knowledge. There is no consideration in the *Muqaddama* of the use of hyperbole as displaying the skills of a poet, nor any attempt to differentiate between different types of hyperbole. This is in contrast to manuals of rhetoric, such as Sajjad Mirza Baig's *Tashil al-balaghat* (The facilitation of rhetoric), which do make such distinctions, and treat different types of hyperbole in terms of the poet manipulating various degrees of probability (*imkan*) in verse (Baig c. 1940: 176).

Thus, Hali attempted to replace the lyrical world of the *ghazal*, and its self-conscious sense of artifice and symbol,[16] with mimetic realist literature. Interesting here is Hali's anxiety about the gender of the beloved in the *ghazal*. Because the word beloved (*ma'shuq*) is of the masculine grammatical gender in Urdu, it often takes masculine agreement, even when some feminine attribute of the body or dress is mentioned (see Naim 1975: 121–2). Hali is critical about this because, first, he feels the biological gender of beloved should be clear and, second, the beloved, if a woman, should be depicted in morally uplifting terms, rather than suggestively erotic terms, and third, the depiction of a feminine beloved should be appropriate to the respectable mores of society (Hali 1953: 209–13). In Hali's *Muqadamma* poetic symbol becomes 'nature', hyperbole becomes realism, and grammatical gender is confused with biological gender.[17] The self-referential world of the *ghazal* is opened up to a mimetic reference to nature, and in part natural poetry means depicting 'natural' differences between sexes in morally uplifting ways.

A number of scholars have pointed out the vagueness of the key term 'nature' in Hali's work (Steele 1981: 19, Pritchett 1994: 165–6). Hali uses synonyms such as '*adat, ka'inat, fitrat, tabi'at*, and the term 'nature' itself phonetically transcribed from English. However, the transcribed term is used at crucial points in the text, so that the Perso-Arabic terms mentioned above are oriented around the English term 'nature'. Thus, the section on natural poetry in the *Muqadamma* is actually entitled 'nechral *sha'iri*' (Hali 1953: 184). He also uses the transcribed term when describing Goldsmith's poetry as '*sachi* nechral *sha'iri*' (truthful natural poetry), and when he analyses a couplet of Mir's as both 'nechral' and '*anokha*' (extraordinary) (Hali 1953: 124, 176). The transcribed term is also used when discussing the difference between Ibn Rashiq's and Milton's poetry, and when he recommends the study of *nechar* to poets (Hali 1953: 178, 182). Hali also extends the use of the term nature to mean 'second nature'. He refers to this twice, once as *tabi'at-e thani* when he discusses how the poetry of past masters should become second nature to a poet, and the second time he uses the transcribed term *sekand nechar* when he refers to the idiomatic everyday language (*rozmarra*) of a country (*mulk*) as second nature to the speakers of a language (Hali 1953: 148, 184). Although Hali's use of the word nature seems vague, the fact that he uses the English term nature transcribed phonetically into Urdu, around which possible Urdu equivalents are grouped, suggests that the term for him has a specificity which is linked to its European context.

Sayyid Ahmad Khan also uses a variety of terms for nature in his work, but he provides a clue as to the specificity of the transcribed term 'nature' in both his and Hali's work. The title of one of Sayyid Ahmad Khan's essays is 'Tabi'ion, ya necharion ya fit'ration', in which he argues that the three terms are synonymous (Khan 1984: vol. 3, pp. 277–82). However, this is not borne out by the argument of the essay itself, which makes it clear that by 'nature' the author means nature as the object of study of nineteenth-century natural science (throughout the essay he uses the transcribed term '*nechral sa'ins*'), as opposed to the Greek sciences of the past (Khan 1984: vol. 3, p. 279). In other words, the importance of the category 'nature' in Hali's poetics and Sayyid Ahmad Khan's thought derives from the valorization of the nineteenth-century natural sciences. Hali himself hints at this view of nature, when he argues that contemporary science has opened up a variety of possibilities for a realist poetry. He argues that science and mechanics (both terms are transcribed from the English) have opened up a permanent treasury (*lazaval dhakhira*) of metaphors and similes (*tashbihat aur tamthilat*) (Hali 1953: 109–10). Similarly, he speculates as to the adequacy of the resources of the Urdu language, especially given the daily increase in people's knowledge and information (*ma'lumat aur ittila'*), and the corresponding availability of new poetic conceits (*khayalat-e jadid*) (Hali 1953: 154).

Hali's contention that the study of nature is crucial for poets (Hali 1953: 182), suggests that Urdu poets need to cultivate what might be called 'scientific' habits of observation. In the *Musaddas* this is applied to the Indian Muslim community as a whole, when the eagerness to travel which distinguished the early Islamic world is contrasted to the present disinclination among Indian Muslims to undertake journeys (Hali [1879]: vv. 125–6 [p. 36]). There is an implied link between the status of the Muslim community as a subject population, and its indifference to travel. Furthermore, travelling is seen as one of the ways of not just broadening the mind, but of actually verifying the existence of things mentioned in books and, more importantly, of learning how to distinguish between legendary place and geographical fact. As the poet asks, unless things mentioned in books (names such as Paradise and Iram, Salsabil and Kausar, mountain and jungle, island and ocean) are seen, who can be sure whether they exist in heaven or on earth? (Hali 1953: v. 126 [p. 36].) There is thus also an implied link between the disinclination to travel and the Muslim community's ineptitude in what might be called 'scientific' habits of observation and verification.

Thus, the category of nature in Hali's and Sayyid Ahmad Khan's work, which often appears in its transcribed form, is closely connected to the nineteenth-century natural sciences as conceived of by them. What stands behind Hali's poetics is less Wordsworth (Pritchett 1994: 166), whom he does not mention by name in spite of mentioning other English poets, but rather the natural sciences of the nineteenth-century. It is important to remember here the huge prestige that the natural sciences enjoyed in late nineteenth-century India, as these sciences were associated with the power of the British Indian state and the general expansion of the European powers (Washbrook 1982: 158). In broader terms, Hali's and Sayyid Ahmad Khan's valorization of science can also be seen as part of what Habermas has called 'scientism' as the ideology of modernity: '"Scientism" means science's belief in itself: that is the conviction that we can no longer understand science as one form of possible knowledge, but rather must identify knowledge with science' (Habermas 1986: 4). We can conclude here that the category of 'nature' for Hali and Sayyid Ahmad Khan was a redemptive one, but not in the style of European Romanticism as discussed by M. H.

Abrams in his *Natural Supernaturalism*. Abrams' theory, put simply, is that the Romantic apotheosis of the imagination and nature derives from two processes; first the secularization, displacement, and reconstitution of inherited theological ideas and ways of thinking in response to the challenges of the Enlightenment and, second, the retreat from the political realm following the failure of the French revolution into an alternative aesthetic realm in which millenial hopes might be fulfilled (Abrams 1980: 12–13, 350–1). In contrast to this, the category of 'nature' was redemptive for Hali and Sayyid Ahmad Khan, precisely because it represented the transformative and empowering presence of the natural sciences, not because, as in English romanticism, it represented a displacement of the political (McGann 1983),[18] nor because it represented an attempt to recover and reintegrate a unity lost through habits of analytical thinking.[19] By defining an Islamic modernism and a new poetics around this presence, the powers of science would theoretically become available to Indian Muslims in their enterprise to reconstruct Islam in conditions of modernity.

Science, religion, and magic

Sayyid Ahmad Khan's work represents just such an attempt at reconstruction. His essay 'Tabi'ion, ya necharion ya fitration' can be read as a contradictory attempt to stake the claims of religion both against and on the basis of nineteenth-century natural science. On the one hand, the author tries to show that natural science and its discoveries are in fact compatible with Islamic faith, by arguing that science and religion relate to completely different areas—and so they neither contradict nor conflict with each other (Khan 1984: vol. 3, pp. 281–2). On the other hand, the author also states that the adoption of a natural scientific view entails the acceptance of God as the creator of the universe (Khan 1984: 281), although throughout the essay the author points to the other possible positions on this, namely agnosticism and atheism. This contradictory stance to natural science will be discussed further below.

Sayyid Ahmad Khan makes a more far-reaching attempt to establish a compatibility between the modern sciences (*'ulum-e jadida*)[20] and the Qur'an in the course of defining his fifteen principles of Qur'anic exegesis. These principles were adumbrated in a series of letters written to Nawab Muhsin al-Mulk in 1892, and were collected under the title *Tahrir fi usul al-tafsir*.[21] To sum up here, there seem to be two main points that the author wishes to make, namely that the work of God (which he sometimes transliterates as 'werk af gad') or *qanun-e fitrat*, is in fact synonymous with the natural laws of modern science, and that the criterion employed to decide whether a given Qur'anic passage is to be interpreted metaphorically or not is truth as established by natural science.[22] This also seems to have been al-Afghani's view on Qur'anic exegesis, namely that reason should be used fully when interpreting the Qur'an, and if the text seems to be in contradiction to what is known, it should be interpreted symbolically (Hourani 1983: 127–8). There is some continuity between Sayyid Ahmad Khan's general position here, and his general contention in one of his essays on magic, that from a Qur'anic point of view magic is unreal and false (*batil*). He argues that references to magic and sorcery in the text can be interpreted as references to the perceptions and beliefs of unbelievers. Moses' transformation of his staff into a serpent, as related in *surat al-a'raf*, is seen not as an instance of magic or sorcery (*sihr*), but rather as a manifestation of a natural human power (*quvvat-e nafs-e insani*)—'Sihr-jadu bar haq hai aur karne vala kafir hai—'Enchantment-magic is justifiable and those who perform it are unbelievers' (in Khan 1984: vol. 4, pp. 306–39).

Putting together the general contentions of his fifteen principles of exegesis and his essay on magic, Sayyid Ahmad Khan's view seems to be that miracles are against both reason and the text of the Qur'an (Troll 1978/9: 177–9).[23] There are, of course, precedents for these rationalist views, and Troll has described Sayyid Ahmad Khan as a neo-Mu'tazilite (Troll 1978/9: 173–4; see also Ahmad 1967: 44–5) but he concludes that whilst Sayyid Ahmad Khan revived to a large extent the teachings of the *falasifa* in his writings, he did so within the context of his own distinctive world-view. What made the adoption of a new world-view necessary was precisely the development of modern science (Troll 1978/9: 192–3, 171). As one of Sayyid Ahmad Khan's interlocutors puts it, 'he [Sayyid Ahmad Khan] has considered the hypotheses of science correct (*sahih*), certain (*yaqini*) and irrefutable (*ghair qabil al-i'tirad*) and has given them precedence over the Qur'an itself' (Muhsin al-Mulk to Sayyid Ahmad Khan, 9 August 1892, in Khan 1913: 3).

An Enlightenment narrative?

In broad outline, both Hali's and Sayyid Ahmad Khan's narrative of nature can be illuminated by the dialectic of the European Enlightenment as discussed by Horkheimer and Adorno, the main theme of whose work is 'the principle of dissolvent rationality' underlying that Enlightenment, and the consequent subjugation of nature. Technology becomes the 'essence' of knowledge, with the result that, 'what men want to learn from nature is how to use it in order wholly to dominate it and other men' (Adorno and Horkheimer 1979: 6, 4).

In some ways, nature in Hali and Sayyid Ahmad Khan is very much a controlled, developed and subjugated nature. Thus, in his essay on 'Religious Beliefs in Olden and Modern times', Sayyid Ahmad Khan emphasizes the use of nature as a modern religious belief, as opposed to an older attitude of rejecting nature in order to concentrate on God's transcendental reality (Khan 1984: vol. 3, p. 26). The subjugation of nature figures prominently in Hali's *Musaddas*, where it underlines the narrative of progress in the poem, for which the poet employs images of the cultivation and irrigation of land.[24] This imagery is particularly clear in the verses depicting the civilizing effect of Islam on the Arabian peninsula and the Middle East generally. Thus, the Arabs are described as becoming 'unmatched and unique in agriculture', and as making 'every desolate land flourish' (Hali 1953: vv. 75–6 [p. 26]). Images of greenery are also used in a more general sense to measure the fructifying impact of Islam; so the seeds of spring are brought by the Arabs into the world, and the coming of Islam is described as 'the first wave of liberation by which the garden of the world was to become green' (Hali 1953: v. 76 [p. 26], and v. 57 [p. 22]). Later, when the poet sums up the glories of early Islamic civilization, agriculture is again listed as among its achievements, and the Prophet himself is described as a gardener who had laid out a harmonious, egalitarian garden – 'The gardener had laid out a garden which did not contain any very large or small plant' (Hali 1953: v. 103 [p. 31], and v. 58 [p. 22]).

The importance of gardens, verdure, and barrenness to the imagery of the *Musaddas* is also clearly signalled in the section entitled 'Simile of the nations as gardens' (Hali 1953: vv. 109–12 [pp. 32–3]). Here the ruined garden of Islam is compared to other flourishing gardens, as well as gardens which although not actually flourishing, are ready to bloom. The decay of agriculture and of the garden of Islam forms a contrast not just with earlier glories, but also with the present achievements of British rule itself—amongst whose benefits is included a reference to cultivation. Under the British, 'In the jungles, every corner is a rose garden' (Hali 1953: v. 285 [p. 68]). The use of garden imagery would of course have had Qur'anic resonances for Hali's Muslim readers. The garden in the Qur'an is used as an image of paradise. The abode of the Just is variously referred to as 'al-janna' ('The Garden', Qur'an XI:108) or 'jannat 'Adn' ('the Garden of Eden', XVIII:32). Paradise is also described as a garden watered by running streams (II:25 and IV:57). The Qur'an also contains a parable of the blighted garden, which is meant to warn mortals of the consequences of heedless arrogance (LXVIII:17–33).

Whilst these resonances must be borne in mind, the use of garden imagery and images of cultivation and irrigation in the *Musaddas* is significant in a number of other ways.[25] Here there is space to deal with only one possibility; namely that schemes of agriculture, land reclamation, and irrigation in British India furnished Hali with a contemporary example of imperial power and its command over water for agricultural purposes. It was in the decade after the *Musaddas* appeared that the economy of the Punjab was reshaped by unprecedented expansion in agricultural production brought about by canal colonization. This colonization signified an important experiment in social and economic engineering, which reflected an increasingly confident and interventionist colonial state.[26]. However, prior to this, there were important developments in canal engineering concentrated in the Doab, with irrigation in the grand manner beginning with the Ganges Canal, which was opened in 1854 (Whitcombe 1972: 64). In 1875, one colonial observer was to describe this canal as 'the most magnificent work of its class in the whole world' (cited by Whitcombe 1972: 85). Thus, even before canal colonization got seriously under way in the Punjab, there were a number of significant examples of colonial hydraulic engineering and its impact on agriculture. Such monuments of the colonial state's schemes of public works (and the *Musaddas* does depict the benefits of British rule at least partly under the heading of public works) may have sharpened Hali's interest in images of cultivation and irrigation. Thus, the emphasis on controlled and subjugated nature in Hali's work might also reflect the controlling and subjugating policies of the colonial state itself, but behind this stands the transformative and sub-jugating powers of the natural sciences and their technologies themselves.

Horkheimer and Adorno have also argued that the programme of Enlightenment rationality and the sciences that are derived from it, 'was the disenchantment of the world' and 'the dissolution of myths' (Adorno and Horkheimer 1979: 3). Myth is seen as anthropomor-phic, that is, as the projection on to nature of the subjective in the form of the supernatural, demonic and spiritual (Adorno and Horkheimer 1979: 6). As we have seen above, the thrust of Sayyid Ahmad Khan's exegesis of the Bible and the Qur'an is an anti-miraculous one, and there seems to be no place for the supernatural at all in his view (Troll 1978/9: 177–9). Furthermore, as we have also seen above, he tries to argue that the Qur'an is free from any verses that reinforce a magical view of the world ('*Sihr*' in Khan 1984: vol. 4, pp. 306–39). In his *Muqaddama*, Hali discusses how science (*sa'ins*) has cut the roots of Urdu poetry, and how civilization (*sivila'izeshan*) has broken its spell (*tilism*) and erased its magic as though it were of no substance (like an erroneous word, *harf-e ghalat*) (Hali 1953: 179). Similarly, when he dis-cusses narrative poetry (*mathnavi*), he stresses that the stories related should no longer be based on improbable and supernatural (*fauq al-'adat*) events. Such stories were current when human knowledge was restricted, but now science ('*ilm*) has broken this enchanting universe (*tilism*) (Hali 1953: 279). Hali's concern with the demystifying effects of science and its undermining of the magical quality of literature helps us to add another gloss on his rejection of hyperbole. It is as though in the Enlightenment scheme of things, hyperbole is akin to mythologiz-ing, which distorts the clear, observable quality of the nature that ought to be the subject of the modern poet's verse. One can conclude here that Hali and Sayyid Ahmad Khan were, in part, trying to find a place for Muslims in a post-magical world, a world rendered disenchanted by both Enlightenment reason and the success of European imperial-ism.

Returning to nature and the consequences for scripture

A number of scholars have pointed to the problems in Sayyid Ahmad Khan's notion of nature, such as the vacillation between a mechanical

and a teleological view of it, the confusion between laws based on empirical, statistical data, and normative laws, the conflation of the God
of Islamic faith with the God of natural law, and so on (Ahmad 1967:
44–5, but see especially Troll 1978/9: 174–6, 217–18, 226). Albert
Hourani, writing of Afghani, 'Abduh and Wajdi, describes how Islam
becomes identical with civilization and the scientific norms of nineteenth-century Europe, and how in fact it almost dissolves into modern
rationality (Hourani 1983: 144, 162). Aziz Al-Azmeh has also extensively discussed 'Islamic liberalism' and its exegesis of scripture as a
code 'open to the modernist interpreter, which yielded ideas in keeping with science, with evolutionsim, and other ideas in currency'
(Al-Azmeh 1993: 33).[27] Much the same could be said about Hali and
Sayyid Ahmad Khan in the context of their Islamicizing of the category of nature.

However, the focus here will be different. Far from an easy incorporation of modernity into a liberal Islam, this Islamicization of nature
teases out the problematic character of some of the central categories
of modernity itself. Furthermore, there is much evidence in the texts
examined here of doubt and uncertainty regarding some of the key
categories and narratives of modernity. The pairing together of various notions from tradition with matters of contemporary relevance, to
use Aziz Al-Azmeh's phrase (Al-Azmeh 1993: 80), is certainly part of
a self-conscious polemic of modernization; but this polemic is called
into question by some powerfully eloquent ambivalences and tensions.
This is especially true of Hali's work, in which the apparent eulogy of
a narrative of (modern) progress is undermined by the multiple levels
of meaning in his texts and by hints of alternative possibilities.

In dealing with the Islamicization of nature, I shall make six general points about Sayyid Ahmad Khan's, and to a lesser extent, Hali's
work. The first three relate to the category of nature or reason in his
work, and the last three relate to the role of scripture in a post-magical
world.

First, as mentioned above, Sayyid Ahmad Khan vacillates between
the claim that Islamic faith can be reconciled with modern science,
and the claim that their spheres are so different (since one deals with
spiritual and the other with the mundane), that there is no need to
reconcile them. These contradictory claims reflect the shifting nature
of the terms of science and faith themselves. This shifting of key terms

captures something of the protean nature of modern Enlightenment reason. Sayyid Ahmad Khan often refers to how modern science bears no resemblance to Greek science, as well as to new sciences which had no precedents in the Greek world. In his essay '*Ulum-e jadida*' he categorizes the modern sciences according to those which did not exist among the ancient Greeks, those which did exist among the Greeks but whose principles have been completely recast (such as chemistry and astronomy), and those whose principles have developed to such an extent that they no longer resemble what they were in the Greek world (for example, geometry, mechanics, and algebra) (Khan 1984: vol. 7, pp. 211–12). In his introduction to *Tahrir fi usul al-tafsir*, he argues that the main difference between the modern and the Greek sciences is that the former are based on experiment and practice (*tajruba aur 'amal*), while the latter were based on analogical and fanciful proofs (*qayasi aur fardi dala'il*) (Khan 1913: 2). At the same time, he admits the possibility that just as the nineteenth-century sciences have supplanted the Greek sciences, so the latter too may one day be supplanted by new forms of science. This would necessitate a reinterpretation of the holy text once more (Khan 1913: 35).

For Sayyid Ahmad Khan, then, there is a close connection between the shifting nature of scientific truth itself and the need to reinterpret the Qur'an anew. What interests us here, however, is that, in spite of the valorization of the natural sciences in his work, he is aware of the changing nature of scientific truth. There is a sense in which the shifting term 'science' in his work exemplifies Popper's remark that science rests on shifting sands. As Giddens goes on to argue, 'In science, *nothing* is certain, and nothing can be proved. ... In the heart of world of hard science, modernity floats free' (Giddens 1994: 39). In other words, the shifting nature of the term 'science' in Sayyid Ahmad Khan's work is part of that crisis of science to which Lyotard has called attention, signs of which have been accumulating since the end of the nineteenth century (Lyotard 1986: 38–9). Indeed, Sayyid Ahmad Khan's valorization of science can be more fruitfully read in terms of the problems attendant upon legitimizing science for religious world-views in late nineteenth-century India.

Second, Laurel Steele has argued that Hali's *Muqadamma* is arranged in a series of circles (Steele 1981: 18). Furthermore, the structure of the *Musaddas* is cyclical in accordance with subtitle of the poem referring to tidal cycles. Thus, the poem opens with a simile of a boat in danger during a storm at sea (representing the sorry state of Indian Muslims at the time) (Hali 1953: v. 3 [p. 11]), and the concluding section of the poem reintroduces this simile:

> There is a boat being caught in a whirlpool, putting the lives of young and old at risk.
> There is no way out or room for escape. Some of them are asleep, while others are awake.
> Those who are asleep stay intoxicated with their profound slumber. Those who are awake mock the others.

> (Hali 1953: v. 275 [p. 66]).[28]

Also both Sayyid Ahmad Khan's and Hali's work contain a number of circular definitions. In general terms it can be said that in *Tahrir fi usul al-tafsir*, Sayyid Ahmad Khan's argument is that the Qur'an is 'true' because the natural sciences are consonant with it, and the natural sciences are true because they are consonant with the Qur'an. Similarly, Hali's argument on a modern poetics may be summed up as: hyperbole is the equivalent of lying because it violates nature, while nature is 'truthful' because it stands in opposition to the falsity of hyperbole.

These circularities in their work point to a feature of modernity itself, which Giddens has called reflexivity: 'What is characteristic of modernity is not an embracing of the new for its own sake, but the presumption of wholesale reflexivity—which of course includes reflection upon the nature of reflection itself' (Giddens 1991: 39). He further argues that this reflexivity necessarily subverts reason itself, because we live in a world which is constituted through 'reflexively applied knowledge', but 'we can never be sure that any given element of that knowledge will not be revised' (Giddens 1991: 39). It is in part because of this 'circularity of reason' that modernity is 'unsettling' (Giddens 1991: 49).

Third, Hali's *Muqaddama* in particular is markedly eclectic. It invokes a large variety of figures from Persian and Arabic writers and thinkers, to Macauley, Milton, Goldsmith, Shakespeare, Byron, Virgil, Homer, and Plato. Laurel Steele has argued that this plethora of references is a reflection of the intellectual and literary confusion of the nineteenth century, and a portent of the problems of the twentieth (Steele 1981: 1). Pritchett has also pointed out that it is difficult to establish how well Hali controlled his sources (especially his English ones), and how much he was at the mercy of his translators, but she goes on to suggest that he manipulates his English sources in order to make his own very distinctive arguments (Pritchett 1994: 151). What can be said, though, is that it is not always clear what purposes this eclecticism serves in Hali's work. Ecleticism was to reach its apotheosis in Iqbal's *Reconstruction of Religious Thought in Islam* (1934) whose most striking feature is the contrast between the depth and range of its eclecticism, and its lack of any clearly articulated conclusions (as I argue in Majeed 1993). Eclecticism becomes a substitute for argument, perhaps because it is no longer clear what the criteria are for undertaking and judging an argument. It is as though a logic of argumentation has to be constructed anew with each encounter, and the ground rules have to be drawn up as the protagonists go along.

Fourth, the terms of faith are themselves fluid. W. C. Smith has argued that the term scripture refers to a text being given special status by a community. The term is bilateral, since no text is a scripture in itself; rather, a given community makes a text into a scripture by treating it in a certain way (Smith 1993: 11, 17–18). In other words, they impose meanings on the text, and this is also made clear by the variety of interpretations a scripture receives throughout its history (Smith 1993: 5). Sayyid Ahmad Khan, by taking the Qur'an out of pre-existing relationships of exegesis, and re-inserting it into a new set of relationships determined by the watch words of European modernity, namely reason, nature, and progress, unwittingly lays bare the arbitrary nature of the relationship between scripture and the meanings imposed on it. This emerges from Sayyid Ahmad Khan's admission that should the sciences of his day be superseded by new forms of science, then the Qur'an will need to be reinterpreted anew. Whilst he dismisses the objection that this would mean that the Qur'an will become a 'plaything' (*khilona*) in the hands of people (Khan 1913: 35), it does seem as though the text becomes a blank screen onto which the current intellectual and scientific trends of the age can be projected.

Fifth, by substituting chains of authoritative commentaries with these Enlightenment categories, the result is also a naive view, namely that individuals can grasp the meaning of scripture without recourse to the constraint of preceding authorities. This is in keeping with Francis Robinson's argument about the impact of printing on Indian

Islam; whereas before the reading of theological students was closely
controlled by their teachers, and the issuing of *ijaza*, with large scale
printing, such constraints were no longer possible (Robinson 1993).
This results in what Aziz Ahmad has called 'exegetical fundamentalism' (Ahmad 1967: x),[29] namely the invoking of an original text to the
exclusion of the traditions of commentary it is embedded in. There is
a parallel argument in Hali's *Muqadamma*, when he suggests that poets
ought to substitute the imitation and refinement of the verses of preceding masters with observations of nature, and when he seeks to
replace the *ustad-shagird* relationship with a notion of the poet as his
own teacher, or, more accurately, with nature as his teacher. Thus, he
argues that it is only if the poet acquires the habit of studying the text
of nature (*sahifa-ye fitrat*) that he will be able to escape from the limits
of his predecessors' conceits (*mahdud khayalat*) (Hali 1953: 145). This
note is sounded elsewhere, when Hali argues that the drift away from
natural poetry occurs when poets remain circumscribed by imitation
of the ancients (*qudama ki taqlid*) and the circle of their imaginings
(*khayalat ke da'ira*) (Hali 1953: 187). Hali also questions the usefulness
of the *ustad-shagird* relationship, and it is in this context that he ranks
the study of the poetry of past masters after ability or capacity (*isti'dad*)
and the study of nature (*nechar ka mutala'a*) as the prerequisites for a
successful poet (Hali 1953: 182). Just as Sayyid Ahmad Khan sought
to release the Holy Text from pre-existing networks of exegesis, so
Hali in his poetics seeks to supplant pre-existing hierarchical relationships with a different set of connections.

The result in the case of Sayyid Ahmad Khan's hermeneutics is
that scripture becomes almost infinitely interpretable, and so comes
close to losing its sacredness and ceasing to be scripture. Thus, whereas
Smith has spoken of the 'human propensity to scripturalize' (Smith
1993: ix), we also need to consider those possibilities of 'de-
scripturalization' opened up by thinkers attempting to recast some of
the fundamental categories of Islamic faith.

Finally, in the context of discussing the development of the notion
of scripture in the West over the past two centuries, Smith has also
discussed what he calls the 'de-transcendentalizing of the concept of
scripture and the emergence of its plural' (Smith 1993: 11). This entailed recognising that scriptures are texts upon which readers impose
meanings, and that there is not just one unique scripture (the Bible),

but rather a collection of scriptures occurring in a variety of cultures. We see tentative elements of this view in Sayyid Ahmad Khan's *Muhammadan Commentary on the Bible*, and in his measurement of the Qur'an by nineteenth-century views of rational nature. At times, his work can be seen as hovering between a singular view of the Qur'an as unique and transcendental, and a post-scriptural view of a plurality of texts that were once scriptures but have now been rendered mundane by the secularizing and historicizing imperatives of modernity.

A narrative of progress?

Robert Nisbet has argued that during the period 1750 to 1900 'the idea of progress reached its zenith in the Western mind in popular as well as scholarly circles. From being one of the important ideas in the West it became the dominant idea.' He goes on to say that this period also saw the 'secularization' of the idea of progress; as a historical process it was detached from its previous relationship with God, making it a historical process 'activated and maintained by purely natural causes' (Nisbet 1980: 171–2). We might say that part of the aim of Hali's *Musaddas* and *Muqadamma* and Sayyid Ahmad Khan's essays is to connect Islamic history with the master narrative of European progress. This is done in a variety of by now familiar ways.

The Prophet of the *Musaddas* is a liberal figure embodying moral and economic virtues which are necessary for an Islamic narrative of progress to get underway.[30] He strikes the reader as somewhat similar to the stereotype of a Victorian social reformer. Much of the moral polemic of the *Musaddas* stresses the virtues Samuel Smiles emphasized in *Self-Help* (1859), a popular text in Victorian Britain which promulgated the contemporary spirit of self-help and personal initiative in an idiom of political and social reform (Dennis and Skilton 1987: 50–7). That Hali was aware of the term self help is indicated by the fact that he uses it, transcribed into Urdu, when he discusses how Urdu poetry can progress in accordance with contemporary trends (Hali 1953: 179). In a sense, the Musaddas can be seen to repackage, through the model of classical Islam, an ethic akin to the one Max Weber so famously described in *The Protestant Ethic and the Spirit of Capitalism* (1904–5). This is slightly ironic, given Weber's own views regarding the sensuality of Islamic culture (on which, see Turner 1994: 98).

Hali was also at pains to point out the debt that Europe owes to
the achievements of classical Islam in a variety of sciences, and anxious
to ensure that the European narrative of progress should not suppress
the memory of Arab contributions to that narrative. In contrast to the
ruined architectural monuments of Islamic culture, Hali points to the
hadith—with its laws of substantiation and invalidation, which prefig-
ured their use in the sense of modern critical history—as a complete
body of learning that testifies to the intellectual glories of past Islam
(Hali 1953: vv. 92–7 [pp. 29–30]). Furthermore, when the poet deals
with the 'cooperative sympathy of people of Europe (*ahl-e yurap ki
hamdard*)' he posits another historical irony, namely that they have got
where they have because they, rather than Muslims, have followed tenets implicit in the *shari'at* (Hali 1953 v. 171 [p. 45]).

Thus, in Hali's handling, the European narrative of progress becomes an extension of an earlier Islamic narrative of progress. Ironically,
the European narrative works out the true values of an essential Islam,
which Muslims themselves have forgotten.

However, there are a number of problems with Sayyid Ahmad
Khan's and especially Hali's formulations of progress, which bring out
the problematic nature of the notion itself. In the case of the *Musaddas*
there are three images of historical process, a linear narrative of progress,
a cyclical image of natural tidal forces, and a narrative of vicissitudes of
fortune.[31] The poem ends on a bleak and fatalistic note which undermines the narrative of progress. The last section of the poem lists
civilizations which were once great but have since fallen, and suggests
that the sate will befall the British. The last verse stresses the transi-
tory nature of the world and the abiding transcendence of God, while
the penultimate verse reads:

> The end of every movement of progress here is this. The conclusion of
> every people and community is this.
> The way of fate has always been this. The true state of this wonderful
> world is this.
> That many springs have welled up here only to dry, many gardens have
> bloomed and blossomed only to be cut back.
>
> (Hali 1953: v. 292 [p. 69])

There is a similar instability of temporal images in Sayyid Ahmad
Khan's essay on 'Principles of Progress and Causes of Decline'. Here
he exhorts his readers to concentrate on the present moment, but in

doing so repeatedly invokes past decline and future progress as incitements to concentrate on the present. While trying to define the shape of present progress (*taraqqi ki surat*), he also has to invoke past narratives of progress—that is, there is a hint of the plurality of historical narratives which the European notion of progress has edged out of the picture ('Taraqqi ke usul aur tanazzul ke vujuh', Khan 1984: vol. 12, pp. 265–84).

In Hali's *Musaddas*, too, the present is constantly fusing into both an imagined past and an imagined future. This is related to the circular structure of the *Musaddas*, which has been referred to above. This structure reflects the predominance of the cyclical character of history in the poem, which in part stems from the fact that in some ways the *Musaddas* is a revivalist poem. It draws its imaginative strength from the imagined pristine simplicity of classical Islam. This is, of course, problematic, and here Gustav von Grunebaum's view of classical Islam, although markedly Orientalist, might be illuminating: 'The classical represents a model. It is, in fact, a model whose reconstruction is by definition an obligation and an impossibility' (cited in Turner 1994: 69). Aziz Al-Azmeh has also discussed revivalism in terms of retrieval of pristine beginnings and in this context, he argues that for revivalism 'the past is the accomplished future, and the future is the past asserted' (Al-Azmeh 1993: 48). There is something of the temporal circularity of revivalism in Hali's *Musaddas*.

In some ways, this narrative of temporal circularity is also history as repetition with a difference. Thus, Sayyid Ahmad Khan frequently points to parallels between the reception of Greek thought and science in classical Islam, and the tussle between contemporary science and nineteenth-century Islam (Khan 1913: 1–2). Indeed, in his essay 'The Progress of the Sciences', he argues that there are two ways in which Muslims could make progress in the modern sciences, and both ways can be derived from the lessons that classical Islam in its engagement with Greek philosophy and sciences teaches us ('Taraqqi-ye 'ulum',in Khan 1984: vol. 7, p. 215). In some ways, then, the drama of Greek science and philosophy in classical Islam is seen as a rehearsal for the contemporary drama of modern science and Islam. At the same time, though, Sayyid Ahmad Khan is anxious to stress the epistemological break which modern science has made, so that the discontinuities between Greek and modern science are stressed in order to convey the urgency of the need to take on modern science. This usually takes the form of pointing to the new principles on which modern science is based, and emphasizing its experimental practice and observational character (Khan 1913: 2; and 'Taraqqi-ye 'ulum', in Khan 1984: vol. 7, p. 215). It is worth pointing out here that in the *Musaddas* when Hali delineates the stagnant intellectual condition of Indian Muslims, he points to the infatuation with Greek sciences and thought as just one symptom of this state (Hali 1953: vv. 232–45 [pp. 57–60]).

In this context, it is worth pointing to two opposed views of 'Islamic' history. Gustav von Grunebaum has described the 'Islamic' world-view as least able to accept the ontological reality of change, while W. C. Smith has described modern Islamic thought as elevating dynamism or fluidity as a principle in its own right (von Grunebaum 1962: 209, and Smith 1957: 89). To some extent both formulations point to features in Sayyid Ahmad Khan's and Hali's rhetoric of temporality, in which continuity and discontinuity reinforce each other. Continuity serves simultaneously to justify and measure the enormity of change, whilst change itself is seen as returning to a point of pristine origin.

Hali's ambivalence towards modernity's narrative of progress comes to the fore at one point in the *Musaddas* where he describes progress as a carrion bitch (*murdar kuttiya*) (Hali 1953: v. 138 [p. 38]). Furthermore, the verses praising Europeans are sometimes ambiguous. Thus, when their restless energy and hard work are praised, the picture is unappealing and slightly comic. The description of European peoples racing so far along the way as if they still had far to go, carrying on their heads every kind of load and burden, is a little reminiscent of an undignified and rather childish game (Hali 1953: v. 131 [p. 37]). In contrast, picturing Indian Muslims in languorous pose becomes almost appealing (Hali 1953: v. 133 [p. 37]). This is also evocative of the fatalistic mood which the poem never quite manages to shake off. Indeed, there is a sense in which the poem suggests that decline imparts a wisdom which the British, at the zenith of their powers, cannot hope to have.[32]

These ambivalent strands in the *Musaddas* merge in the depiction of the *jahiliyat*, which serves as a foil to the narrative of Islam as progress. It also represents savage and chaotic nature as opposed to controlled, ordered, and subjugated nature, but, more importantly, there is also a suggested overlap between the degenerate state of pre-Islamic Arabia and contemporary Muslim India.[33]

However, there are other aspects to the depiction of pre-Islamic Arabia and the degenerate state of Indian Muslims which need to be highlighted. The hedonism of both can come across as bright and lively, in spite of the poet. There is a festive energy to the picture of young blades roaming around fairs, visiting wrestling pits and taverns, indulging in the sports of quail-fighting and pigeon-racing, loitering around affecting the pose of languorous lovers, and uttering curses in the 'gatherings of the base' (Hali 1953: vv. 259 [p. 62], 261 [p. 63], 257 [p. 62], 263 [p. 62], and 258 [p. 62] respectively). There is a similarly energetic edge to the description of the anarchic state of pre-Islamic Arabia. One particular instance of this occurs where the quarrelsome energy of tribal habits is combined with an evocation of the appealing simplicity of a pastoral and tribal lifestyle, again in spite of the poet's moralising (Hali 1953: v. 18 [p. 14]). In effect, the anti-hedonistic moral rhetoric of the *Musaddas* magnifies the ludic quality of the pleasurable activities it condemns.[34]

In this regard, it must be stressed that Hali's poetic sensibility was decidedly divided. There is much evidence that he identified closely with the classical Urdu poetic world that he sought to reform.[35] One is left with feeling that like all modern reformers, Hali and Sayyid Ahmad Khan were not just deeply intimate with the world they sought to reform, but that, in some way, they carried this world within themselves. They were, in fact, more conversant with those magical, hyperbolic worlds than they dared to admit either to themselves or to the colonial state. In the end, perhaps, their ambivalence to the values of modernity stemmed from their ambivalence to the British Indian state itself. The simple fact was that the British Raj had brought to an end Muslim ascendancy in India, and it is no surprise, therefore, that the reflections on decline and exhortations to embrace modernity in Hali's and Sayyid Ahmad Khan's work should sometimes convey elements of strain. Furthermore, the British Raj's rhetoric of modernization can hardly be taken at face value itself. As David Washbrook has argued, the British Indian state's ambiguous attitude to change is revealed in its agrarian policies during the period from the 1850s to the 1920s, when it established the context for the capitalist development of Indian agrarian society. At the same time it felt threatened by the possible

social transformations which such a development would bring about.
These transformations would have undermined the Raj's reliance on
existing agrarian structures and corporations for its authority and le-
gitimation. It therefore had to obstruct the unfolding of the logic which
it had set in motion in the first place (Washbrook 1981). Hali's and
Sayyid Ahmad Khan's ambivalence to the values of modernity which
they strove to incorporate into a redefined Islamic world-view, therefore, also needs to be placed in the context of the British Indian state's
own contradictory stance to modernization in India.

A concluding image

As mentioned above, there is one image which appears at the beginning and at the end of Hali's *Musaddas*, thereby reinforcing its circular
structure. This is the image of a ship adrift on a storm-tossed ocean,
approaching a whirlpool, with its sleeping crew oblivious to imminent
dangers. Hali says this is representative of the state of the Indian Muslim community:

> Precisely this is the condition in the world of that community whose
> ship has entered the whirlpool and is surrounded by it.
> The shore is far away and a storm is raging. At every moment there is the
> apprehension that it is just about to sink.
> But the people in the boat do not even turn over, as they lie asleep and
> unconscious.
>
> (Hali 1953: v. 3 [p. 11])

Why is this image so resonant? It conveys a sense of the Indian
Muslim community, and perhaps the global Muslim community, cut
adrift from the world of modernity in tempestuous circumstances.
Their listing ship needs to be brought into safer waters, and Muslims
need to be reconnected to the world from which they have been expelled by European modernity. But the image of a ship of fools has
other resonances. Foucault has discussed the significance of this image
in fifteenth-century European literature. He elaborates on the figure
of ships carrying a cargo of insane men expelled from towns and cities
in a ritual of both exile and purification, and he connects this with
madness as a manifestation in man of a chaotic aquatic element
(Foucault 1989: 9, 17). Dols has stressed that medieval Islamic society
permitted wider latitude and freedom to the mentally ill than modern

Western society, and also that madness was not always perceived as something to be treated or healed—the mad lover, the crazed mystic, and the holy fool were seen by some to possess a deeper insight into reality, hence the visits to hospitals by philosophers and others to listen to their 'wisdom' (Dols 1992: 4, 390–4, and chs 11 and 13). In the *Musaddas*, the gathering of aristocrats and poets seems like the madcap gatherings of a lunatic assembly, their poetic outpourings a babble of nonsense which Hali is trying to convert into the sense of modernity. It is as though Hali is both listening to and expelling those voices from the past that threaten to subvert the incorporation of modernity into his poetics.[36] In his effort to translate the poetic babble of the past into modern sense, the voices preceding Enlightenment rationality become more and more difficult to catch, but they remain vibrant in the noise of the storm which forms the background to the listing ship in the *Musaddas*.

Notes

I am indebted to Christopher Shackle for his comments on matters of transliteration.

1 The standard work on the Aligarh movement is Lelyveld 1978.
2 The standard work on this is Ahmad 1967.
3 See also Baljon (1949), but for a masterly study see Troll (1978/9).
4 For a full translation and commentary on this poem, see Shackle and Majeed 1997.
5 See Aziz Al-Azmeh's salutary reminder that 'there are as many Islams as there are situations that sustain it' in Al-Azmeh 1993: 1, and Hasan 1997: 25–52. See also Chiriyankandath 1996 on the problems encountered by Hindu nationalists in their attempts to define an all-Indian Hindu identity, and Khory 1995 on similar problems encountered by the state in Pakistan in its attempts to play an Islamic card in defining a national identity.
6 The literature on this is vast, but for some illuminating studies see Hardy 1972, Robinson 1974, Brass 1974, Page 1981, Freitag 1989, and Pandey 1990. The issue is also discussed in Shackle and Majeed 1997.
7 For Sayyid Ahmad Khan's journalism in this respect, see Lelyveld 1978: 80, 115, Troll 1978/9: 13–15, Aziz Ahmad 1967: 38, and Hijazi 1988: 20–1. See also Minault 1986: 13, and Hali 1890: 3, where Hali refers to how translations from English into Urdu, especially those undertaken

under the aegis of the Aligarh Scientific Institution, transformed literary taste.

8 A government grant provided 20–25% of the annual expenditure of the college; Lelyveld 1978: 141.

9 For a recent, more sophisticated view of loyalism, see Bayly 1994: 12, 21.

10 See Smith 1957, von Grunebaum 1962 and Ahmad 1967. The most sophisticated expression of this view is to be found in Al-Azmeh 1993.

11 See also Pritchett 1994: 93–105 for a lucid exposition on the art of rendering conceits in classical Urdu poetry (*madmun afrini*).

12 For an exposition of the notion of *rozmarra*, see Hali 1953: 250–5.

13 See his categorical statement 'There is no doubt that when lies and hyperbole entered our poetry, from that time onwards its decline began.' (Hali 1953: 182.)

14 For his comments on the decline of Islamic culture and poetry due to sycophancy (*khush-amad*) and servile flattery (*ghulamana' tamalluq*), see Hali 1953: 119–21.

15 For an illuminating account of the *qasida*, and a reconstruction of its history as a genre, see Sperl and Shackle 1996.

16 On the symbolic universe of the *ghazal* see Pritchet, 1994: 63–122.

17 On the distinction between the two, see Corbett 1991. Corbett cautions that 'it is not at all straightforward to establish links between grammatical gender and the relative status and treatment of those classified by the different genders' (p. 322). In technical terms, Hali would have seemed to have also confused the syntactic and semantic principles of gender resolution, for which see Corbett, pp. 269–306.

18 McGann argues that English Romantic poetry is marked by 'dramas of displacements and idealization' (McGann 1983: 1).

19 Abrams 1980: 182: 'Romantic philosophy is ... primarily a metaphysics of integration'.

20 For Sayyid Ahmad Khan's elucidation of what he means by modern science, see his essay 'Ulum-e jadida' in Khan 1984: vol. 7, pp. 211–12.

21 The text I have used is Khan 1913.

22 For a full discussion of Sayyid Ahmad Khan's method of exegesis, see Troll 1978/9: 160–70, and Ahmad 1967: 42–8.

23 See also Sir Sayyid Ahmad Khan, 'Madhhabi khayal zamana-e qadim awr zamana-e jadid ka', in Khan 1984: vol. 3, p. 27, where he contrasts the older belief that prophets are confirmed by miracles with the new principle that they are confirmed by nature (*naichar*).

24 This is discussed fully in Shackle and Majeed 1997.

25 This is dealt with in detail by Shackle and Majeed 1997.

26 This is fully discussed in the standard work by Ali 1988.

27 See also Al-Azmeh's superb essays 'The Discourse of Cultural Authenticity: Islamist revivalism and Enlightenment universalism' and 'Islamist Revivalism and Western Ideologies' in the same volume, pp. 39–59 and 77–88 respectively.

28 This translation is taken from Shackle and Majeed 1997, which also discusses the cyclical character of the poem in more detail.

29 See also on this type of exegesis, Al-Azmeh 1993: 136-7.

30 Cantwell Smith has discussed the virtues with which Indian Muslim biographers in the nineteenth and twentieth centuries invested the figure of the Prophet. In this context, he notes that these virtues are typical of 'early capitalist society' and that the 'entire axiology may be subsumed under the liberal conception of duty'. The Prophet of these biographies is a 'liberal Muhammad within a capitalist society'. See Smith 1985: 74, 76.

31 This is discussed fully in Shackle and Majeed 1997.

32 For a more detailed account, see Shackle and Majeed 1997.

33 For which, see Shackle and Majeed 1997.

34 For a more detailed discussion, see Shackle and Majeed 1997.

35 For which, see the illuminating comments in Pritchett 1994: 43-5.

36 Madness was close to Hali in a number of ways. His father died when he was young, and as his mother became insane, he was raised by his older brother and sister (see Hali, 'Ap biti', in Hali 1964: 282; and Minault 1986: 5). Later in his life, Hali was to look after his mad grandson at Panipat (see Abdul Haq, 'Hali', in Haq 1950: 143).

2

The Limits of the Sacred
The Epistemology of 'Abd al-Karim Soroush

JOHN COOPER

Within the larger context of the meeting of Islam and modernity, the absorbtion of the natural and social sciences and technologies into Muslim societies has provided a particularly resonant example of the intellectual conflicts that have arisen over the last two centuries.[1] The history of debates within Muslim societies around Islam and science clearly shows various phases, of which one of the most recent has centred around the slogan of the 'Islamization of knowledge' (see Al-Azmeh 1996: 120–2). In the last half century, a variety of circumstances has forced this particular debate to the centre in many areas in the Islamic world, nowhere more evidently than within the Shi'i world and specifically among Iranian writers. At the core of the problems discussed is the perception of an anxiety-laden dichotomy between a Muslim's individual and social life, strongly influenced on many levels by science and technology, and what is expressed as the civilization or culture of an almost by-gone era, many of whose elements continue to influence that Muslim's personality and way of thinking (see, e.g., the remarks of Iran's recently elected president in Khatemi 1997: 2ff). In this connection, one Western writer has drawn attention to the desire of many Muslim religious intellectuals 'not to "suffer" modernity but actively accept and foster modernization, and to do so in a religious context that is in harmony with the indigenous culture' (Stowasser 1994:5).

Of the several contemporary Iranian contributors to this debate, perhaps the most outstanding and controversial has been 'Abd al-Karim Soroush. He came to prominence in Iran in the 1980s in the wake of the educational reforms following the 1979 Islamic Revolution, but has only recently attracted attention outside his own country. This has in great part been due to a shift in his lecturing and writings from epistemological considerations to a more overtly political discourse on the nature of government within Islamic, or, more generally, religious, societies. One of the consequences of the controversy this shift has inevitably courted within Iran has been that he has spent, albeit reluctantly, more time in Europe and America, presenting his ideas not only to audiences with an Iranian or Islamic background but also to a larger public through the press (see, e.g., his interviews in *The Guardian*, 6 and 7 June 1996, and the article in *Time*, 23 June 1997). He has thereby started to attract greater international attention, and has become one of the small group of Muslim scholars who have come to represent, both within the Muslim world and to those beyond, what might be called a 'critical Islam'. However, this essay is less concerned with Soroush's recent writings,[2] and more with earlier concerns in which he focused on the nature of the relation between science and religion.

In common with most of the writers who aim to open up a critical debate within Muslim societies on epistemology, interpretation, and historicity, Soroush wishes to situate himself within a tradition, not break with it. It is, as it were, a matter of reclaiming a portion of the past long relegated to the margins, but now in urgent need of being brought to the centre, into the main body of the text. Hence the common complaint from such figures that they have to deal with attacks from two opposed quarters: the 'modernists', who accuse them of ultimately doing no more than reinforcing the prejudices of the past; and the 'Islamists', for whom they represent yet another fifth column for the ambitions of Western expansionism. Their claim to belong to an (alternative) Islamic tradition is thus at once part of a rhetorical argument and of an intellectual strategy which aims to achieve a conceptual unity wherein individual and social experience come at least to speak on the same terms as the cultural. It is therefore with an examination of the way in which Soroush perceives his intellectual genealogy and with his depiction of a typology of Islamic reform that this essay is mainly concerned, and, in this context, with the tensions in his writings between the reclaimed past and the realities of the present.

'Abd al-Karim Soroush[3] was born on 'Ashura (10 Muharram/15 December) 1945 in south Tehran. He followed a conventional pri-

mary education, and after one year of secondary education enrolled in
the 'Alavi High School, newly founded by two pious bazaar merchants
under the influence of clerical figures who were becoming concerned
at the marginalization of religious education in the secondary curricu-
lum (see Boroujerdi 1996: 92). It was in this environment, and through
an introduction while still at school to the Husayniyye-ye Irshad (on
the history of this institution see, inter alia, Chehabi 1990: 202–7),
that Soroush first came into contact with Murtaza Mutahhari (1920–
79) (see, inter alia, ter Haar 1990, Dabashi 1993: 147–215) and 'Ali
Shari'ati (1933–77) (see, inter alia, Dabashi 1993: 102–46, Rahnema
1994, and Boroujerdi 1996: 105–15). The atmosphere of the
Husayniyye-ye Irshad did not apparently greatly appeal to him, although these two figures deeply influenced, and continue to influence,
him. He went on to Tehran University, where he read pharmacology,
obtaining a PhD in 1968. He also privately studied philosophy during
his university years with a religious scholar and bazaar merchant to
whom he had been recommended by Mutahhari.

After national military service, and a brief period in the Public
Health Department in Bushehr, and later in Tehran, Soroush pro-
ceeded to Britain, where he enrolled in the MSc course in analytic
chemistry at London University in 1973. Upon completing this degree, he decided to pursue interests which had been preoccupying him
for some time in the history and philosophy of science by becoming a
PhD student at the Chelsea College of Science and Technology, later
amalgamated into King's College London. His thesis, however, remained incomplete, as events in Iran drew him back in 1979.

While in London, Soroush was, like many of the Iranian expatriate
student population, actively involved in religio-political activities, first
in the Muslim Youth Association (MYA), and later in a breakaway
group who set themselves up in the Hammersmith Imambara in West
London, which, after the Islamic Revolution in Iran, became the centre for an Iranian student organization, the Kanun-e Tauhid. The
Imambara became a vibrant centre of Iranian student activism in the
period leading up to the Revolution; and it was here, in 1977, that the
body of Shari'ati was brought when he died suddenly at Southampton
almost immediately after arriving in Britain, his wife having been prevented from leaving Iran by SAVAK (see Rahnema 1994: 242–3).
Soroush was involved in the reception of Shari'ati's remains in Lon-

don, from where they were taken for burial at the Zaynabiyya, the tomb of the Imam Husayn b. 'Ali's sister near Damascus, with Musa al-Sadr leading the prayer (see Chehabi 1990: 209–10).

It was also during this period in London in the seventies that Soroush began lecturing and writing. A book attacking the Marxism of the Sazman-e Mujahidin-e Khalq-e Iran[4] (Soroush 1977a) was one such work, compiled from lectures, while another on ethics, in particular, the 'is/ought' fallacy (Soroush 1979), and a work which approached the subjects of monotheism and resurrection through Mulla Sadra's metaphysical theory of substantial motion (harakat-e jawhari) (Soroush 1977a) were both conceived and published as books. The Safavid philosopher's magnum opus, the Asfar, was one of the few books which Soroush had brought with him from Iran when he came to study in Britain.[5]

Upon his return to Iran in 1979, Soroush took up a post at the Daneshkade-ye Tarbiyat-e Mu'allim (Teachers' Training College), and began the private study of Islamic jurisprudence (usul al-fiqh). His appointment as Director of the College's Islamic Culture Group, set up in the first wave of Islamicization after the Revolution, prepared the way for his inclusion in the Mu'assase-ye (later Shura-ye) 'Ali-ye Inqilab-e Farhangi (The Supreme Cultural Revolution Institute/Council). The Cultural Revolution had been announced by Khomeini in April 1980, and was a venture with which both the Islamic Republican Party and the liberal wing of the Revolution, which included such figures as Mehdi Bazargan and Bani Sadr, were in agreement, although the liberals eventually lost out to the IRP and in turn became the object of the Cultural Revolution's attention. The beginning of the Cultural Revolution also, incidentally, provided the occasion for some of the first outings by violent bands of 'club-wielders' on university campuses, whose slogan 'Hizb faqat hizbu-'llah, rahbar faqat Ruhu-'llah (The only party is God's party, the only leader is Ruhollah [Khomeini])' gave the name Hizbollah to such 'impromptu' shows of mob force, instrumental in Bani Sadr's demise as well as later in events in Soroush's life. The Cultural Revolution Council was set up by Khomeini in response to the occupation by radical students of the universities, initially Tehran University and the Teachers' Training College, and the subsequent closure of the universities by the Revolutionary Council. Its formation was thus a way of both institutionalizing this protest, and limiting its demands. In the end, despite predictions of twenty or even thirty years' closure, the universities opened again in 1983, and the large part of the work of the Council became that of revising syllabuses and producing new textbooks, not only for the universities, but also for elementary and high schools (on the Cultural Revolution, see Moaddel 1993: 212–13).

Soroush resigned from the Cultural Revolution Council in 1984, when its membership was augmented to seventeen, thus ending his involvement in government organizations apart from an occasional consultative role. He also resigned from the Teacher Training College, and took up a post, which he held up to 1997, as Research Fellow at the Institute for Cultural Research and Studies. He set up the department for the philosophy and history of science at the Humanities Research Institute, and, following the default trend among academics in Iran to occupy a bewildering number of positions, he has held posts as university professor, researcher at the Iranian Academy of Philosophy, and member of the Iranian Academy of Sciences.

Beyond his official teaching, he has lectured both within the universities and outside on a wide variety of subjects, and has become associated with 'kalam-e jadid', a modern theological trend which arose out of the perceived need for Muslim scholars to provide a credible response to modernity and secularism. Mysticism has also been a focus for his lectures and writings, with two books providing commentaries on sermons by the first Shi'i Imam, 'Ali (Soroush 1992 and 1994b), a work on devotional literature, and, recently, as a fitting monument to his attachment to the poetry of Jalal al-Din Rumi which pervades all of his works, an edition of the latter's Mathnavi (Soroush 1996) based on the earliest Konya manuscript. Some of Soroush's lectures end up in collected volumes, but many of them are distributed in the form of audio cassettes and videos, long a popular medium in Iran for the transmission of intellectual debates.

As a result of the contestative nature of much of his writing and lecturing since he began the publication of a series of articles under the general title of Qabd-u-bast-e ti'urik-e shari'at (The Theoretic Contraction and Expansion of the Shari'a: a theory of the evolution of religion) in 1988,[6] Soroush has increasingly drawn the enmity of certain clerics, government figures, and the popular mob. A group calling itself the Ansar-e Hizbollah (Supporters of God's Party) violently targeted his

lectures, forcing him to suspend them in 1996, and ideological problems also led to the curtailment of his popular lectures at the Imam
Sadeq Mosque in north Tehran. Since then, Soroush has spent much
of his time outside Iran, although it is rumoured that he has been required to remain there since his return from a lecture tour of North
America in the spring of 1997.

The best entry into Soroush's ideas is perhaps via the 1990 collection *Qabd-u-bast-e ti'urik-e shari'at*. *Qabd* and *bast* are two terms used
within the Islamic mystical tradition to refer respectively to the con-
striction and dilation of the mystic's heart, its depression and elation,
and the expression of its fear and hope (see Schimmel 1994: 251).
Soroush uses this terminology to refer to the alternating moments of
epistemic openness and closure of Islamic societies. The main thrust
of Soroush's argument in these articles is directed towards situating
the religious sciences within the larger framework of human knowledge in general, and in particular within the context of philosophy and,
more recently, the natural and social sciences in particular. The theoretical basis for this endeavour lies in what he sees as the crucial
distinction which must be made between two layers of any religious
discourse: at one level there is the religion itself, immutable, essential,
and sacred; while at the second level there is the human understanding
of religion, about which there is nothing sacred, and nothing which
cannot be the object of questioning and criticism. At this second level
are the texts of Islamic scholarship throughout the centuries. Moreover, the Islamic religious sciences, like any other product of human
understanding, are in a constant process of evolution and perfecting,
an advance in one passing on in turn to affect the others (see, in general, Soroush 1990). As several authors have remarked, the problem
with this pragmatically a priori division is where precisely to draw the
boundary between the two levels, a problem which Soroush leaves
largely undetermined (see, for example, Rajaee 1993:114, and Schirazi
1997: 282–3).

The various ideas which Soroush develops in the course of his argument bear upon the problems which faced those grappling with the
educational reforms of the Cultural Revolution, among whom was
Soroush himself. In particular, some way had to be found for dealing
with the legacy of the confrontation that had been building up since
the middle of the nineteenth century between the millennium-long tra-

ditions of the religious schools and the ethos of the more recently established universities and technical colleges which lay at the apex of a
state educational system, a system which had become increasingly associated with the various political reforms which the country had
undergone. Soroush started to publish these articles four years after
leaving the Cutural Revolution Council, and they clearly reflect his
soul-searching over these problems and the conclusions to which he
had come. They also clearly demonstrate his increasing despair over
the possibility of a meeting-point being found for these two wielders
of cultural capital where each could strengthen the other. It would
seem that the debate was already resolving itself into two opposed
stances: either the state educational and research system should be
under the guidance of the religious schools (the *hawza*), which would
of course have to adapt themselves formally to the requirements of a
modern educational system in terms of syllabuses and examinations,
or the religious schools would have to submit themselves to the supervision of the state system. A conflict had been thus set up in which the
victor would carry off the prize of cultural hegemony.

It seems right to see Soroush as moving towards an alternative approach, sidestepping the dichotomy of the running debate, and seeking
a different kind of solution in which neither side need lose face; but he
inevitably drew the swords of the religious establishment. Too much
was at stake to leave unchallenged a public discussion which could sow
seeds of doubt about the claims made by the religious schools to religious knowledge. The religious sciences as studied within the religious
schools are the product of the accumulated effort of centuries of scholarly activity, and are organized into an impressive epistemological
structure whose claims to certainty are uncompromising and strenu-
ously defended. If that certainty was to be undermined, so would the
authority of the religious schools within society and their very existence would be threatened. Gradually Soroush's lectures and articles
acquired more and more of the character of polemic, and the search
for a solution turned into an increasingly acrimonious confrontation.
He began to present a more personalized discourse, in which his intellectual autobiography came to figure prominently, and as part of this
strategy he came to construct in the late 1980s a kind of Islamic reformist genealogy for his own positions. Several lectures and essays
containing his reflections on the figures of the past and present who

had had the greatest influence on him were eventually collected and published in 1994 in *Qisseh-e arbab-e ma'rifat* (The Tale of the Masters of Knowledge). Eight chapters were devoted to Ghazali, Fayz-e Kashani,[7] Rumi, Hafez, Khomeini, and Shari'ati, and to comparisons between them, but many other figures were included incidentally.

In a chapter entitled 'Yesterday's sun, today's elixir' ('Aftab-e diruz va kimiya-ye emruz') previously delivered as a lecture in 1989 as a memorial to Khomeini, who had passed away only ten days previously, Soroush set out the framework for a taxonomy of religious reform. He defines revivalists (*muhyiyan*) as those who, although they see nothing missing or deficient in God's revelation, nevertheless perceive weaknesses in the temporal, geographical, historical manifestations of religion, that which is 'in the hands of men' (Soroush 1994a: 362). Such revivalists may see their task in a variety of forms. It may be that they have to perform a trimming (*pirayishi*) function, removing extraneous, foreign elements and restoring the purity of the religion. This is accompanied by the feeling that the reality or truth of religion has somehow become hidden to man. Or it may be that they have to perform an enriching (*arayishi*) function, neglect and abandonment of religion having led to the need for a restoration of health and vitality. Here it is a question of the need to return to the completeness that religion should manifest within itself (Soroush 1994a: 362–3). He specifically mentions Abu Hamid Ghazali, Fayz-e Kashani, Muhammad 'Abduh, and 'Ali Shari'ati as examples of revivalists in these two modes.

Beyond these two functions, however, a revivalist may see himself as having to restore the capability and power (*tavana'i*) of religion, and this can be done in two ways. From within, the task is one of perfecting religious understanding and knowledge, and this can be done through concentrating at one level on the *furu'*, the legal aspects of the religion, or, more profoundly, on the *usul*, the fundamentals. From a more external perspective, it can be done by a kind of bricolage (*iltiqat*) from different sources, although this approach can meet with varying degrees of success (Soroush 1994a: 362–3). Further still, the revivalists may perceive that religion has become weak not because of anything intrinsic to it but because its practitioners, the believers, have. This, he says, is what prompts figures like Jamal al-Din Afghani/Asadabadi (1838 or 39–97) to turn towards political activity.

All revivalists are responding in their different ways to the presence of stagnation (*rukud*), rigidity (*jumud*), and laxity (*rikhvat*) within the religious community, a state of affairs which has come about as a result of a threat to its religious integrity. This stagnation leads in turn to the setting in of a kind of dogmatism (*dugmatism*) in which the door to reasoning is closed. In one of his typical turns of phrase, Soroush characterizes this as a moment in which sanctity (*taqaddus*) is sought in petrification or fossilisation (*tajahhur*). The very notion of thinking things through becomes an abomination, an audacity in the face of the 'law-giver' (*Shari'*). This is how he understands the historical contexts which gave rise to the Hanbalis amongst the Sunnis and the Akhbaris amongst the Shi'a (Soroush 1994a: 365). Also associated with religious stagnation and the rise of dogmatism is fatalism. Religious thought, albeit possessing its own realm, is nevertheless intrinsically related to all other branches of knowledge, principally metaphysics, but also knowledge of the natural world and human society.[8] When these links become severed as a result of the supposed profanity of reason and thought, the events of the natural and human, social worlds come to be seen by people as the result of direct celestial intervention. Consequently the idea that human action may improve situations gives way to an attitude in which God is expected to redress injustices and avert disasters (Soroush 1994a: 365).

In the same lecture Soroush throws light on his understanding of the relation between mysticism (*'irfan*) and revivalism, a relation particularly to the fore in any consideration of Khomeini. He criticizes the tendency among mystics to use retreat from the world as a kind of vaccination against the diseases of this life. In this context he inscribes Muhammad Iqbal into his revivalist genealogy by quoting him on the contrast between the mystic and the prophetic types of consciousness: the former would ascend to highest heaven, but only the latter would return (Soroush 1994a: 367 quoting Iqbal 1982: 127). Again, a one-sided mystical approach to religion leads to a fatalistic attitude towards society and human history, for it encourages a view of the social order as natural and unchanging, ever thus. Ghazali, he remarks, was inclined to take the position that we have no responsibility for history; to stand aside from its flow will not cause the world to collapse (Soroush 1994a: 374).

The ideas represented above have, of course, been taken out of their context. This lecture was intended to mourn the passing of, and celebrate the unique qualities of, the founder of the Islamic Republic of Iran, who, for Soroush, displayed the characteristics of a religious revivalist as he had outlined them, including a mystical aspect which seems for Soroush to approach the prophetic type of consciousness. In another commemorative lecture given two years earlier in 1987 to mark the tenth anniversary of the death of 'Ali Shari'ati, however, the same considerations can be seen to be influencing what he has to say. Not perhaps worked through so systematically, but bringing out another aspect of revivalist psychology which, by the way it is expressed, seems to find its echo within Soroush's own autobiography.

The Shari'ati of this lecture, 'Doctor Shari'ati and the Opening up of Religious Thought', is a much more of a human individual than any other figure Soroush has depicted, apart perhaps from Rumi. The emphasis is on the existential qualities of the man, and Soroush remarks on Shari'ati's ability to look at himself from the outside.[9] His first observations are of a general nature, and on the propensity of religious societies to view themselves from the inside. It is much more arduous for them to see outside themselves, and even more so to look from outside at themselves. Here he uses the term 'religious enlightened thinkers' (*rowshanfikr-e dini*) to refer to those who have this capacity (Soroush 1994a: 384). Such people are necessarily ahead of their times and consequently benefit future generations more than their own, presumably because they map out a kind of path through their own personal struggles which can illuminate ways others will subsequently find easier to follow.

Adjectives which are used frequently in this lecture to refer to Shari'ati are *dardmand* and *dardshinas*, the first denoting the experience of anguish, specifically here the anguish arising out of the crisis of the times, the second the recognition and understanding of that anguish, perhaps what in English would be called 'dealing with' it. This understanding, *dardshinasi*, is not at the level of everyday life and its problems, but at a much deeper level where events are experienced which the majority do not even see. Furthermore, Shari'ati was not merely able to deal with this anguish, but, as it were, to take responsibility for it and face the consequences of the knowledge thereby attained (Soroush 1994a: 386–8). This lends to Shari'ati's life a heroic quality (*diliri*), the

living through of religious anguish, drawing inspiration as he often did
in his own lectures and writings from the lives of the Imams, particularly 'Ali b. Abi Talib and Husayn b. 'Ali. Shari'ati's inner struggle
arose, however, from a conflict peculiar to his times, and thus he becomes a model for those who experience within themselves the conflict
between deep religious faith and the knowledge sought and attained
outside the confines of a traditional Islamic culture. Stressing the aesthetic qualities of Shari'ati's thought and writings, Soroush calls for an
understanding of him, even an honouring of him, for those actions of
his which he freely chose to do (*af'al-e ikhtiyari*) rather than his native
qualities (*awsaf-e tabi'i*) (Soroush 1994a: 389).

For Soroush, the tensions experienced by Shari'ati which lend his
life its heroic qualities are mirrored in post-revolutionary Iranian society by the two tendencies, or 'flanks' (*janah*) as he calls them, which
characterize its response to the difficulties posed by the sudden projection of Islamic law into the arena created by the need to find new
and acceptable answers to that society's social and political problems.
These 'flanks' have come to be known as *fiqh-e sunnati* and *fiqh-e puya*.
Fiqh-e sunnati is the traditional approach, and regards the provision of
new rulings in Islamic law as being governed by the same methodological parameters that have governed their provision in the past and
that have been developed and elaborated on over the centuries. *Fiqh-e
puya* might be translated as dynamic *fiqh*; it maintains that the methodology of the past cannot by itself provide rulings for situations which
arise within a modern Islamic society. The traditional methodology is
outdated, and solutions based on it will inevitably be out of step with
the changing requirements of a society whose culture has been radically transformed by new modes of understanding of itself and the
natural world. For Soroush the difference between these two tendencies is a clear one. Traditional *fiqh* is in a kind of retreat, fearful of
contamination by foreign, non-Islamic thoughts and values, while 'dynamic *fiqh*' is forward-looking. It frames itself within the larger
perspective of questions such as: Can religious thinking have an hon-
ourable status among other ways of thinking (*makatib*)? Is it well
founded? Can it effectively solve the contemporary problems of mankind? (Soroush 1994a: 390.) It is thus an attempt to deal in broader
terms with the kinds of questions Shari'ati dealt with within himself.

In the context of Soroush's treatment of traditional and dynamic *fiqh* it is interesting to compare him with another intellectual of post-revolutionary Iran, Muhammad Mujtahid-e Shabistari. Some ten years his elder, Mujtahid-e Shabistari is a cleric from the religious schools, who held the position of director of the Islamic Centre in Hamburg in the seventies. This period in Europe allowed him to develop a proficient knowledge both of European languages and of Christian theology (Boroujerdi 1996: 168-9). His views on the discipline and practice of *fiqh* are similar to those of Soroush: he is highly critical of the present inability of the religious schools to come to terms with the findings of the modern sciences, particularly the social sciences, and with the questions raised in contemporary philosophical discourse (Schirazi 1996: 278). He bemoans the lack of a philosophy of civil rights in Muslim societies, or of any moral, economic, or political philosophy. Like Soroush, he rues the inability of Iran and other Islamic societies to take their place within international scientific communities, an inability born of their failure, as he sees it, to universalize their values and legal system (Boroujerdi 1996: 168). Yet his standing as a respected cleric allows him sometimes to be more outspoken than Soroush. He is daring in his categorical assertion that Revelation's primary function is to communicate divine values, not laws. Although Islam traditionally expresses itself through the legal endeavours of the *fuqaha'*, this is an accidental rather than an essential connection; the purpose of these endeavours is to constantly subject the laws and political decisions of society to arbitration before divine values (Schirazi 1997: 279-80, and the quotes therein). Such ideas clearly show his concern to confront the difficulties posed by the emergence of a political regime in Iran founded on the ideological premise of the *shari'a* and governance by the *faqih*, yet which is faced with a lack of specifically *shar'i* legislation to satisfy the legal demands of the society it governs. Mujtahid-e Shabistari's approach is through theology, both Christian and Muslim, rather than the natural sciences, though the social sciences play a central role in both his and Soroush's writings. He is also more articulate than Soroush on the boundary between what is purely religious and the human understanding of religion, but it is difficult not to contrast his status as a cleric with that of Soroush, the lay religious intellectual, and speculate on the relative freedom each experiences to express his ideas.

The first, and longest, essay in the *The Tale of the Masters of Knowledge* is a discussion of, and comparison between, Ghazali and his *Ihya'* and Fayz-e Kashani and his *Mahajja*,[10] two leading scholars separated by five centuries, the one a Sunni, the other a Shi'i. The first composed his *Revival (Ihya') of the Religious Sciences* as a compendium of the Sunni orthodoxy of his day into which he brought Sufism as the uniting thread breathing life into religious knowledge; the second reworked the text to reflect the mysticized Shi'ism of his day. According to Soroush the *Mahajja* is roughly three-quarters the text of the *Ihya'*, with certain omissions, and one quarter new material; many of the Sunni Traditions are replaced with Shi'i equivalents. Soroush returns to these two figures in his Shari'ati lecture and inserts them within the larger context of his reformist genealogy. Although we look back to Ghazali's time as one of the great periods in Islamic history, Ghazali saw it as one of decline in the religious sciences. There was observance of religious practices and application of the law; but 'all those jurists, theologians, and transmitters of *hadith*, all those schools, books, religious debates, [Ghazali] saw all of this, yet he said that these externals had had their innards squeezed out and destroyed, and that the reality of the *shari'a*, what he called *fiqh-e akhirat* (knowledge of [the law of] the Afterlife), had altogether been ignored' (Soroush 1994a: 402–3).

Soroush plays on the ambiguity of the words *zahir* and *batin*, at once the exoteric/esoteric dichotomy of Islamic thought, and an object's physical, material outward surface and inward parts, to supply his metaphor of squeezing the life out of religious form. In the terms of his theoretical framework, this is the mistake of taking the human understanding of religion to be religion itself. Ghazali, having perceived this malaise, sought to breathe life back into (again the literal meaning of *ihya'*) the empty skin of the Islamic religious sciences. Or again, in terms of Soroush's trimming/enriching metaphor, Ghazali saw the need to reform through a nurturing of the parts that had been abandoned and neglected. One specific way he chose to do this was by restoring to religious terminology the meanings current in the first Islamic century; Soroush explicitly mentions Ghazali's treatment in this fashion in the first book of the *Ihya'* of the words *fiqh* and *tafaqquh*, which originally denoted a much broader sense of religious understanding and investigation than merely that of what is lawful and what is unlawful (Soroush 1994a: 403).

Soroush then invokes Fayz-e Kashani as the reviver of Ghazali's revival (ihya'), but by transforming the locus of reform and revival from the Sunni schools of the Seljuqs to the Shi'i schools of the Safavids, Soroush authentically inserts reform into the context in which he needs to legitimate it for his argument to work. He is simultaneously undermining any claim by Shi'i ulama to exemption from the need for reform; any special claim, such as that they derive their authority from the Shi'i Imams and are thus without the circle of reform, now loses its power since four centuries ago a respected Shi'i scholar had insisted on the need for religious reform. What motivated both Ghazali and Fayz-e Kashani was the need to reform through enriching; they were both faced by a caricature (karikatur) of religion in which some parts were cancerously enlarged and deformed and others severely undernourished (Soroush 1994a: 404).

Returning to the Sunni sphere and moving nearer to the present, revival, although of the trimming rather than the enriching variety, is to be found in the Salafi movement started by Jamal al-Din Afghani/ Asadabadi and Muhammad 'Abduh, but again this used the strategic tool of a return to the origins of Islam, to a revival of its ethical, inward, esoteric dimensions (Soroush 1994a: 404).

All this has been an elaborate mining of the organic images of the gardener cultivating his plot, pruning, fertilizing, reviving his plants and restoring them to health; but when Soroush turns to consider Muhammad Iqbal he transposes his argument from revival (ihya') to reconstruction (baz-sazi), moving, as it were, from the title of Ghazali's Ihya' to that of Iqbal's The Reconstruction of Religious Thought in Islam (Iqbal 1982). The imagery then changes from that of horticulture to that of architecture, which seems to betoken a shift from the innocence of the past to the starker realities of the present day. 'Imagine,' he says, 'that you live to the end of your life in one building, and never leave it. Of course, you know all the rooms and corridors; perhaps, bit by bit, you get to know its bricks, lights, ceilings, floors, heights and dimensions, and count and measure them. Yet, despite all this, there is one thing you clearly do not know, and that is the architecture of the building, its external appearance, and its situation vis-à-vis other buildings around it' (Soroush 1994a: 405). Now imagine that you go up onto the roof and see these other buildings; and if you were to go beyond that and leave the village or town in which you live, you would then have a completely different idea of your own house, an external perspective, not an internal one. The idea of reconstruction would now come to you with this view from outside, for at this moment you begin to realize what can be done with the same materials; you see how others have constructed their buildings (Soroush 1994a: 406).

Reformers such as Ghazali and Fayz-e Kashani operated on the inside of Islam, opening locked doors to hidden apartments, but the likes of Iqbal have the view from outside looking in, watching Islam in the larger context and seeing all the comings and goings. It is this which gives the Muslim in the modern world his unique understanding and responsibilities, which makes his situation so different from that of his forebears, and it is this which should inform our understanding of Shari'ati, who took so much of his inspiration from Iqbal (Soroush 1994a: 407).

Soroush now inserts a remark on the way in which thought is passed on from generation to generation, and returns to the horticultural imagery he used before. Thoughts are like seeds; they come to fruition, are broadcast, and settle in the minds of others where they are watered and grow in their turn into plants (Soroush 1994a: 407–8). Having established one line of his genealogy—Ghazali, Fayz, Iqbal, Shari'ati—he now invokes another—'Ali b. Abi Talib, Rumi, Iqbal, Shari'ati. If the first stressed the scholarly aspect, the second serves to accentuate the spiritual. In these genealogies, each figure acts as a mirror reflecting the previous, or, in terms of his horticultural imagery, as the seedbed in which the seed sown by the previous figure germinates and grows. The Iqbal–Shari'ati link provides an apt example for how the seed from one place, i.e. India, can end up germinating in another, Iran; Iqbal, one of the engineers (*mohandesan*) of new Islamic thought finds his apprentice in Shari'ati (Soroush 1994a: 409).

Reconstruction is an endless process, but not one of deriving new legal rulings. It is the outcome, the 'crop' (*mahsul*), gathered from knowledge of the structure of a religion, the relationship between its parts, its historical development, and its position with regard to other religions and systems of thought (Soroush 1994a: 409). Reconstruction is re-comprehending, re-understanding, and may not always be comprehensible to the ordinary person. It requires a certain level of understanding to recognize the important and great ideas that spring up in the process of reconstruction, and it is essential to realize that what matters is the questions that a great thinkers raises in society, not the answers, which is what we may want as the result of our laziness and bad habits (Soroush 1994a: 410). Although answers are important, it is the correct formulation of questions which is of greater significance. When Shari'ati is criticized it is usually for his answers, but what makes him an important figure is the questions he asked—dig here in the garden, he says, not out there in the desert (Soroush 1994a: 411).

In the rest of the lecture on Shari'ati, the focus changes, and from the establishing of genealogies Soroush now switches to a different kind of argument of which it is only necessary here to give the outline. The purpose is to defend the objective study of religion, primarily against the accusation that such an approach somehow evinces lack of faith. Soroush moves through a brief exposition of the difference between instrumentalist and realist theories in the philosophy of science to defend Shari'ati against the criticism that he regarded religious beliefs merely as a means to the reconstruction and empowering of religion, and that he was ultimately entirely indifferent to their truth or falsity, whether they correctly described reality (Soroush 1994a: 412–13).

Two kinds of thinking are required, Soroush says, in reconstructing religion. On the one hand there must be knowledge based on one's love of, and respect for, religion, imbued with the awe of the sacred; on the other one must have an analytic, anatomical knowledge. The difference between a religious 'alim (sing. of 'ulama, but here Soroush uses the plural 'aliman) and a religious roshanfikr (enlightened thinker, i.e. a reconstructing intellectual) is that the former only permits the former kind of knowledge and understanding of religion. The roshanfikr can, or rather has to, have both kinds of knowledge, and this is because the 'alim only sees religion from the inside whereas the roshanfikr has the perspective of one looking in from the outside as well. All of which imposes on him the difficult but necessary responsibility of bridging the gap between the sacred and the profane, between heaven and earth (Soroush 1994a: 414–20).

This reading of Soroush's lectures on Khomeini and Shari'ati has endeavoured to gain some insight into his main epistemological concerns and into his manner of argumentation. Certain aspects of his style have not been mentioned, specifically his use of poetry, mainly that of Rumi;

and there are other aspects of the language he uses—his employment
of obscure literary words and phrases, for example— which it would
be impossible to examine in the context of this essay. It has to be said
that there are those who find his style laborious and uninspiring; it
does combine the love of both novelty and tradition which is characteristic of his thought as well, and this can be tiresome when translated
into style. But it is also the case that others find the style of his lectures
and writings exciting and attractive. He has created a new rhetoric to
convey his ideas, and it would be difficult to deny that the rhetoric and
the ideas do complement each other.

Although Soroush has his defenders among the more adventurous
clergy, his main audience is the large number of young university and
college educated Iranians with a commitment to Islam, yet who have
not received much, if any, formal religious education within the religious schools. More often than not their religious commitment comes
from reading and listening to tapes and videos by writers who use a
language they can understand, one which formulates ideas in ways
which they have access to and can employ themselves. The religious
schools remain remote and the language used by its students difficult
to assimilate and master. Soroush bridges the gap for this audience
between the language of their everyday lives and the language of the
religious culture which provides the larger context. He uses Arabic
expressions which help to link his ideas to that larger context, yet he
employs a creative Persian idiom which coveys the excitement of his
ideas. However, underlying this facility the tension between the old
and new remains, exposed but never quite resolved.

Soroush's discourse always seems to be striving for legitimacy; hardly
surprising as the odds against him speaking and publishing freely mount
up. Criticism of his earlier writings in which he presented the main
ideas in his theory of the expansion and contraction of religious thought
brought him to reconsider the manner in which they were to be defended. There was a move from a more 'scientific' to a more rhetorical
exposition. Although he had always written and spoken about poetry
and mysticism as well as the more philosophical and theological subjects, the two became more and more entwined. Imagery comes to serve
as a principal vehicle in his works. A certain kind of harmony is achieved,
but there is a new tension between the organic world of gardens, seeds,
and plants and the more artificial world of construction, buildings,

towns, engineers, and architecture, reflecting the *roshanfikr*'s knowledge from the inside and knowledge from the outside. His fundamental ideas remain the same, but the effects of a general lack of acceptance by the religious schools which constantly undermined the legitimacy of these ideas can be detected, as too can the pressure of the increasing animosity of the more conservative revolutionary clerisy who rely on the unquestioning allegiance of their mass supporters.

The shift to the more autobiographical and personal style of *The Tale of the Masters of Knowledge* seems to be a response to this rejection. While continuing with a discourse of reason, Soroush began to construct for himself a legitimating genealogy, overlapping that of the epistemological tradition of the schools, yet uncompromisingly incorporating figures like Shari'ati who had never been entirely acceptable. At the same time, and surely in some part as a result of this newly-created and appealing legitimacy, he found a larger audience, one that could claim his autobiography for themselves and could thereby attach themselves to his epistemological genealogy, at once Islamic yet also including the figures of Western thought whom they had encountered in their university syllabuses. This dimension in Soroush's writings, the dimension of the natural and social sciences and their history and philosophy, has not been examined in this essay, although it has been alluded to. It has, however, been addressed by others (see Boroujerdi 1996, Rajaee 1993).

It might perhaps seem inevitable, given the combination of rejection and latterly animosity from parts of the religious establishment and an increasing popularity among the young, that Soroush should have moved in the last few years towards a more political kind of writing. Yet it is one of the leitmotifs of *The Tale of the Masters of Knowledge* that what counts of a person's actions are those he voluntarily chooses, not those which circumstances and his nature force upon him. It would also seem that a society like that of present-day Iran presents a striking and contemporary locus in which to observe the way in which the epistemic realm is closely intertwined with religion and politics; one of many, it is true, but one with its own very specific characteristics. Writings such a those of Soroush can be seen as attempts to unravel this skein, and the examination of them as avenues to understanding the interdependence of these three dimensions of human life.

Notes

1 The literature on this subject is now considerable, but for a stimulating, if somewhat unsystematic, account see Hoodbhoy 1991.

2 Several writers have discussed Soroush's political ideas, among which attention should be drawn to those of Boroujerdi (1994, rev. 1996), Vakili (1996), and Schirazi (1997: ch 16).

3 The information on the biography of Soroush was collated mainly from the 'Biography of Dr Soroush' on the Seraj Internet Home Page (http:/dspace.dial.pipex.com/town/parade/ac889) and the brief details in Boroujerdi 1996: 158–9, confirmed and elaborated on in a personal discussion with Soroush in London on 18 November 1996.

4 On the Mujahidin, see Abrahamian's critical work (1989).

5 The other three were Fayz-e Kashani's *al-Mahajja al-baida'* (a Shi'i reworking of Ghazali's *Ihya 'ulum al-din*), Rumi's *Mathnawi*, and the *Divan* of Hafiz (Soroush 1989: xxi).

6 The first article, 'Bast-u-qabd-e ti'urik-e shari'at: nazariyye-ye takamul-e dini', appeared in *Kayhan-e Farhangi* 5/ii (1988); the collection was published in book form in Soroush 1990.

7 Muhammad b. Murtada, Fayz-e Kashani (c. 1598–1680), a noted Safavid religious theologian, philosopher, scholar of *hadith*, and poet, who studied under, and was the son-in-law of, Mulla Sadra.

8 Soroush is elsewhere much more precise about his understanding of the interpenetration of human knowledge. He summarizes his position in three principles (Soroush 1990: 278): (i) the understanding of religion (*shari'at*) both affects and is affected by human knowledge, the whole being characterized by coherence, continuous dialogue and give and take; (ii) any contraction or expansion in human knowledge entails a corresponding contraction or expansion in religious understanding; (iii) human knowledge—of nature and existence, science and philosophy—is constantly evolving and subject to contraction and expansion. This third principle he calls the Principle of Evolution (*tahavvul*).

9 This is Soroush's reading of Shari'ati's famous anti-alienation slogan 'baz-gasht bi khish' (return to the self), which itself forms the subject of another lecture (1994a: 441–62). On Shari'ati's *'baz-gasht'* see Dabashi 1993: 144.

10 'Jame-ye tahdhib bar tan-e Ihya': tatbiq-e naqdana-ye al-Mahajja al-baida' va Ihya' 'ulum al-din' ('The Clothing of Revision on the Body of Revival: a critical comparison of *al-Mahajja al-baida'* and *Ihya' 'ulum al-din'*), in Soroush 1994a: 1–133; previouly published in the magazine *Farhang*, nos 4 and 5, 1989.

3

Islamic Scholar and Religious Leader:
Shaikh Muhammad Sa'id Ramadan al-Buti

ANDREAS CHRISTMANN

I ask myself, what is it that keeps me writing and writing? As for my
fame I got more of it than I had hoped and expected. As for my
property and wealth Allah blessed me with more than I need. And
as for the respect of people I got more than I deserve. In the end I
found out that all this is fruitless and tasteless unless it is an individual prayer for me by an unknown brother in Islam. (Muhammad
Sa'id Ramadan al-Buti)

Introduction

In the light of his high reputation and great influence on life in modern Syria, it is surprising that Shaikh al-Buti's work and thoughts are
highly under-represented and almost unknown in European academic
literature. He appears in all the media—as the weekly Qur'an and
hadith-exegete on TV frequently as preacher on the radio and as the
author of several dozen books and polemics in bookshops. In his Friday sermons in the Jami' Mawlana al-Rifa'i Mosque, and in his lectures
held twice a week at the Jam'i Tinjiz Mosque, al-Buti addresses hundreds of people each time, many of them standing in the mosque
courtyard following his speech over the loudspeakers. A professor at
the University of Damascus, al-Buti has a considerable formative influence on future generations of teachers who will teach religion and
shari'a in state primary and secondary schools. Even people who do
not practise religion actively have come across al-Buti's name, and know
where and when he can be heard. Also non-Muslims admit to having
attended one or another al-Buti session to find out what distinguishes

this scholar from the others. Indeed, Shaikh al-Buti synthesizes spiritual leadership and Islamic scholarship in a unique way. Just consider his function as *the* Muslim TV-preacher, who popularizes Islamic knowledge and ideals in the political context of Syria, where any public statement which is different from the official Ba'th-party line may lead to imprisonment or even torture. Of course, there are other 'ulama', too, who appear on Syrian TV as religious authorities, like, for example, Shaikh Marwan Shaikhu, a senior officer in the Ministry of Endowment who holds sermons every Friday on radio, weekly *fatawa* and Qur'an programmes on television, as well as daily *iftar*-speeches during Ramadan. But al-Buti's fixed broadcasting time (Wednesday 7 pm) and the thematic series of lectures, in which he walks the tightrope to verify *shar'i* rules in the light of secular law and society, have turned al-Buti into a widely accepted—sometimes fiercely questioned—public institution, advising Syrian Muslims, even in the country's remotest parts, on current issues of mainstream orthodox Islam.[1]

This essay is, in a way, the first attempt at a broader European appraisal of al-Buti's life and work. It will paint a portrait of a thinker who represents the majority in Sunni Islam—or 'middle path Islam'—in Syria finding its place between the current realities of a secular state and an ideal Islamic society. To begin with, the essay introduces the biographical details of al-Buti's life and the main intellectual influences from people and events arround him, then his *oeuvre*, style and personality. Second, it will explore the main thoughts and views of al-Buti, taking into account the fact that he writes and speaks in two different roles, as an Islamic scholar and as a religious leader, which is perhaps a unique situation in contemporary modern Syria.

Life

Muhammad Sa'id ibn Ramadan 'Umar al-Buti was born in 1929 in the small Turkish village of Jilika on the island of Butan (Arabic: Jazira Ibn 'Umar) in Western Anatolia, which 'suffered from the spread of ignorance and the need for culture (*thaqafa*) and knowledge (*ma'rifa*)' (Buti 1995: 14). He was the second child and only son of the Kurdish scholar Mulla Ramadan al-Buti. His ancestors had all been farmers and so it was al-Buti's father who—supported by his mother, a woman 'full of piety (*salah*) and devotion (*taqwa*)' (Buti 1995: 14)—had studied Islamic sciences (*al-'ulum al-islamiyya*) against his father's will and established the family's scholarly traditions—continued by Shaikh al-Buti and his son Muhammad Tawfiq Ramadan al-Buti. All we know about al-Buti's mother is that she gave birth to three girls who all died very young, whereupon she fell ill herself and died when al-Buti was 13 years old. By that time al-Buti's family had been in Damascus for several years. In 1934 they fled from the secularization measures of Kemal Ataturk, who—as al-Buti put it—'insulted Islam',[2] through Halwat, al-Hasaka, Deir az-Zor, ar-Raqqa, al-Hama, and Homs to Damascus, where they settled down in the Kurdish quarter of Rukn al-Din. al-Buti began to study religion, Arabic, and mathematics in a private school in Suq al-Saruja, an old city neighbourhood, then—at the very early age of eleven—the Qur'an and the Prophet's biography with Shaikh Hasan Habannakah and Shaikh al-Maradini in the Jami' Manjak Mosque in al-Midan, and, eventually, when the mosque was transformed into the Institute of Islamic Orientation (Ma'had *al-Tawjih al-Islami*), he studied Qur'anic exegesis, logic, rhetoric, and the fundamental principles of Islamic law (*usul al-fiqh*)—until 1953. And yet his main and most influential teacher was, until that time, his father.

According to al-Buti's memories, his father was a most pious man, who, unlike most of his contemporary fellows, already as an undergraduate did not see Islam as a source of emotionless casuistry (Buti 1995: 17) but as a way to inner perfection, through unremitting Qur'an recitation (*tilawa*), night prayers (*tahajjud*), hundredfold repetitions of *dhikr* and *wird* formulas (invocations of Allah), and unremitting communion with Allah (*munajah*), discipline (*wara'*) and asceticism (*zuhd*). His father's habitual performance of these extensive religious rituals, in spite of his lifelong proneness to a mysterious illness which caused temporal paralyses, was an important part of al-Buti's family life. The *Ya-sin* sura was read every morning and evening, and at meal times the children were expected to behave as if 'they were eating together with Allah'; every Monday and Thursday morning, after morning prayer, the father called the family together for *dhikr* to chant out the *tahlil*-formula '*La illaha ila Allah*' and the word '*Allah*' a hundred times each, as well as any other intercessions, hymns of praise and beseechings of refuge—all of which al-Buti has performed till the present day.

The overwhelming influence of al-Buti's father, who was born in 1888 and died in 1990 at the age of 102, was by no means restricted to al-Buti's religious education. The father decided almost all biographically relevant events in the life of his only son. When al-Buti turned 18, his father married him to the sister of his second wife, who—though considerably older than al-Buti—was still 'a good catch' as the family was very poor at the time.[3] Al-Buti's reluctance to marry so young was met by the father with references to the necessity of marriage as described in al-Ghazali's *Ihya 'ulum al-din*, so that al-Buti soon recognized his rejection as 'disobedience and reluctance' towards his father and 'contentedly' agreed to the engagement. The father also decided on al-Buti's professional career. When, in 1956, on the completion of his three-year degree course at the al-Azhar[4], al-Buti returned to Damascus with a *shari'a*-teaching qualification (*ijaza*) and an education diploma, he refused to take part in an aptitude qualifying contest (*musabaqa*)[5] for future *shari'a* teachers decreed by the Ministry of Education, because he knew his father considered a career in the civil service for religious affairs, i.e. 'any pursuit of religion for the sake of money', a great sin. Yet for 'inexplicable' reasons and to al-Buti's 'great astonishment' his father consented to and even ordered his participation in the competition, in which he did very well. So al-Buti became a *shari'a* teacher at a secondary school and, later, at the Dar al-Mu'allimin al-Ibtida'iyya in Homs. His academic career began in 1961, when he became an assistant at the newly founded Shari'a Faculty of Damascus University. After he had completed his doctorate at the al-Azhar in 1965 he became a lecturer in comparative law (*al-fiqh al-islami al-muqarin*) and religious studies (*al-'aqa'id wa l-adyan*) at Damascus University; for some time he was also the Dean of the Shari'a Faculty. Al-Buti was professor of comparative law at the Department of Islamic Law and its Schools (*al-Fiqh al-Islami wa-Madhahibi-h*), and works today as lecturer in the 'sources of Islamic law and the methodology for its development' (*usul al-fiqh*), Islamic dogma (*al-'aqida al-islamiyya*), and the Prophet's biography (*al-sira al-nabawiyya*).

Influences

When al-Buti's intellectual development began, his family had already undergone a process of 'Syrianization', whereas at the early stage of his life their Kurdish ethnicity had dominated their social and cultural background.[6] Yet, al-Buti never denied his Kurdish origins and maintained his interest in the Kurdish language and its literature. At that time, when he was in his twenties, for example, he translated the tragic story by the Kurdish poet Ahmad al-Khasani of the love between Mamu and Zain, a love 'which was sown on earth and ripened in heaven'[7] and transformed the story written in verse into narrative form.[8] Also, the deprived rural milieu of Anatolia and the poverty of his parents' house developed in al-Buti a strong sense of social justice, which repeatedly induced him to denounce the social, economic and financial defects of Syrian society. This, and his father's lifelong resistance to secularization tendencies—first in Turkey and then in Syria—could have led al-Buti into contacts with the Syrian Muslim Brotherhood, which was politically very strong during al-Buti's formative years.[9] The leader of the Syrian Brotherhood, Mustafa *al*-Siba'i, had been appointed Dean of the Faculty of Law and Professor of Islamic Law at the University of Damascus in 1956, and was still there when al-Buti began work there as an assistant in 1960. We learn from the biographical sources that both families exchanged frequent visits, and that the father showed great sympathy with the profoundly physically handicapped Muslim leader. During the early fifties, al-Buti was seen as an enthusiastic listener (Buti 1995: 127) at weekly rhethoric performances held by the Rabita al-'Ulama' al-Diniyya (League of 'Ulama'), which had, at that time, close links to the Syrian Muslim Brotherhood. However, it seems that a stronger influence on al-Buti's intellectual and personal life was his teacher at the Ma'had al-Tawjih al-Islami in al-Midan (at that time headquarters of the Ikhwan al-Muslimun [Muslim Brothers] in Damascus) Hasan Habannakah. During the protests of 1964, 1967, and 1973 Shaikh Habannakah was one of the leading clerics who manifested their resistance to the secular government of the Ba'th party —which came to power in 1963 (see Munson 1988: 89; also Hassan 1980: 91–108, and Hinnebusch 1982: 138–69). For example, in 1967, as the president of the League of 'Ulama', he organized demonstrations in protest against a nationalistic, anti-religious article in an army magazine (see Schaikh 1992: 233, Mayer 1983, and Reissner 1980), and in 1973 he led protests in Damascus against the first draft of a new constitution that made no mention of Islam except as a main source of legislation (see Munson

1988: 88–9, and Hudson 1983: 82–6). Al-Buti, full of admiration for
the Shaikh, gives a full report of how his father suddenly abandoned
his lifelong seclusion from public affairs in order to support Hasan al-
Habannakah, who was a Shafi'i, in his election to be Grand Mufti of
Syria. The father's endeavour was to convince other *'ulama'* that, because of Habannakah's 'juridical brilliance', the rule, which demanded
succession of a Hanafi scholar, should be abrogated. Moreover, al-Buti's
father not only joined study circles in Hasan al-Habannakah's house,[10]
he was also the only *'alim* who 'prayed publicly for Habannakah's health
and stayed with him the whole night, when the Shaikh fell terribly ill'
(Buti 1995: 130–2).[11]

During that time another intellectual and spiritual guiding figure
emerged in Ramadan al-Buti's life: Badi' al-Zaman Sa'id Nursi. One
of the most influential religious and political propagandists in late Ottoman and Republican Turkey, and founder of the intellectual-religious
movement 'Nurculuk', Sa'id Nursi was arrested and banned several
times—both by the Ottoman and the Republican governments (see
Mardin 1982: 65–79; also *EI1*, vol. 7, p. 143). After translating Sa'id
Nursi's autobiography, published in 1958, from Kurdish into Arabic,
al-Buti published the article: 'Sa'id Nursi: the miracle of the Islamic
revolution in Turkey.' The following paragraph not only reveals his
admiration for Sa'id Nursi's *da'wa* (Islamic missionary call), but also
reflects al-Buti's own aspirations at that time.

> When I hold this pen to write down his life on these few pages, I feel an
> immense emotion moving within the depth of my being. When I write
> these words I feel that I am illustrating how the life of a Muslim who is
> faithful to his Islamic belief, and of a preacher who is honest in his mis-
> sion, and of a scholar who is dedicated in his work, ought to be—whether
> that be from the social, the political, the ethical, or other aspects ... How-
> ever, this is not the only reason why I am engulfed with this immense
> sense of emotion and happiness as I narrate the life of this great mission-
> ary. It could be that I find in his great life, which is characterized by
> dedication, pious efforts, and selflessness that which we no longer find in
> the lives of most other Islamic *'ulama'* and preachers today. It is no exag-
> geration that my happiness when writing about the life of Badi' al-Zaman
> exceeds that of a man dying of dehydration whose liver has dried up from
> thirst in a remote desert, when he sees the glimmer of the Euphrates'
> water (Buti 1972a: 240).

It seems that Shaikh al-Butiʾs sympathy for the cause of a viable and politically conscious Islamic movement was considerable. Yet sympathy with some ideals of the Muslim Brotherhood is not the same as collaboration or complicity when it comes to militant actions. He witnessed with growing opposition the assassinations of prominent ʿAlawis and the attacks on government and Baʿth party offices, police stations, and army units by Muslim Brothers and members of smaller Islamic groups. After the gunning down of eighty-three ʿAlawi cadets at the Artillery Academy at Aleppo in June 1979, Shaikh al-Buti condemned the killing on television as juridically illegitimate—at the request of the Ministry of Information.[12]

This event could be regarded as al-Butiʾs breakthrough as a public figure and high ranking *ʿalim*. Only a few years later—at the climax of violent upheavals all over Syria in 1982—he was asked to give a speech on the occasion of welcoming the next century (the fifteenth of the *hijra*), in which he was obediently to address the President of Syria, Hafiz al-Asad—at that time the official target of the Islamists' fight. The Shaikh assented (Buti 1995: 140–1). Some years later, when the government removed strict censorship on Islamic publications, the total ban on religious broadcasting, and the prohibition against wearing the *hijab* and *niqab* (types of womens' coverings) in state institions, al-Buti accepted an invitation to thank the 'hidden hand of these achievements', President Asad, on television (Buti 1995: 141).

The more al-Buti became a public figure, the less he could retain his revolutionary impetus. Previously, he was shown great respect because of his long dissociation from the state's rigid reaction against the Islamic opposition. After 1979 he lost much of his credit by becoming, increasingly, a recipient of President Asad's benevolence, in particular after accepting the latter's offer to become a regular lecturer on Syrian television. Many Sunni Muslims expected him to be a mouthpiece of Islamic criticism in broadcasting, but were extremely disappointed when they found him very cautious and diplomatic; yet he seems to have been sensitive to the critical voices around him. The reader of his biography *This is my Father* is constantly given the impression that al-Buti himself was always reluctant, and even unwilling, to fulfil the official tasks of the state authorities. He tries to show that it was always his father who advised him, rather obliged him, or, better, demanded of him to do everything. 'In fact, everything that I said at that time was led and ordered by my father, may the mercy of God be with him' (Buti 1995: 140).

Works

Al-Buti's works are numerous and varied. First of all, more than twenty voluminous treatises have appeared since al-Buti's first publication some thirty years ago. Then there is his series of (so far ten) pamphlets on crises in the Islamic world over the past twenty years, which appears under the somewhat odd title *Summit Analysis* (*Abhath fi'l-qimma*)[13] and is very popular amongst Muslims. With these A6-booklets al-Buti means to 'administer the most effective medicine for the treatment of the problems of the Muslims', and if some people do not perceive their world problematic—he continues—he is going to show them 'that they do require this medicine' (Buti 1971: 2). Furthermore, there are hundreds of religious instructions, lectures, and sermons held by him in mosques, which are regularly taped by a team of young Muslims who sell them in their thousands in front of mosques.[14] In the study rooms of *shari'a* students I saw, for example, the 27-piece lecture series about 'Islamic doctrine' (*al-'Aqida al-islamiyya*), on which the students had spent a fortune (L1080)[15] as well as the several-part commentary on al-Nawawi's book *The Gardens of the Virtuous* (*Riyad al-salihin*). Since January 1990, the medical and scientific journal *Tabibuk* has published occasional *fatwas* from Shaikh al-Buti, in particular on *'ibadat* and *mu'amalat* issues (e.g. rules for the *arkan* rituals, problems of circumcision, perforation of the hymen, homosexuality, masturbation, AIDS, and so forth) (see Houot 1996). Finally, there are his lectures on comparative Islamic law, which are now available as books (Buti 1970, 1968a, 1965, 1975a, and 1994a) and video cassettes, his religious TV instructions and his numerous articles in periodicals like *al-Ijtihad* and *al-Nahj al-Islami*.[16]

It is almost impossible to see in al-Buti's work any limitation of topics. As an Islamic scholar who has climbed the ladder to more and more highly ranked positions in his academic and public life, and who is, for many Syrian Muslims, the leading religious authority in the intellectual disputes in Islam about modern life, he has made statements on all the most relevant and explosive topics of the day. These appear in the form, 'What does Islam say about ...', e.g. slavery, the veiling of

women, female labour, education, Islamic *da'wa*, revivalism, radicalism and reformism, *jihad*, secularization, Marxism, nationalism, etc. (
Buti 1978, 1993, 1990a, 1969, and 1988) His work even includes comments on topics such as abortion, the mass media, macro- and
micro-economics, and Arabic literature (Buti 1976b, 1972a, 1993, and
1958). His choice of subjects does not follow a consistent pattern, and
nowhere is there the same definitive answer to the same question. Many
of his publications are ad hoc statements about topics widely discussed
at a certain time, or disputes with his opponents published as books
(Buti 1990b, 1994c, and 1994d); for example the very controversial
interview by Nabil Fayyad, who wrote *Yawm inhadara'l-jamal min al-
saqifa* (Fayyad 1995; see also, for further details, Wörtz n. d.), which
was banned in Syria—according to the author of the book—after a
visit to President Asad from al-Buti himself.

Style and personality

The remarkable thing about al-Buti's academic style is his personal
tone. He does not correspond at all to Michael Gilsenan's 'ideal type'
of an *'alim* who defines his authority purely through the knowledge
(*'ilm*) he has acquired and not through his individual character, and
who has usually gone through a depersonalized and objectified educational process (Gilsenan 1982: 31–2). Al-Buti, however, presents his
Islamic erudition with a strikingly individual tone, not least through
the revelation of very private spheres of his life, as can best be seen in
his father's biography. The introductions to his books are also very
personal. His emotional outbursts—not to say eruptions, in the middle of a sermon or a prayer of supplication (*du'a'*), which will often end
in sobs or even bursts of crying—are well known.[17] Al-Buti is admired
for his open speaking, his extemporizations, his rasping voice, his vivid
facial expressions and gestures. His Arabic is certainly pure *literary*
Arabic, yet his usage of the Levantine dialect is remarkable, for example, when he almost systematically replaces the more formal
interrogatives *'madha', 'hal', 'man huwa'* with *'shu', 'ma',* and *'meen',* or par-
ticles like *'faqad'* and *'idhan'* with *'bas'* and *'teeb'*. What is unique about
al-Buti, in comparison with other Damascus-based scholars I inter-
viewed, is his ability for self-reflection. Al-Buti is fully aware of his
position and his influence as a public figure on his environment. He is

capable of differentiating between the various currents, groups, and
followers within Islam, and argues with them in a provocative and polemical way. His books, speeches and sermons read like a never-ending
disputation in which al-Buti tackles a 'just published treatise', a 'book
written by certain scribblers', an 'odd question received yesterday over
the phone', or a 'peculiar response to my last book'. He tackles divergent opinions, often proves the others 'definitely wrong' or 'completely
unscholarly'. Now and then he calls them liars or fools, or he even dis-
criminates against other authors an account of their 'Western' or 'Jewish'
background. In summary, one can say that al-Buti's rhetorical style,
which is marked by his endeavours to be at all costs superior to his
spiritual opponents, could be called 'competitive academicism'.

Unlike many modern Muslim thinkers, al-Buti is specialized in the
shari'a-sciences and, in particular, in their main discipline, *usul al-fiqh*.
He is outstanding in his knowledge of all relevant sources of Islamic
jurisprudence, which gives him an enormous advantage over his rival
in debate. Most of his arguments and ideas are put forward within the
framework of traditional legal scholarship, frequently refering to
Qur'anic verses, Prophetic traditions (*hadith*), and the opinions of the
leading classical authorities, in particular Imam al-Nawawi, Ibn al-
'Arabi, al-Ghazali, and al-Shafi'i. Due to his profession, al-Buti regards
Islamic law as the core of the Islamic religion; whenever he speaks of
Islam he means the principles, injunctions, and practical implications
of the *shari'a*. When talking about juridical matters, he never overem-
phasizes the originality of his conclusions, but tells people that he does
not want to change what has already been carefully established.
'Rearrangements of the law of Allah mean only the abuse of it, do they
not?' (Buti 1994d: 63.) However, at the same time, al-Buti shows an
interest in overriding the boundaries of the classical legal casuistic, treating Islamic law from different perspectives. He writes on philosophical,
cosmological, and historical underpinnings of Islamic jurisprudence
(Buti 1968b, 1992, and 1994b) He also deals with specific areas of secular positive law, for a detailed comparison (Buti 1976b). Like many
modern scholars, he takes a particular interest in differences of juristic
opinions (*ikhtilaf*) and defends them in his books and lectures about
comparative jurisprudence (*al-fiqh al-muqarin*) (Buti 1970, 1968a, 1965,
1975, and 1994a). In this regard, al-Buti does not stick to his Shafi'i-
background, but offers a balanced treatment of the views and

contributions of all the prominent schools of law without the sectarian bias that can be found in premodern *usul al-fiqh* works (see Kamali 1991: xiv).

His teaching style is appealing, logical, and didactic, and the contents of his books are clearly written. The reader of his works or the listener to his lectures is always asked to follow the logic of his arguments, the way he uses the legal sources, and therefore to catch the stages through which a particular ruling is reached. This reveals the paramount aim of his writings and lectures about Islamic law, which is to educate Muslim laymen in the general principles of the *shariʿa*. For al-Buti, it makes no sense to turn to the Islamic religion without knowing the rules and requirements of Islamic law. His endeavour is to give people the chance to understand the underlying principles of an *ijtihad* process (reasoning to derive laws from the legitimate sources), but he always demands that followers know the specialized technical terminology of Islamic jurisprudence, thus avoiding the impression that anyone not sufficiently qualified can reason juridically for himself. 'It is absolute nonsense to claim that Islam and Islamic law is nothing more than a couple of uncomplicated rules!' (Buti 1969: 42.)

Shaikh al-Buti as an Islamic scholar

In his defence of the traditional, scholarly way of Islamic jurisprudence against overly liberal or relativist positions, his main concern as an Islamic scholar can be discerned. His major and most sophisticated works are dedicated to attacking radical salafiyya positions which try to simplify the complicated demands of Islamic reasoning. In his book *Non-Madhhabism: the greatest bidʿa threatening the Islamic shariʿa* he criticizes the anti-School-of-Law trend—which promotes a more flexible and less constrained *ijtihad* system, rejects the hairsplitting by the *fuqaha'*, encourages every individual not to rely on the judgements of religious experts, seeks to merge the different Schools of law into one single School, and finally emphasizes the *Qur'an* and *sunna* over the consensuses of the four Schools of law as authoritative sources for beliefs, ritual practices, ethics, and law. Al-Buti does not deny that modern conditions demand a flexible *ijtihad* system and that the gate of *ijtihad* should be kept open. He says: 'It is absolutely necessary to study conditions and problems that are new in our time. We have seriously and honestly to study values and customs which are different from what they used to be. No doubt this is one of the central duties Allah has imposed on us' (Buti 1990c: 177). Elsewhere, he had previously stated that he would always promote *ijtihad* rather than *taqlid* (imitation of the rulings of *mujtahids*) if Muslims are faced with issues that could not have been dealt with by previous generations of the Muslim community (Buti 1970: 10–16). In fact, Shaikh al-Buti encourages people to use their individual opinion (*ra'y*) so they may study the authoritative sources extensively. 'If a person finds a different understanding of a particular issue, conflicting textual proofs or a divergent *hadith* to that of his school, then he is bound by the results of his own *ijtihad* and should not follow his Imam' (Buti 1969: 85). The Shaikh also strongly supports the famous idea of the 1984 Conference of Islamic Thought in Constantine to establish an independent board of the most prominent *'ulama'* of the Islamic world to give institutionally collective *ijtihads* about newly emerging issues (Buti 1990c: 178). Metaphorically, he compares this idea to two boats, one containing Islam and its law, the other all signs of modern civilization, which are driven parallel through the constant work of the *mujtahids* (Buti 1990c: 143).

However, despite his enthusiasm for regaining the flexibility of the pre-classical *ijtihad* system, al-Buti rejects what he calls 'selfish arbitrariness in looking at *ijtihad*'. 'Some [modernists] believe that *ijtihad* is a kind of a secret recipe to fulfil all their dreams, to open all gates and to pull down all barriers, a kind of permission to do forbidden things' (Buti 1990c: 143). For him, it is unacceptable that every individual should have the right to exercise his or her own *ijtihad*. On the contrary, the process of *ijtihad* demands deep knowledge of all the relevant sources and the capability to apply rules from authoritative texts to modern circumstances. As long as the *muqallid* (imitator) does not reach the level of knowledge of the *mujtahid*, the former has to follow the latter. Supporting his strong hierarchical view on religious knowledge with a saying of al-Shatibi, al-Buti claims that in the case of intellectual inferiority the ruling of the *mujtahid* is binding for the *muqallid*; as binding as the Qur'an and *sunna* for the *mujtahid* (Buti 1969: 73).

Al-Buti feels the threat of modernists challenging established authority: 'How is it possible for the *muqallid* to replace his Imam every day, who will be then followed by another Imam? Or should that happen every month or every year? If the *muqallid* is obliged to do that, where is the legal proof to back this necessity?' (Buti 1969: 76.) What happens, asks al-Buti next, when people stop following their Imams? And he gives the answer: It is as if people were to ignore the knowledge of engineers in building their houses, or that of physicians in healing their illnesses, or that of specialists in running factories. There is no doubt what will ensue: a dangerous chaos. People will destroy their houses, suppress their souls, and produce poverty. 'And all that, because people displaced *ijtihad* from its rightful place and applied it without any condition, and because people ignored the normative practice of Allah which consists of mutual cooperation, help, instruction, and counseling among different groups of people' (Buti 1969: 73). When he compares the science of deriving rulings with that of proper medical diagnosis, he is informing the reader that he lives today in an age in which specialization has become essential: 'Is it not a sin when the father of a seriously ill child gives him the wrong medicine only because he looked in medical textbooks for himself instead of consulting a trained medical practitioner?' (Buti 1969: 104.) And thus it is, he concludes, in matters of religion: it would be foolish and hazardous for everyone to study the sources in order to become his own *mufti* .

Furthermore, al-Buti warns his readers against exercising eclectic *ijtihad*, which he observes among Islamists who are 'not well versed in Islamic law, the principles of jurisprudence, or early Islamic history'. They become convinced of the islamicity of the issue and then attempt to justify their position by selecting texts which support their preconceived position. But, traditionally, each new problem should be seen in isolation and not considered as a means to fulfilling a purpose. Shaikh al-Buti defends the traditional method of linking new problems to authoritative scripture or a text of the Imams in order to make a decision as to the permissibility and non-permissibility (or *bid'a*: condemned innovation) of an action. In this respect, he strongly argues against the 'trend to revitilize al-Tufi's concept which authorizes *maslaha mursala* (considerations of public interest) to take precedence over all other considerations; that is to say: if the Qur'an and *sunna* and other proofs of the *shari'a* happen to conform to the *maslaha* of the people in a particular case they should be applied forthwith, but if they oppose it *maslaha* should take precedence over them.' Those 'fantasies', polemicizes al-Buti, give free rein to all sorts of abuse. For him, a concept that authorizes recourse to *maslaha* without the existence of a *nass* (explicit text) is unthinkable (Buti 1965: 178–89).

Against the background of Muslim modernists' attempts to 'disqualify a whole corpus of ritual actions and religious institutions as un-Islamic', he develops in his book *The Salafiyya: a blessed, historically limited period, not an Islamic school* an 'academic method towards knowledge of, and commentary on, texts' ('manhaj 'ilmi fi l-ma'rifa wa tafsir al-nusus') (Buti 1988: 55), or, as he calls it later on, 'a comprehensive method' (*al-manhaj al-jami*') (Buti 1988: 60). Here al-Buti revitilizes the classical apparatus of textual analysis and criticism in order to correct the Salafiyya movement in its 'hasty eliminating of all "that had slipped" into the Islamic Tradition'. He emphasizes the fact that not all the *ahkam* (injunctions) of the *shari'a* are equally important or permanent, and therefore that different interpretations can be permitted. There are hypothetical judgments which mainly deal with transactions, customs, and manners. These are open to *ijtihad*. Disagreement based on authentic *ijtihad* on these issues represents no harm or threat. On the other hand, there are *ahkam* dealing with matters of faith, belief, and *'ibadat*—which are firmly established in the Qur'an, *sunna* and *ijma'* (consensus)—that are definitive, categorical, and not open to *ijtihad*. Overly ambitious Muslims should be fully aware of which issues are open to disagreement and which are not. More importantly, they should know the standard norms of behaviour practised in settling differences and disagreements. They must learn the ethics of disagreement (*adab al-khilaf*) in Islamic jurisprudence. 'The "essence" of Islamic law is not to prescribe absolute certainty' (Buti 1970: 6).

Again, the Shaikh is harsh in his criticism of the classical Salafiyya and young modernists today who have 'no deep understanding of classical Islam, the methodology of *usul al-fiqh* and other such skills in Islamic scholarship', but tend to classify other *mujtahids* as *kafirs* (unbelievers). In his view, the lack of understanding of the 'true meaning of Islam' among Muslims has led them also to condemn what are intrinsic parts of Islam, such as Sufism or specific types of Islamic worship. Through applying traditional terminology, al-Buti reaches a much less radical view and a more differentiated picture of valid Islamic practices. He teaches his reader to apply the old reliable differentiation between what is just divergent opinion (*khilaf*), what is deviation (*shudhudh*), what is departure from or distortion of the truth (*inhiraf*), and what is in fact godlessness (*kufr*) (Buti 1988: 109–30). Furthermore, Shaikh al-Buti argues against modernists that intuiting the intention of someone who is performing a certain ritual 'only by watching his outward ritual behaviour' is misguided. Some rituals mean true worship of Allah, even if they were not explicitly ordered or performed by the Prophet Muhammad.

As for Sufism, Sa'id al-Buti shares the modernist criticism that the establishment of Sufi orders, the sacralization and blind obedience of Sufi Shaikhs by their followers, worship at tombs, and the exclusive and emotionalized way of reciting *dhikr* and *tasbih* have led to 'a distortion of true Islam' (Buti 1988: 117–30, and Buti 1971: 17–45). This is what he calls 'emotional Sufism' (*al-tasawwuf al-wijdani*) (Buti 1971: 79), which he rejects. According to al-Buti, it is true that many Sufis do not follow the aims of the Islamic *da'wa*, but only selfish interests. 'I know a lot of Sufi shaikhs who do not preach honestly, but do it professionally. They want to earn money, political influence, and power as spiritual leaders. They do it just so that others may say: Look at how many students and *muridun* (followers) they have!' (Interview by the author, 2 February 1996.) At the same time, al-Buti points out that he does not accept the zealous demand that Sufism should be condemned and expelled from Islam. 'I am greatly puzzled by a Muslim who joins his brothers in the *ruku'* and *sujud* of their prayers, who feels their turn to Allah in God's places of prayer, but runs away from *dhikr*-meetings. Is it not astonishing that he flees if he spots Muslims who stretch out their arms towards Allah as if he has seen a revolt against God?' (Lecture, held on 22 February 1996 in the Rukn al-Din Mosque—recorded by the author.) Al-Buti warns against mixing sentimental Sufism with ethically oriented Sufism (*al-tasawwuf al-akhlaqi*), which consists of activities based on the Qur'an, *sunna* and Islamic law.[18]

Al-Buti's main books and ideas aim to condemn 'those people who not only assume that they know the whole truth, but who also try to coerce other people to follow them, believing that they can eradicate all *madhhabs* and disagreements and unite all people in one single stroke' (Buti 1970: 15). They tend to forget that their own understanding and interpretation of the texts are no more than hypotheses which may be right or wrong. However, in spite of his harsh criticism of 'overambitious' Salafiyya adherents, he is very cautious not to condemn them all. While, for example, he shows his disapproval at the Salafiyya attempt to establish their own school 'creating adherents of a new *madhhab* (school) as a result of partisanship and sectarian egoism, thus splitting up the Islamic community' (Buti 1988: 244–6), he cannot on the other hand deny their contribution in having introduced a new, fresh and radical impulse towards a rejuvenated Islamic society (Buti 1988: 5). Shaikh al-Buti supports their call for adherence to the texts and their new interpretations and understandings of the Islamic past. His final statement is, therefore, rather vague: 'We do not want them to give up their opinions about *ijtihad*. We only want to remind them that they should not consider themselves the only true representatives of Islam ..., but we do not exclude theirs and others' opinions from our programme of *ijtihad* outlined here' (Buti 1988: 258).

Shaikh al-Buti as religious leader

The higher al-Buti climbed up the academic ladder of Islamic scholarship, the more his thoughts turned towards the concerns of the whole Muslim community (*umma*) and the theoretical premisses of a modern Islamic civilization (*al-hadara al-islamiyya al-mu'asira*). Unlike many other modern Muslim thinkers, he transcends the modernist debate about Western progress (*taqaddum*) and Islamic backwardness (*takhalluf*). When the Shaikh talks about the reasons for the crisis of Islam in our century, he does not blame Islamic religion as the main cause. He argues that 'almost all of the social, cultural, and other problems from which the Islamic community (*umma*) has been suffering, arise from one single source: that Muslims felt attracted to Western civilization' (Buti 1990c: 33). Their turn away from Islam during the first decades of our century was due to the fact that they interpreted European progress and superiority as a result of secularization, that is to say the success in restraining the influence and power of the Christian Church. The angry outburst of Westerners against the Church, their turning away from all religious activities, and their focus on a purely materialistic way of life had a tremendous effect on Muslims, who then thought that progress was only possible without religion. Totally ignoring the importance of religion, al-Buti continues, they rejected all Islamic prescriptions and rules of conduct; they were convinced that Islam was insufficient for all the areas of social life and was unable to solve the question of power. Today, however, one can clearly recognize the 'end of blindness and a de-mystification of European progress'. Every Westerner now feels in his soul and his mind the results of the total absence of religion, which again has had an immense influence on Muslims and their attitude towards religion (Buti 1980: 9). Unlike previous generations of reform-minded Muslim scholars, Shaikh al-Buti rejects the feeling of inferiority to the West. In his preaching and writing is an implicit optimism and a feeling of the superiority of Islam. He writes repeatedly that Islam has now returned to the Islamic world, and that there is no Muslim who would doubt whether Islam had political and social sufficiency, whether Islam was compatible with the sciences or not, because Muslims have put a stop to some of the traditional scholars' retrogressive perception of the modern intellect and modern knowledge. Muslims are now ready to accept Islam as a comprehensive system of worship (*ʿibadat*) and authoritative legislation (*shariʿa*).[19] At the back of the West's own deep social, moral and spiritual crisis—or moral inferiority—Shaikh al-Buti discerns a new attractiveness of Islam. 'Young Muslims react to recent developments in the Western world, the collapse of the family, the destruction of culture, morality, and health, through drugs, venereal diseases, and neuroses. Muslims who thought that the Western way of life was the best way to live, are now disappointed and return to Islam' (interview by the author, 2 February 1996). The Shaikh even thinks of a postmodern mutual dependence between Islam and the West: 'In the name of Islam and its Law Muslims have the right to adopt that of Western civilization which has proved to be good and useful' (Buti 1990c: 47). Westerners for their part could adopt from Islam what they need to escape spiritual devastation and attain salvation. This mutual exchange follows the new insight into the global character of the destruction caused by civilization and that this sickness can only be healed by religion (Buti 1980: 12–13).

However, despite this appealing analysis of recent developments concerning Muslim mentality, he is less clear and straightforward about how to achieve an Islamic society based on Islamic worship (*ʿibadat*) and law (*shariʿa*). In his most controversial book, *Jihad in Islam: How we understand it and how we apply it*, the Shaikh basically rejects *jihad* (self-exertion in the cause of Allah) as a violent means to change the balance of power and society. Against today's mainstream Islamism, he declares the ultimate reason (*ʿilla*) for *jihad* to be the prevention of robbery or brigandage (*daf' al-hirabah*) and the defence of existing things, and not as a mean to fight against unbelief (*qada' al-kufr*). Furthermore, he differentiates between those *mujahids* who have committed *baghi* (false or evil endeavour) and those who have committed *hiraba* (highway robbery). Whereas the former (*al-bughat*) do not obey an Imam's or a *khalifa's ijtihad* but have their own *ijtihad* which is *methodologically* valid, the latter (*al-muharibun*) attack the ruler without any juridical legitimacy. Looking around the Islamic world, he complains: 'If we could only apply the conditions of *baghi* to those who proclaim their attacks on their rulers, who are dedicated to kill, to assassinate treacherously (*fatk*), and to steal (*khatf*). If only they could differentiate between those who called the Prophet obedient (*al-ta'i'*) and those who called him sinful (*fajir*)!' (Buti 1994d: 35.) However, al-Buti's differentiation has harsh consequences: if *mujahids* are accused of being *muharibun*, then the ruler is allowed by Islamic law to treat them as such, as *murtaddun* or *kuffar* (people actively against Islam), which could lead to their execution (see Doi 1984: 252). Because of this judgment, al-Buti was criticized for being in the same camp as the currently ruling despots. One of his critics said: 'The reader of his book gets the feeling that the author was not succesful in dealing with some of the problems of our contemporary world, as he flatters the rulers who call themselves "Imams of the Muslims" but do not apply the *shari'a* of Allah. For him [al-Buti], they are not unbelievers and attacks on them are forbidden' (Buti 1994d: 48). In fact, the Shaikh is very reluctant to condemn rulers as *kuffar*. Even if they have ordered the closure of mosques, *shari'a* schools and institutes in order to prevent the Islamic mission (*da'wa*), attacks on them are not allowed. The *da'wa* can take place somewhere else: in squares, courtyards, or gardens! (Buti 1994d: 36–7.) However, at the same time Shaikh al-Buti is aware of the fact that he could easily be accused of being corrupted and patronized by the authorities. He himself has always blamed other '*ulama*' of having lost the courage to disagree with rulers, of being silent about the rulers' atrocities and their negligence of the *shari'a*, and of glorifying and commending them for such deplorable actions. That is why he emphatically adds: 'Obviously it is necessary to repeat and stress that an attack on the ruler, that is a revolution against him, is one thing, and a rebellious disobedience against him ('*adam ta'ati-hi fi l-ma'siyya*) is another thing. How often people obliterate the distinction!' (Buti 1994d: 54.) He regards patience in the face of the injustice of the ruler or in the face of suffering, and perseverance in the face of deviance or provocation as the highest values of an honest and sound *da'wa*, which is free of violence (*qahr*) and force (*ilzam*) (Buti 1994d: 37). Al-Buti makes clear that a forceful *da'wa* does not mean fanatical, violent actions, and although he repeatedly indicates that he feels some sympathy with those who are suffering from oppression and exploitation, he can never accept violence. Inspired by Gandhi's concept of non-violent resistance, his thoughts are preoccupied with the Islamic mission as educational and non-violent (Buti 1990a: 135). We can infer from his writings that he considers the complete return to the Islamic way of life and the establishment of the Islamic state as a gradual process, taking into account that right belief (*iman*) is a precondition for an Islamic way of life. 'Only when all individuals in a society or most of them have choosen Islam and declared their obedience to its rules and principles, can an Islamic society based on the contract of obedience to Allah (*'ubudiyya Allah*) emerge' (Buti 1994c: 68).

According to al-Buti, Islam needs to be rooted in every Muslim mind and heart, otherwise fetters of disbelief, superstition, and ignorance will remain. A Muslim *da'i* (missionary) should concentrate his effort on teaching monotheism (*tawhid*) and the *shar'i* injunctions, purifying the heart from doubts, sins, and distractions, so that the heart which embraces the right faith constitutes a nucleus of the correct Islamic way of life. We read elsewhere: 'If a person commits himself to worship and applies all its rules and *adabs*, this will urge him to complete obedience to Allah. He will automatically be turned into a garden of different virtues where the seeds of righteous politics, social cooperation, and justice will grow. All good things will grow there reaching a perfect state' (Buti 1980: 78). At the same time, the Shaikh continues, this will enable the individual to turn against all symptoms of tyranny (*zulm*), abuse of power, acquisitive greed, and oppression of the weak (Buti 1980: 78). It will prevent people from self-idolization (*ta'alluh*) and from considering themselves superior to others (*takabbur*), moreover the weak and deprived will overcome humilation and inferiority, thus regaining freedom, dignity, power, and pride (Buti 1980: 81). The *hikma* (underlying purpose of a rule) of worship is that the emotions are being constantly purified as human life is being constantly observed by Allah. It is evident that, for Shaikh al-Buti, ritual acts

have extra-religious values; that is that worship means a personal awareness of the well-being of society, since it is prescribed as social
events—the five daily prayers as a meeting of the neighbourhood, the
Friday prayer as a weekly meeting of the whole city or village, and the
pilgrimage as an annual gathering of the whole Islamic community.
Hence, al-Buti concludes, the mosque—as the place of worship—is
the foundation of the Islamic state (*al-hajr al-asasi al-awwal fi bina' al-
dawla al-islamiyya*), a symbol of unity, equality and harmony between
the individual and the *umma*, and between the *umma* and the ruler of
the country. 'There is a natural growing up of our souls, but only provided that these souls are moulded together within the melting pot
(*budaqa*) of the mosque' (Buti 1980: 83–4).

However, what makes al-Buti different from orthodox preachers
who stress the importance of individual piety and public religiosity for
the well-being of society is that he attaches great importance to the
power of the nation state. His main interest is to convince his readers
and listeners that a strong nation state guarantees the best way of establishing a true Islamic civilization. At the same time, an Islamic *da'wa*
that promotes 'a purified soul' and 'an enlightened, conscious and educated heart' (interview by the author, 2 February 1996) would
strengthen the nation state against neo-colonialist attempts to regain
control over the country. In the light of this post-colonialist setting we
have to understand the Shaikh's sermonizing stand: his crusade against
superstition, ignorance, materialism, and sectarianism. He carries out
an energetic polemic against some of the phenomena of popular religion, e.g. *tasha'um* (taking things as evil omens), certain fertility rites
and talisman cults 'under the guise of true religion' (Buti 1990a: 109).
'In fact, superstition not only damages religion but all pillars of society:
religion (*din*), culture (*thaqafa*), patriotism (*wataniyya*), and nationalism (*qawmiyya*). That is why foreign enemies often seed superstition'
(Buti 1990a: 110). If one stops propagating and teaching clearly and
comprehensively 'an undistorted, true picture of Islam' (Buti 1980: 11)
then, so we are assured, the enemies of Islam immediately come and
brainwash Muslims with something different. This causes the latter to
have doubts about the competence of Islam to adopt reason and science and fight the evils within Islamic civilization. When Muslims are
constantly presented with an irrational, superstitious, and sentimental
Islam, they will be tempted to give up Islam again. Good examples of

his endeavour to fight ignorance are the sermons in which he accuses his Muslim fellows of 'regressive attitudes', e.g. when they extort the *mahr* (bridal gift) from their daughters, when they deny their wives the right to attend prayers and Islamic instruction in mosques, when they keep them in public places half a metre behind themselves or when they are ashamed of hearing their wives' names spoken. 'All of these are acts of ignorance (*jahiliyya*), not of Islam!' (Lecture on television, 24 January 1996—recorded by the author). As for materialism and moral decadence, he states that the modern world is full of materialistic desires, passion, and seduction ('the modern weapons of the ideological war') (lecture on television, 24 January 1996—recorded by the author), which are mobilized by neo-colonialist forces to keep people from getting closer to God, as has already happened in the West. Finally, even the fragmentation of the national community is, according to al-Buti, clearly a colonialist phenomenon. A distorted picture of Islam is spread among the population—causing the total ignorance of Islamic ideals such as magnanimity, unity, and cooperation—thus creating sectarianism and unrest within the nation (Buti 1990a: 123–32).

Since he perceives superstition, ignorance, materialism, and sectarianism as the main obstacles to creating national unity (*al-wahda al-wataniyya*) and an Islamic civilization (*al-hadara al-islamiyya*), it has become Shaikh al-Buti's preoccupation to denounce all phenomena and practices which he regards as their preconditions or results. In positive terms, he believes that 'knowledge' creates in the hearts and minds of Muslims a kind of a shield against 'all signs of these evils'. 'We need literature that does not distort Islamic truth, but spreads an honest morality. We need spiritual and emotional food to satisfy thirst, to keep them [the Muslims] from being attracted to the slippery ground of meanness and the precipice of their ruin' (Buti 1958: 9). He announces himself as a spiritual guide who leads his followers to the truth, and to full harmony with Allah's creation (*fitra*). 'The aim of my work is to provide a key for the locks of Islam, a simple path to correct knowledge about the truths of our majestic religion, to right belief, judgement, society, and morality' (Buti 1972a: 6).

Conclusion

As for the debate about his role as an influential Islamic figure, many Syrians see in al-Buti *the* representative of a modern and self-conscious Islam, whose religious and social affairs are rationally determined, of a moderate and non-violent Islam in the post-revivalist era, of a problem-oriented, socially pragmatic, and denominationally ecumenical Islam in an unstable Syria attempting to open itself, politically and economically, to the outside world. Others, however, think that al-Buti represents those thinkers whose attempt at comprehensive Islamic reform has failed, being stuck halfway between the traditional, socially-conservative legacy and a modern, socially and politically progressive Islam. Yet, in his role as a Muslim leader, al-Buti seems always to have tried to present Islam as a modern, rational, enlightened, and self-aware religion. He adopted the Muslim Brotherhood's appeal to the Syrian nation to devote themselves to reading and studying Islamic knowledge for the development of a self-confident and self-sufficient Islamic civilization. Like them he empasizes principles such as social justice, social solidarity, mutual social responsiblity, strengthening the national economy, and increasing national prosperity. Yet unlike them, he attempts to prove that real progress can only be achieved through a synthesis of Islamic faith, ethics, academic research, and support by the (existing) state, adopting the idea that absolute faith (*iman*) in God is the basis of a moral society.

As a Muslim *'alim* and *faqih* he is challenged by the modernist view on traditional scholarship and the literalistic understanding of authoritative scriptures. Not that he feels threatened in his position and status as a religious expert (like many traditionalists before him), rather that he regards the decline of the *'ulama'* as the loss of an important part of the Islamic tradition. He believes that Muslims lack a proper methodology for comprehending and developing 'the essence of Islam', which is much more than merely a literal understanding of the scriptures. This can only be achieved when there is a deep and wide knowledge of the texts, especially the Qur'an and the traditions of the Prophet—in addition to an insight into the reasons, the events, the circumstances, and the purposes of each text—as well as an ability to distinguish between eternal and unalterable injunctions and those formulated to meet a temporary need, an existing custom or tradition, or certain circumstances (which can be changed when the latter change). Fulfilling the legacy of Mulla Ramadan al-Buti—as well as that of his teachers Hasan Habannakah, Mustafa al-Siba'i, and Sa'id Nursi—Shaikh al-Buti's paramount project has been, therefore, to build sound and independent institutions of Islamic learning capable of producing excellent scholars steeped in the Islamic tradition, and keeping abreast of the demands and dilemmas of the modern age.

Concerning his place as a 'culture broker' of Islamic tradition, his statements on the Salafiyya movement illustrate the potential conflict between his role as Islamic scholar, who must watch over proper and sound juridical reasoning, and his role as religious leader, who regards religious fervour and conscious interest in Islam as more important than an overcorrect observance of all rules. It is this ambiguity, and his role as a buffer between the Syrian secular authorities and the Muslim community, that has made him one of the most controversial figures in the contemporary Middle East. Certainly, it is too early to make a final statement about Shaikh al-Buti's place, as his independence and intellectual integrity are today much more at stake than when he was a middle ranked *'alim*. However, he still enjoys great respect for his charismatic teaching, and an enormous popular legitimacy envied by others. In his various roles as preacher, *mufti*, teacher, and spiritual mentor he continues to attract millions of young Muslims all over the Islamic world. Considering the fact that Kurdish scholars have always benefited from President Asad's special patronage in achieving high position within the religious establishment, Shaikh al-Buti could become an even more public figure. Al-Buti is of the right age, and has the proper Islamic *shari'a* background and a very close relationship to President Asad, which could enable him one day to become the successor of the current Grand Mufti of Syria, Ahmad Kaftaro.

Notes

1   It was during my field studies in Damascus in the months of Ramadan 1995 and 1996 that I learned about al-Buti's great significance and reputation. To my question as to which of the *'ulama'* in Damascus gives the best Ramadan sermons, everybody answered in unison: Shaikh al-Buti. Seeking advice about which of the scholars in Damascus I should primarily consult about the relationship between Islam and social change in Syria, I was again referred to al-Buti: 'Talk to him first', I was told.

'You will then realize that you need not see anybody else!' Having thus become aware of al-Buti's leading position in Syria's spiritual life I was anxious to meet him personally. In 1995 I encountered al-Buti only briefly after one of his sermons, whereas in 1996 I succeeded in conducting an interview with him in his university office.

2   The father is described as furious about such measures as the abolition of the call to prayer in Arabic, the replacement of the Arabic by the Latin alphabet, the prohibition against reciting the Qur'an publicly, the translation of the Qur'an into Turkish, the prescription to wear European clothes and the prohibition of women wearing the *hijab* and *niqab*— all of those 'acts of dangerous sabotage undertaken under pressure from British hegonomy'. Buti 1995: 29–32.

3   Because of the family's poverty (the father had to work as a trader of Islamic books, which he delivered mainly to the Kurdish Jezira region, beside his profession as Imam and *khatib* of the al-Rifa'i Mosque in the al-Harat al-Jadida neighbourhood) the father had to sell quite a large number of his own books, otherwise he would not have been able to hold the wedding celebration. Buti 1995: 62.

4   Al-Buti only escaped from being called up to the Syrian military service by becoming a student at a high school, since in the fifties the law that the only son of a family is freed from conscription had not been passed. Buti 1995: 63.

5   By means of a qualifying test the Ministry of Education has been trying to establish a short-list system, where teaching jobs are given to graduates in accordance with their place on the list. Candidates on the lower end of the list have no chance of getting a job and have to repeat the qualifying test in the following year.

6   Al-Buti's first encounters with religious scholars were exclusively with Kurdish '*ulama*', such as Mulla 'Abd al-Majid, Mulla 'Ali, Muhammad Jazu, Mulla Sa'id, Mulla 'Abd al-Jalil, and Mulla Khalid.

7   This is the subtitle of the book *Mamu Zain*: (Buti 1958).

8   Other activities included the editing of *Nahj al-'anam* (a manual of religious and ethical behaviour) and *Nu bahr* (a dictionary of juridical terminology). I am very grateful to Sandra Houot for these details.

9   In 1949, the Brotherhood won 23% of the parliamentary seats in Damascus, 19% in 1954, and 18% in 1961; see Batatu 1982: 17; also Abd Allah 1983: 88–95, and Kelidar 1974: 16–22.

10 Al-Buti could not himself take part at the gathering, but remembers the participants: his father, Hasan Habannakah, Ahmad al-Dakar, 'Abd al-Karim ar-Rifa'i, Amin al-Misri, and the study subjects: *al-Risala* by Imam al-Shafi'i and *al-Majmu'* by Imam al-Nawawi: Buti 1995: 130.

11   During my talk with al-Buti he did not seem reluctant to praise him as
      a warm-hearted and pious teacher with an enormous influence on him
      and other students. Looking back to his own life al-Buti reports that he
      learnt Islamic knowledge mainly from 'two mentors and spiritual lead-
      ers' (*ustadhain wa-murshidain*): from his father and from Hasan
      Habannakah al-Midani: Buti 1995: 62.

12   He argued that the assassination was neither 'killing because of apostacy'
      (*qatl al-murtadd*), nor 'killing because of retaliation' (*al-qatl qasasan*), nor
      'killing because of unjust war or robbery/brigandage' (*al-qatl bi-sabab al-
      siyal aw al-hiraba*): Buti 1995: 140; see also Binswanger 1981.

13   (i): Buti 1971; (ii): Buti 1973b; (iii): Buti 1972b; (iv): Buti 1975b; (v):
      Buti 1973a; (vi): Buti 1973c; (vii): Buti 1976a; (viii): Buti 1977; (ix):
      Buti n.d.; (x): Buti 1994b.

14   They are sold under the trademark: 'Hafith Records: Production and
      Distribution of Qur'an Recitations and Hymns of Praise on the Prophet'
      (*Tasjilat al-hafith: intaj wa-tawzi' khitam al-Qur'an wa-'l-mada'ih al-
      nabawiyya*).

15   In 1996 a cassette cost 40 Syrian pounds (50 pence), which is about a
      quarter of the price of a book with religious content.

16   Most of al-Buti's books are now reprinted in their 4th, 5th, or, in two
      cases, even 8th and 10th editions; thus hundreds of thousands copies
      must have been sold up until now even if one takes into consideration
      that in the Arab world only a few copies are printed per edition. Al-
      Buti's enormous productivity ocassionally still seems to astonish Ara-
      bic booksellers. When I asked one of them which works by al-Buti he
      had and he discovered the huge stock of al-Buti-works on his shelves he
      exclaimed: '*huwa majnun*'—'This man is mad!'

17   Weeping during religious speeches is a historically widespread phenom-
      enon, which can be seen as a rhetorical means to emotionalize the audi-
      ence, as Christian (1982) has shown for Christianity.

18   He advocates a new interpretation of *dhikr*-performances: '*Dhikr* means
      spiritual mobility of the heart towards Allah. In its outer appearance it
      could be *tasbih, tahwid, tahlil,* and *tawhid* (invocations) of Allah or recita-
      tions of Allah's book, it could be an individual prayer to Allah to pro-
      tect him from what he fears, a medidation on Allah's attributes, indi-
      vidual or collective seclusion, and it could be a mutual reminder not to
      forget the remembering of Allah. Each of these activities means *dhikr*
      and is in accord with the habit and tradition of the Prophet.' Lecture,
      22 January 1996.

19   Al-Buti deliberately refuses to speak of '*din wa dawla*' (religion and state).

4

Islamic History, Islamic Identity and the Reform of Islamic Law

The Thought of Husayn Ahmad Amin

NADIA ABU-ZAHRA

Husayn Ahmad Amin is a liberal writer on Islamic topics.[1] He is a retired diplomat who was educated in Egyptian schools and later graduated from the Faculty of Law at Cairo University. He followed his legal training with the study of English literature at London University. Amin worked for Egyptian radio and the BBC Arabic World Service. He also wrote two plays for the BBC (personal correspondence with Husayn Ahmad Amin dated 28 May 1996).

Amin has written articles as a journalist in various magazines published in Egypt and other Arab countries, short stories, plays, and satire in prose and rhyme (the latter in Egyptian colloquial Arabic). The bases for the consideration of his Islamic thought presented here are three of his published works. Firstly, *Dalil al-muslim al-hazin ila muqtada al-suluk fi'l-qarn al-'ishrin* (The Sad Muslim's Guide to Required Behaviour in the Twentieth Century), which first appeared in 1983, and was awarded the prize for the best book at the 1984 Cairo International Book Fair. In this book, Amin treats the various misconceptions Muslims have added to Islam over the centuries. Amin maintains that these misconceptions and additions have veiled the real message of Islam, ossified it, and hindered Muslims from responding to the changing needs of society. The second work is *Hawla al-da'wa ila tatbiq al-shari'a al-islamiyya wa dirasat islamiyya ukhra* (On the Call to Apply *Shari'a* Law, and other Traditions of Islamic Learning), which first appeared in 1985. This book is composed of seventeen articles which had all been published before in various Arabic magazines (details of when and where are not given). Six articles are on the subject of the reform of the *shari'a*. The rest deal with a variety of subjects, ranging from the historical development of secularism in the West to the *Salaf al-Salih* (The Pious Forefathers) and misconceptions concerning them, which he treated earlier in *The Sad Muslim's Guide*. There is also a chapter on 'Ali 'Abd al-Raziq's *al-Islam wa-usul al-hukm* (Islam and the Bases of Political Authority). The other articles are on a variety of subjects, such as the place of dogs in Islam and Muslim societies. In the more light-hearted journalistic essays, he humourously criticizes the behaviour of some Muslim groups in Texas and Los Angeles who consider that sitting on the floor is a tradition of the Prophet to be emulated even when attending a public lecture; they also forbid watching television, which they regard as religiously unlawful, and believe in the segregation of the sexes and the wearing of the veil even for small girls. Another article is an account of the persecution of Muslim thinkers in the Soviet Union. These two works were re-published in one volume in 1987, and this is the text used in this work. Amin's arguments in *The Sad Muslim's Guide* and *The Call to Apply the Shari'a Law* are supported by the relevant Qur'anic texts and by historical references, but the specific publication details of the sources he uses and the pages from which he makes his quotations are not indicated.

The third work I have used is his *al-Islam fi 'alam mutaghayyir wa-maqalat Islamiyya ukhra* (Islam in a Changing World, and other Essays on Islam) (1988) As a polemical work, the book is interesting, but it is based mostly on long quotations, many of them from Western sources or translations of these sources. The book deals with a variety of subjects, ranging from historical accounts on the subject of the Muslims' response to the West, to journalistic articles, satire, and creative writing in the form of a short play. In this book Amin reaffirms most of the arguments developed in the previous two works, but omits the cornerstone of his thesis: Islamic identity. This leads to some inconsistency in his argument, as will be discussed below.

Amin's argument

Amin's thesis, extracted from the first two books, is that the Muslim world should develop and change in order to join the global community. This desirable change is hindered by the Muslims' wish to return to the past, rather than to look forward and adapt the *shari'a* rules to present social conditions. Amin maintains that correct knowledge of the history of Islam, the biography of the Prophet, the lives of the Pious Forefathers, and the history of the development of the *shari'a*, would enhance Muslims' confidence in their Islamic identity and heritage. This would enable them to accept change, comfortably incorporate within their Islamic heritage elements from other civilizations, and thus join the global community and avoid isolation. According to Amin, to achieve correct knowledge of Islamic history able historians, who can differentiate between what is authentic and what is a superfluous addition to the Islamic message should have the courage to promote these facts (Amin 1987: 27). But he does not explain how a historian might acquire this confidence before commencing the historical investigation. Amin, however, maintains that correct knowledge of the history of Islam requires the elimination of additions to the Islamic message, and the the avoidance of omission and apology. Thus Muslims should accept authentic historical accounts of the life of the Prophet, the lives of the Pious Forefathers, and the history of Islam. These would show Muslims that the historical figures they venerate were ordinary human beings who had their human shortcomings. Correct knowledge of the history of Islam also indicates that *shari'a* law developed centuries ago, and that, due to social and political circumstances, its stipulations have not been amended to accord with new social conditions. According to Amin, this knowledge would encourage Muslims to innovate, to adapt to new social conditions, and to convince people to agree to the modernization of *shari'a* law. Muslims would thereby be encouraged to adhere to their Islamic identity, and consequently regain their self-esteem, confidently accept change, and adopt Western technology and thought. This would not harm the integrity of Islam and its heritage.

Amin maintains that ignorance of the Islamic tradition leads to loss of direction, identity, and diginty, and to intellectual contradictions. On the other hand, adherence to the Islamic heritage—and social traditions relating to Islamic festivals and occasions—helps to avoid confusion and the indiscriminate importation of bits and pieces of Western thought and fashion (Amin 1987: 137). He also states that the superficial adoption of Western ways does not last. For instance, the removal of the veil by some high-class women had no lasting effect.

The social conditions and cultural contradictions prevailing in Egypt indicate this lack of direction and self-esteem. Educated people and thinkers produce unsuitable material. For instance, a philosopher uses an elementary American textbook while writers often dwell on the work of secondary Western figures such as Oscar Wilde or Somerset Maugham. Meanwhile important Arabic works, like those of al-Jahiz, Abu Hayyan al-Tawhidi, Averroes and Ibn Tufayl, are ignored and ridiculed, being called 'the yellow books' (a reference to the poor quality paper they are printed on); and those who read them are also ridiculed. Islamic and social traditions are criticized in the newspapers. The media diminshes the Arabic heritage. Egyptian movies and TV programmes ridicule literate people, and the teaching of Arabic is made boring. Arabic books taught in schools are badly printed, while foreign language books are well produced and appeal to the reader.

Amin describes the negative effect on the Egyptian people of this cultural disorientation, and the corresponding economic difficulties and social upheavals. Educated people are faced with contradictory values. Amin gives the example of the diplomat (supposedly an educated person) who goes to court in order to force his wife to return to 'the house of obedience'. According to Amin, due to economic pressures and lack of planning, young people are also disoriented. Thus the ambition of university graduates is to work as waiters in fashionable restaurants and cafeterias. Other young people have lost their faith in Islam and its heritage, and when they can they emigrate to the West. Youth who come from lower, deprived classes and are surrounded by corruption reject their society. Citing the Qur'anic verse 'whoever does not rule in accordance with what God has revealed, they are unbelievers' (V:43), they accuse the society of *kufr* (unbelief in God). According to Amin, though, they are ignorant of Islam; they have the courage to oppose the government and to demand the application of the *shari'a* and a return to the past, but at the same time they deny others the right to renew and innovate in order to respond to the realities of Egyptian society, while the *'ulama'* do not have the courage to oppose corrupt governments, which exploit their passivity to tarnish the image of the *'ulama'* in the eyes of the public.

Amin argues that members of the Islamist groups are, with a few exceptions, ignorant of Islamic history and the social circumstances of the development of *shari'a* law. Their desire to apply the rulings of the

Medinan *umma* to contemporary society isolates Muslims from the rest of the world, and hinders social change and economic development. Such sweeping fundamentalism, he argues, also runs counter to *hatmiyat al-tarikh*, the unalterable course of history (Amin 1987: 140; and 1988: 188, 279), ordained by the divine will, which can be discerned in it, and the fact that a successful Muslim society may be established on the basis of knowledge of this divine will. Amin also argues that for *shari'a* law to be adapted to new social conditions, Muslims should be guided by the spirit of Islam, which he vaguely explains as follows: Islam means submission to the will of God, and according to Amin, if events are the expression of divine will, observing their direction will help Muslims to discern the end result of a course of events which may oppose the divine direction, such as the Islamist programmes. According to Amin, then, the compass that direct us to God's will is to follow the spirit of Islam (Amin 1987: 138–41).

Amin maintains that the flourishing of Islamist groups in Egypt is associated with oppressive social and economic conditions, and regrets that, in response to these conditions, such groups, who know neither Islamic history, the *shari'a* nor *fiqh*, demand the application of *shari'a* law as it was practised in early Islam. Amin argues that this militates against any reform of *shari'a* law. Thus, in his second work, *The Call to Apply Shari'a Law*, Amin demonstrates the necessity of such reform. In this respect Amin follows the ideas of Muhammad 'Abduh, who differentiated between the *shari'a* as the rulings of the Qur'an and the sound *sunna*, and *fiqh* as the deductions of the jurists. 'Abduh maintained that the four schools of Sunni legal thought reached their conclusions on the basis of Qur'anic and *sunna* research centuries ago, and that their rulings do not apply to present social conditions. Thus new Islamic rulings are needed to deal with new conditions and social problems. 'Abduh also claims that the jurists failed because they did not understand politics, and could not make the rulers follow *shari'a* law. The rulers despised them, used them for their own purposes, and made them produce the *fatawa'* they needed. The jurists compiled the rulings and considered them *ahkam shar'iyya* (*shar'i* rules) (al-Tanahi 1963: 208, 212–18).

Amin opposes the argument that the *shari'a* is unchangeable and, agreeing with Muhammad 'Abduh, maintains that *shari'a* law was formed several centuries ago, and that many of its rules and regulations are not applicable to present social problems. Nonetheless, the issue of adherence to the *shari'a* is used for political advantage. The government, according to Amin, uses the subject of the application of *shari'a* law to cover its own weaknesses and distract the public's attention from real political problems, such as its bans on political parties or the postponement of elections. The government also displays interest in applying *shari'a* law as a means to getting aid from a certain wealthy Arab country which pretends to favour the *shari'a*, when in fact it is contributing aid in order to encourage hostility between the recipient country and its neighbour, whose politics do not suit those of the rich country (Amin 1987: 221). In addition to such pressures, there is also the public who claim that they respect the *shari'a*. The government responds to all this by forming parliamentary committees to consider how to implement the *shari'a*.

Amin urges Muslims to acknowledge the obstacles to the application of *shari'a* law. He states that objective historical studies show that it developed in accordance with Islamic events; this knowledge, he maintains, would convince people to accept the validity of developing *shari'a* law so as to be applicable to the social problems of the twentieth century and prevalent social conditions. Amin also argues that the *'ulama'* should re-examine the *shari'a* rules and regulations to adapt them to present social conditions.

According to Amin, to reject Islam as Kamal Ataturk did is not the solution,[2] nor is it viable for legislators to make excuses and develop lengthy explanations in order to prohibit polygamy, as they did in Tunisia and South Yemen. Amin considers that it is better to assess the social conditions pertinent to a particular rule, and, if its application is no longer suitable, to replace it by a new rule inspired by Islam (Amin 1987: 239–40). Amin does not, however, give any examples to illustrate how to create a new rule independent of *shari'a* law but inspired by Islam.

Social stagnation and the Shari'a law

Amin maintains that social stagnation is associated with some Islamic beliefs, some additions to Islam, and to the lack of reform of *shari'a* law. Regarding Islamic beliefs, Amin discusses people's attitude of resignation, in the light of their belief in the Islamic tradition that the advent of the Mahdi would transform society and bring justice and prosperity. As a result of this belief, he argues, people passively wait and hope that a new government can solve all their problems. Egyptians rejoice at the advent of a new government, become disappointed soon afterwards, then resigned to their fate and await the advent of a new government. According to Amin, additions to Islam include the development of Sufism, Sufi orders, and the common Islamic belief in *awliya'* (friends of God/Muslim saints). He maintains that belief in the miracles of these saints has no Islamic foundation and is based on indigenous traditions.

Amin devotes most of his discussion to the subject of the reform of *shari'a* law. He considers that the objective study of history reveals that the *shari'a* developed over time, and that, as Islam spread amongst other nations who had different cultures, their local customs were incorporated into Islamic practice. He argues that the Qur'an was revealed to the Prophet over a period of 23 years. Some verses, therefore, refer to specific events like the campaign at the time of the battle of Badr, and specific acts of the Prophet, such as his marriage to Zaynab bint Jahsh.[3] He points out that some Qur'anic verses also abrogated others, whilst some were replaced by prescriptions more suitable to the unfolding events. Moreover, various Qur'anic prescriptions relate to the practices of pre-Islamic society and were in response to the social circumstances prevalent then, and these practices no longer have the same social implications. Over the centuries Muslim societies have changed and now have new problems, which need new *shar'i* legislation.

According to Amin, the misconceptions which hinder the reform of *shari'a* law are the following: Firstly, that the Prophet and the Pious Forefathers are infallible. This misconception is based on the omission of certain early events from the Prophet's *sira* and the lives of his Companions, or on apology for them. Such omissions and apologies help to depict them as infallible, intimidating Muslims and deterring them from formulating new Islamic rules. The Prophet and the Companions were human beings. Historical accounts show that some of the Prophet's actions did not win the approval of his Companions, and that certain Islamic rules, stipulated at the time of the Prophet, were applicable only at a certain stage in the development of early Muslim society.

The second misconception is that, in the early period of the Prophet's campaigns, the resistance to his mission was only a resistance to a new religion. But in reality the resistance was also driven by political and economic interests. Amin also considers later Islamic disputes to have been struggles for political authority disguised as doctrinal conflicts. Thirdly, Muslims do not appreciate the historical and political events which isolated the jurists and separated their works from the social conditions of their own societies.

The Prophet was a human being who never claimed to perform miracles or know the *unknown* (the realm of God, Qur'an VI:50), nor did he claim that he was infallible. He made mistakes, for which God admonished him in certain Qur'anic verses (LXXX:1–10). Following the Prophet's death, and until the Middle Ages, historians recorded the life of the Prophet without commenting on it (Amin 1987: 33). They believed that God's will was manifest in the historical events of this world, and that it was perhaps possible for future generations to discern this will if events were plainly recorded. 'Urwa b. al-Zuhayr b. al-'Awwam (d. 94/712), Aban b. 'Uthman b. 'Affan (d. 105/723–4), and Musa b. 'Uqba (d. 758 AD) were frank about the life of the Prophet, and made no mention of miracles. Ibn Ishaq, al-Waqidi and al-Tabari recorded without any comments the hostilities between the Muslims and the tribes of Banu Qurayza and Banu al-Nadir, which led to the killing of the captives from the former tribe. According to Amin, these early historians accepted the argument of the military leaders that this was ordained by God (who also ordained the war itself). During the siege of Banu al-Nadir, the Prophet ordered the cutting down and the burning of their palm trees. This was not an accepted practice, and the Prophet's companions were not pacified until a Qur'anic verse was revealed to the Prophet to justify this action (LIX:5).

Amin maintains that with the expansion of the Arabs in neighbouring lands, they encountered other nations and began to debate Islam with Christians and Jews; and, as Christ had performed miracles, Muslims attributed miracles to the Prophet also. Because the Prophet was criticized for polygamy, this was attributed to political goals which were not recorded in earlier biographies. The Muslims also apologized for the events of Banu Qurayza and Banu al-Nadir. The apologetic writing of the biography of the Prophet intensified after contact with the West. In earlier centuries the West denigrated the image of the

Prophet, and in later centuries he was judged according to Western values.

Contemporary Arab authors write the Prophet's biography in order to justify the events in it, as if faith would be shaken if there were no such justification. The most damaging example within this category of Arabic writing is Muhammad Husayn Haykal's *Life of Muhammad*. It omits what the author considers unpalatable, and, as such, acts as a barrier between the reader and the original sources. These readers are subsequently shaken by what they read in Ibn Ishaq, al-Waqidi, or Ibn Sa'd. An honest, proud writing of the Prophet's biography is what is needed today: a biography that does not patronize, omit, or apologize; a biography, according to Amin, that is worthy of the traditions of the writings of al-Tabari and al-Waqidi.

The fabrication of the traditions of the Prophet was a later development which negatively affected the development of *shari'a* law. During the time of the rightly-guided Caliphs, fabrication of traditions of the Prophet did not occur (Amin 1987: 58). Abu Bakr and 'Umar b. al-Khattab did not report traditions from the Prophet and 'Uthman b. 'Affan ordered people not to circulate traditions which were not heard during the period of the rule of his predecessors. With the exception of Abu Hurayra, who was called the 'pious liar', the Prophet's Companions did not attribute false traditions to the Prophet (Amin 1987: 59).

Social conditions and the political climate led to the fabrication of Prophetic traditions. When the Umayyads came to administer new provinces they confronted new problems, the answers to which were not to be found in the Qur'an. In such cases they considered it obligatory to follow the Prophet's traditions (Amin 1987: 53–5). Moreover, the public desired to emulate the example of the Prophet. Traditions were fabricated to satisfy these needs (Amin 1987: 61–7), and if jurists tried to verify them the public accused them of apostasy, preferring to listen to preachers and storytellers.

Traditions were also fabricated to support political causes. Thus the Shi'a fabricated traditions to support the cause of the House of the Prophet. The Umayyads responded by having traditions fabricated to support their own authority, and to condemn factional wars between Muslims (Amin 1987: 55). The fact that the Qur'an states that the Prophet could not know the future did not prevent the Abbasids claiming that the Prophet had foretold their advent. Supporters of Abu Hanifa attributed to the Prophet a prediction that Abu Hanifa would become a prominent jurist, and Muslims from different provinces attributed to the Prophet traditions to the effect that people from these particular provinces were praiseworthy.

Some jurists (for example, Ibn Hanbal) condoned traditions which encouraged virtue and ignored the accuracy of their chains of transmission. This procedure came to be so abused that it ended up as the subject of jokes (Amin 1987: 62). Abu Hanifa objected to the fabrication of traditions, and argued that to answer new problems jurists should use *ijtihad* and *qiyas* (reasoning by analogy) and follow the ideals of Islam; other jurists, however, continued to support *ijtihad* by fabricating traditions in its favour (Amin 1987: 71–2). The ensuing confusion caused some jurists to try to establish criteria by which to verify the accuracy of traditions. They overlooked the text and concentrated on the personal qualities of the scholars of *hadith* and the narrators: their piety, honesty, reliability, and identity. They aimed to assess the historical possibility that narrators lived at the times of those from whom they quoted in the chain of transmission (Amin 1987: 69). Bukhari used this criterion to examine 600,000 traditions, and found that only 7,379 could be correct. If repetition is eliminated, the number is reduced to only 2,762 traditions.

Veneration of the Pious Forefathers also intimidated people, deterring them from innovation because they thought that they did not possess the necessary superior human qualities. Examination of the records of the actions of several of the Companions of the Prophet demonstrates that they were ordinary human beings capable of the mistakes and shortcomings common to all mortals. Amin gives the example of Sa'd b. Abi Waqqas, one of the ten Companions whom the Prophet anticipated would go to paradise in the afterlife. Nonetheless it is known, according to Amin, that he did not fast during the month of Ramadan and, once, was reluctant to repay his debts (Amin 1987: 273–5).

There is also the misconception that certain events were concerned solely with Islam when, in fact, they were concerned with political authority. Thus, according to Amin, during the Prophet's lifetime the state was at the service of religion, and the Prophet did not differentiate between political and religious authority. The rightly-guided

Caliphs' duty was to safeguard the *shari'a*, which was to regulate all aspects of life. Political and social movements were expressed in an Islamic idiom. Amin maintains that the Kharijites' opposition to 'Ali b. Abi Talib originated from the pre-Islamic tribal custom of Banu Tamim, to which the Kharijites belonged. In the pre-Islamic era they lived in small communities which raided caravans and cities. Such raids were replaced by the Islamic campaigns, but when the campaigns ended, the Kharijites resented the sedentary life of the military camps in cities, revolted against 'Ali b. Abi Talib, and reverted to living in small camps on the outskirts of cities, which they attacked. But instead of calling these attacks raids they called them *jihad*. He also claims that the Shi'a struggle was essentially political rather than doctrinal (Amin 1987: 110–12).

According to Amin, political and social circumstances shaped the development of *shari'a* law and, over the centuries, these same social circumstances caused the decline of the social standing and authority of Muslim jurists. For instance, the debate over whether the Qur'an was created or eternal was a debate about political authority (Amin 1987: 116–17). It suited the Abbasid caliph, al-Mutawwakil, to espouse the Mu'tazilite argument that the Qur'an is created, because this would enable him to avoid the supervision of jurists like Ibn Hanbal, who argued that the Qur'an was eternal and coexistent with God.

The decline of the status of the jurists contributed to the stagnation of *shari'a* law; the political struggles isolated the jurists and prevented them from adapting *shari'a* law to the problems of society. The Umayyads had ignored the jurists who remained in Mecca and Medina and devoted their energies to the scholarly study of the *shari'a*. Later, jurists supported the Abbasids, who appointed them as judges and tutors to their children. Schools for teaching *fiqh* were established to train graduates for government jobs; thus, to earn their living, the jurists depended on the political system (Amin 1987: 120–3). Over the centuries the jurists became submissive to rulers and, therefore, produced the *fatwas* they required. They engaged in highly formalized doctrinal debates, whilst failing to develop the intellectual foundation which would enable the *shari'a* to deal with changing social conditions (Amin 1987: 125–6). Relations between rulers and jurists, however, were not always so smooth: al-Mutawakkil imprisoned Ibn Hanbal and prevented him from teaching because of his views on the eternity of the Qur'an.

When Amin comes to consider more recent times, he describes how in nineteenth-century Egypt the Azharites weakened their position by collaborating with Muhammmad 'Ali against their leader 'Umar Makram. They became divided as a result, and Muhammad 'Ali took advantage of their weakness to spread rumours against them and humiliate them in the eyes of the people. According to Amin, Muhammad 'Ali also contributed to the continuance of the people's ignorance of their Islamic heritage. He separated the secular and the religious systems of education. In the former the teaching of Islam was marginalized, and consequently its graduates lost touch with their Islamic heritage. 'Ulama' such as Rifa'a al-Tahtawi were dependent on Muhammad 'Ali and, as a result, did not take a stand against Western writing on Islam (Amin 1987: 117, 127, 131, 145-8).

In later decades, because of the political strife in Egypt which affected the al-Azhar university, the renovation of Islamic thought and *shari'a* law which promoted the use of *ijtihad* and was introduced by al-Afghani and Muhammad 'Abduh was unsuccessful because they were opposed by the *'ulama'* (see Crecelius 1978). According to Amin, the failure to revive the concept of *ijtihad* disappointed those who saw the need for Islamic reform. Some renounced religion altogether, while others who were disappointed in the *'ulama'* looked for guidance from secular writers who knew neither *fiqh* nor the *shari'a* (Amin 1987: 133).[4]

The reform of the Shari'a law

In *The Call to Apply Shari'a Law*, Amin endeavours to convince Muslims that *shar'i* rules and regulations can be developed. He quotes historical instances which demonstrate that the same *shar'i* rule was applied differently at different times and in different societies. He also argues that Qur'anic stipulations and traditions of the Prophet were often suspended. For example, jurists have prescribed different rules for marriage in different Muslim societies. Amin also raises the question of the unsuitability of some *shar'i* laws, like the cutting off of the hand of a thief, and points out that, instead of abolishing it, jurists have used various pretexts to avoid applying this punishment. He also questions the validity of attributing the wearing of the veil by women to Islamic prescriptions.

To prove that shari'a law is changeable, Amin gives the example of the punishment for the consumption of alcohol. Although the Qur'an does not stipulate any punishment for the consumption of alcohol, during the Prophet's lifetime a person who committed this offence was beaten, and although the rightly-guided Caliphs were guided by the Qur'an and their immediate knowledge of the teachings of the Prophet, they nonetheless exceeded the punishment stipulated by the tradition of the Prophet (Amin 1987: 201). Abu Bakr stipulated whipping the offender with forty lashes, and 'Umar b. al-Khattab increased this to sixty lashes. The latter also abolished temporary marriage (muta') which had been an accepted Islamic marriage contract.

When the Umayyads vastly expanded the territory of the still young dar al-Islam, their judges incorporated many of the customary laws ('urf) of the newly conquered peoples, and it was left to the judges to follow the Qur'anic stipulations or not (Amin 1987: 202).

Another example is the rules of marriage, in respect of which different shar'i regulations developed in different societies. For instance, Abu Hanifa in Baghdad—which was a mixed community of Arabs, Persians, and Turks—prescribed rules of compatiblity in wealth and status in marriage contracts. In Medina, which was composed of a more homogenous population, such marriage regulations were not needed. For a similar reason, slaves did not have the right to own property in Baghdad, while they did in Medina (Amin 1987: 192–6).

According to Amin, from the era of the Umayyads and Abbasids right up to the present day, the shari'a has not been obeyed; nonetheless the public accept only the shari'a, and though governments claim that they respect and uphold it, they actually fear it, because it represents a check on their political authority (Amin 1987: 207). The 'ulama' defend it because it promotes their powers, and rather than confronting the problem that some shar'i regulations are not applicable, and formulating new Islamic laws, they elaborate all sorts of subterfuges to avoid their application. For instance, they developed the legal ruse that a divorcee whose husband had triply pronounced the divorce formula can lawfully remarry her former husband if she goes through the legal formalities of a marriage contract to a man who divorces her immediately afterwards. Special contracts were also devised in order to receive interest on loans without violating the formalities of *shari'a* law. Tricks were also employed in order to avoid *haqq al-shuf'a* (the right of first option for a partner or neighbour to buy the partner's/neighbour's share). The works of Hanafi and Shafi'i law abound in these ruses, devised to avoid *shari'a* law in situations where it is inapplicable (Amin 1987: 205).

According to Amin, thinkers, reformers, and *'ulama'* ought to confront the Qur'anic text honestly, and rather than making excuses and devising tricks should develop new legislation inspired by the Islamic spirit (Amin 1987: 195–6). To argue this point, he takes the example of the Qur'anic prescription that the punishment for thieves is the cutting off of their hands (V:38). The Prophet confirmed this punishment, and is reported to have said: 'If Fatima daughter of Muhammad stole, Muhammad would cut off her hand.' Amin demonstrates that as the social implication of theft had changed from the days of pre-Islamic society, rather than honestly confronting the problem and legislating a new law, the jurists made excuses and devised tricks to avoid the application of this punishment.

In pre-Islamic society stealing had serious implications. For instance, in the desert, stealing a man's camel, his water supply and food would have resulted in his death, and stealing camels caused years of tribal wars and strife. This severe punishment was needed to put a stop to tribal wars and unite the Arabs into an Islamic nation. With the spread of Islam, the Arabs came to rule over new provinces, and landed property became more important than movable property. This greatly altered the implications of theft. Jurists then variously set about defining what constituted stealing and embezzlement. They did not honestly confront the Qur'anic text and the traditions of the Prophet, and accept that new suitable laws were needed to accommodate the new implications of the theft of movable property. Thus, in order to avoid the cutting off of the hand of the thief, they stipulated thirty eight conditions to exclude many acts from the category 'theft', and supported these conditions by fabricating *hadiths*. Some examples of cases in which the act might be exempt from the punishment of amputation are: stealing books for the purposes of learning, stealing musical instruments, animals, or poultry, and stealing public money (because the thief has a share in it). Poverty, and stealing during periods of excessive heat and cold, also exempt the thief from the punishment of amputation (Amin

1987: 216). In Egypt, according to Amin, a parliamentary committee was formed some years ago to investigate the subject of the application of *shari'a* law. Such committees, he comments, should realize that the crime of the embezzlement of public funds causes the same strife as did the theft of a camel in the time of the *Jahiliyya*.

For the purpose of modernising *shari'a* law, Amin finds great benefit in the concept of consensus (*ijma'*), the third source of the *shari'a*. As social problems are different at different times and in different societies, the consensus of the religious authorities is able to handle new problems. It is also part of the rules of consensus that if people follow a certain practice for a sufficiently long period of time it becomes part of the *sunna*. For instance, until the eighth Islamic century the celebration of the Prophet's birthday was considered an innovation, but then it became part of Islamic life and culture.

Amin also considers the phenomenon of the return to veiling, which really began after the Arabs' defeat in June 1967 by Israel. He links it to political and economic decline. Nasser's regime, he says, destroyed family ties, obscured class boundaries, and consequently wealth became the means to acquire social status. The defeat of 1967 destroyed the population's trust in their government and its proclamation and, together with declining social and economic conditions, it devastated their lives. The emergence of militant Islam was a response to the difficult economic conditions confronting the deprived strata of the society. The middle class and the working class, according to Amin, are the classes which were damaged by Nasser's regime and Sadat's open door policy. He maintains that middle-class women wear the veil to signify their stance against the threat to their social status, and to distance themselves from the corruption surrounding them (Amin 1987: 229–36).

Amin argues that the wearing of the veil is not a specifically Islamic custom, that it was known before Islam, and that today it is known in other parts of the world as part of religious ritual (consider, for instance, the custom of wearing the mantilla in religious processions in Spain) (Amin 1987: 243). He then discusses the development of the Qur'anic use of the word *hijab* (veiling). In the Qur'an, the word occurs in the Meccan period to mean that the unbelievers are separated from God (LXXXIII:14), and to refer to the fact that when Maryam found that she was pregnant she lived in seclusion (XIX:15–16). Amin gives all the Qur'anic usages of the word in this sense in the Meccan period (Amin 1987: 243–4), and maintains that the word *hijab* was used only once in the Medina period (XXXIII:7), where it refers only to the wives of the Prophet, to whom men should speak from behind a curtain.

The Qur'anic texts which deal with the behaviour of women are in the Medinan verses. In sura XXXIII (*al-Ahzab*), verses 32 to 34 refer only to the wives of the Prophet, and in this sura, as well as in sura XXIV (*al-Nur*) verse 60, modest behaviour is recommended. The debate on the subject of the veiling of women focuses on verse 59 in sura XXXIII, addressed to the wives of the Prophet, and verse 31 in sura XXIV, addressed to the women of the believers. XXXIII:59 says: 'O Prophet, say to the wives and daughters and the believing women that they draw their veils close to them, so it is more likely that they would be known and not hurt.' Al-Wahidi explains the historical circumstances of this verse: it was directed against the youth who followed women when they left their compound at night to go to the outskirts of Medina. Slave women who were available to men used to be dressed as free women, so the Qur'anic verse recommends the veiling of the wives of the Prophet so that they would then be distinguished and not hurt (Amin 1987: 245, 247).

Verse 31 of sura 24 states:

And say to the believing women, that they cast their eyes and guard their private parts, and reveal not their adornment save such as is outward, and let them cast their veils over their bosom and not reveal their adornments save to their husbands, fathers or their sons, or their brothers' sons, or their sisters' sons, or their women, or what their right hands own, or such men as attend them, not having sexual desire, or children who have not yet attained knowledge of women's private parts, nor let them stamp their feet so that their hidden ornaments may be known.

According to Amin's research, the command in this verse refers to the fact that women used to wear shirts which had a large opening below the neck and showed their breasts while their head-covering fell on their shoulders. Thus they were advised to draw their head-coverings over their front to cover their breasts. These Qur'anic verses advise, but do not stipulate any punishment—either in this world or in the hereafter (Amin 1987: 248).

Amin goes on to argue that if the veil was meant to cover the face, and that the majority of jurists would not have allowed its uncovering. He also maintains that since slavery is now prohibited, a means of differentiation between slaves and free women is no longer needed. He also refers to the recorded fact that Sakina bint al-Husayn b. 'Ali and 'A'isha bint Talha b. 'Abdullah did not veil themselves. He adds that, in the third century, women prayed in mosques. According to Amin, the influence of Persian culture with its strict rules of veiling, affected the interpretation of the Qur'an and extended the rule of the veiling of the wives of the Prophet to all women.

It is part of Amin's thesis that if a practice justifying a particular *shar'i* rule ceases to pertain, the rule becomes obsolete (Amin 1988: 253, 259, 262). Accordingly, he argues that since slavery has been abolished the use of the veil to distinguish different classes of women is obsolete. However, he contradicts this when he maintains that middle-class Egyptian women wear the veil to indicate that they are defining their status, and dissociating themselves from the corruption surrounding them. This is again contradicted in his work *Islam in a Changing World*, where he maintains that some women are willing to prostitute themselves for the sake of acquiring material goods (Amin 1988: 164).[5] According to my observations, however, veiling in Egypt is not confined to a particular class, and one of the complex implications of wearing the veil is still to claim modesty and virtue, and to differentiate, as was the case in early Muslim society, between respectable and corrupt women. In addition, those who adhere to the veiling of women also argue that, since it is a *sunna* of the Prophet, it is an appropriate social custom to follow.

Egypt and modernity

In the opening pages of his third book, *Islam in a Changing World*, Amin contrasts the superiority of Muslim civilization to that of Europe during the period of the Crusades. He goes on to document the decline of the Muslims when they took their superiority for granted, while Europe developed and became superior to them (Amin 1988: 5-6). Thus, in the first three chapters, Amin describes the impact of the French campaign in 1798 on Egypt, and the Egyptians' realization of the gap between themselves and the advanced scientific, technological and military achievements of the French. Thus al-Jabarti, the Egyptian chronicler, records that he had nothing left to pride himself in except his faith in Islam (Amin 1988: 7). Amin details the cordial relationship between Napoleon and his entourage and the Azhar *'ulama'*, but leaves out the latter's resistance to the occupation, and their persecution and humiliation by the French, as described by al-Jibarti (Ali 1986: 86–118). He also neglects to mention the bombardment of the Azhar quarter by the French artillery (Vatikiotis 1991: 44). Amin describes the impact of the French on Egyptian social life: the rule of the segregation of the sexes was relaxed during the period of the three years of French occupation, and Egyptian women who were subjected to severe *harim* seclusion were impressed by how the French treated their women. Amin also gives an account of the Europeans' social life in Egypt in the nineteenth century; and devotes the fourth chapter to the life and travels of Richard Burton, his life in Cairo, his difficulties in dealing with Egyptian bureaucracy, and an instance of his flirting with an Egyptian woman.

In the following chapters Amin deals with the efforts of Muhammad 'Abduh, in the late nineteenth century, to renew Islamic thought and reconcile Islam with the premises of European civilization—such as liberalism and the modern state. Central to 'Abduh's thought was the notion that Islam is compatible with the bases of scientific method, which is universal and not attached to any particular religion. Today, according to Amin, some followers of this trend overlook the objective study of history, and try to reconcile the life of the Prophet with the values of the twentieth century, thereby hindering objective historical research.

Amin then follows Islamic thought to the present day, concluding that the economic and social difficulties created by Sadat's policies strengthened militant Islamic groups. He argues that Sadat's open-door economic policy increased the gap between, on the one hand, the nouveau riche, and the middle class and the poor on the other. Secondly, the peace treaty with Israel weakened the Arabs, neither fulfilling its promise to the Palestinians nor leading to the bounty Sadat had promised to the Egyptians. These difficulties paved the way for organized militant Islamic movements, whose adherents, according to Amin, ossify Islamic knowledge in rigid forms based on the works of the Pious Forefathers, which include harmful elements.

Amin also treats the same subjects he treated in his earlier two books. He returns, for example, to the subject of the isolation of the earlier jurists from legal procedure and social problems, and argues that dislike of innovation is a *jahili* tradition. It is necessary to encourage *ijtihad*, Amin argues, because it is socially harmful for society to be made up of people who do not question received ideas.

Other chapters deal with the Egyptian government's responses to the Islamist groups' desire to apply *shari'a* law. For instance, chapter fourteen is on the prohibition of alcohol in the United States in the 1930s, which led to crime and corruption. This is a warning to the Egyptian government not to prohibit alcohol in response to the pressures of Islamist groups. In chapter fifteen he issues a warning to those Egyptians who maintain that the opposition of the militant Islamic groups to the government is justifiable on account of the government's inadequate policies, saying that this would contribute to the increased influence of the militant groups. The book also writes satirically on the custom of Muslims and Copts to stick printed slogans on their cars to indicate their religion.[6] Amin summarizes these chapters by stating again that changing social conditions necessitate the reform of *shar'i* rulings, which should be accomplished within the idiom of an Islamic world view, and express Islamic values, religious experience, and social circumstances; yet he does not explain this in any detail.

Amin ends the book with some creative writing in the form of satire and a short play (chapters nineteen and twenty). The satire combines a manifesto of a leader of an Islamic revolution and the repression people would suffer under such a government; the short play is on the same subject.

In this book Amin's historical account emphasizes the gap between Muslim civilization in the past and its present decline, and urges a renewal of Islamic thought and reform. Like other Egyptian writers addressing the lay reader, Amin does not consistently give the details of sources from which he makes quotations. For instance, the section on Burton (Amin 1988: 101–15) contains long quotations (Amin 1988: 103–4, 107–8, 109–10, 112–13, 114–15), but bibliographical and page references are not given. Amin also attributes some quotations to unidentified persons to whom he refers by such phrases as 'one of them has said', but in all such instances the statements are followed by long quotations without proper references (Amin 1988: 147, 169, 246, 261).

In addition, some of the statements are not fully contextualized, which leads to confusion. For instance, he maintains that Rashid Rida, a follower of Muhammad 'Abduh, adopted Arab nationalism (Amin 1988: 13). But Rida's views were advocated within a particular historical context. He held the Turks responsible for the decline of the Muslim World and placed the Arabs at the centre of a renewed Islamic state (Shahin 1995: 411). Amin also refers to important related subjects, but does not expand on them or point out their interrelationships. For instance, he maintains that his research indicates that Islamic stipulations were not followed either in Egypt or in other parts of the Muslim world (Amin 1988: 229), but he gives no details of this research. Furthermore, he states that Egyptians, from the time of the rule of Ibn Tulun in 868 AD until the end of the nineteenth and the beginning of the twentieth century, retained their Egyptian identity and Islamic precepts were ignored (Amin 1988: 117–19). He then maintains that today the majority of Egyptians adhere to Islam (Amin 1988: 159), and that, paradoxically, people are increasingly adopting Western ways (Amin 1988: 150–2, 190, 229–30).

In this work Amin leaves out the subject of Islamic identity, and the necessity of adhering to the social traditions associated with Islamic festivals and occasions. He remains firm, however, in his argument that the objective study of Islamic history, the reform of *shari'a* law, and the assimilation of Western thought would lead to progress. He also asserts the connection between the divine will and the unalterable course of history (Amin 1988:157, 227, 279).

Summary and assessment

Amin writes in an eloquent, witty and brisk style that make his work enjoyable to read. His genuine concern for the decline in the political and economic spheres of Egyptian life, and his candid criticism of the Egyptian government contribute to the value of his work.

In *The Sad Muslim's Guide* Amin shows how economic hardship, combined with the lack of an Islamic identity and ignorance of the Islamic heritage, leads to social and cultural chaos. The work is also informative on aspects of the history of Islam. Some of Amin's arguments, however, are open to debate. For instance, he argues that objective knowledge of Islamic history and of the political and social isolation of the earlier jurists would encourage people to accept the idea of a developing *shari'a* law. But it also can be argued that there are many *'ulama'* and intellectuals who have a sophisticated knowledge of the history of Islam, of the development of *shari'a* law, and of Muhammad 'Abduh's thought and reforms, but this does not alter their essentially conservative viewpoint. Shaykh 'Ali 'Abd al-Raziq was denounced by such *'ulama'*, as Amin explains (Amin 1987).

Amin also maintains that the Islamist groups developed as a result of social and economic decline and corruption in government circles, and that they believe that applying *shari'a* law as it was formulated ten centuries ago would solve these problems. Amin maintains that this would obstruct development and the adoption of Western methods and thinking. It can as well be argued that political and economic decline are also the result of the inability of government to Westernize the economy and the political system. Thus Sa'd al-Din Ibrahim, a sociologist, argues that all Islamic movements, from the flourishing of the Muslim Brotherhood in 1936 until today, are responses to the failure of society to successfully adopt Western thought (Amin 1988: 9–11).

Some items of Amin's thought are difficult to employ for analytical purposes, or to apply in a social context. An instance is his concept of the spirit of Islam, which he defines as the divine will that ordains change: *al-irada al-ilahiyya al-kamina fi'l-taghyir* (Amin 1988: 279). According to Amin, Islam, by definition, means submission to the will of God, which is manifest in *hatmiyat al-tarikh* (the unchangeablility of the course of history) (Amin 1987: 139–40; 1988: 227, 279); therefore social currents which oppose and obstruct the unalterable course of history ought to be resisted. Amin, however, does not give any concrete historical or social examples to illustrate this principle. Furthermore, these notions are inapplicable in concrete social contexts. This is so because there are so many currents of events taking place at any particular time that it would be difficult to find the criteria that Muslims could agree upon, enabling them to identify those changes which manifest God's will and to distinguish them from the opposite case.

In *Islam in a Changing World* Amin contradicts the ideas in his first two books—where he repeatedly stresses the importance of the Islamic heritage and the need for Muslims to retain their social customs

(Amin 1987: 172–6)—by stating, for instance, that it is good that Egyptians no longer perform the naive practice of reading Bukhari in times of drought, believing that it will cause the rain to fall (Amin 1988: 274). Amin does not mention that reading al-Bukhari is part of *salat al-istisqa'* (rain prayers); he had not done the anthropological fieldwork of recording all the prayers people might make on such an occasion, nor did he observe the social context and the social organization within which such a practice takes place. The rain prayers are not so much about the fallacy of rain as a means to emphasize the good-will between members of the community, and to enhance self-awareness and consideration for others in the community (Abu-Zahra 1988).

Regarding the role of the *'ulama'* in reforming *shari'a* law, Amin does not address the problem of how they could effect the reforms he advocates. The authority of Azhar has been a profound problem since the time of Muhammad 'Ali (see Crecelius 1978, and Sa'id Isma'il 'Ali 1986). The teaching of the *'ulama'* at the Azhar forms part of society and does not constitute a separate isolated entity. Some of the *'ulama's* activities and interests are dictated by the people's demand, to which the *'ulama'* respond in their *fatwas*.[7] The reforms needed in the Azhar, therefore, necessitate other social reforms in the educational system in general, government administration, the Ministry of Islamic Endowments and the funding of mosque maintenance.

Notes

I am grateful to Ronald Nettler for his helpful comments on the first draft of this paper. In translating Qur'anic verses I made use of Arberry 1976, but I have followed the Azhar system of numbering of the Qur'anic verses.

1   Husayn Ahmad Amin is the son of Ahmad Amin, a prominent historian of Islam and educator. He was trained at the *madrasa* for Qadis (created in1908), whose graduates were qualified to become judges in Shari'a courts. He soon left these courts, however, and, with the support of Taha Husayn (the famous Egyptian writer, professor of Arabic literature and Minister of Education in the 1950s), moved to the University of Fu'ad al-Awwal (renamed Cairo University after the 1952 revolution), where he took a teaching position in the Arabic Department in the Faculty of Arts, later becoming its dean.

2   In a later work, however, he wrote favourably of Ataturk. See Amin 1996: 55, n. 22.

3 Zaynab bint Jahsh was originally married to Zayd b. Haritha. The
   Prophet saw her and admired her, and when her husband knew of this,
   he left her. The Prophet advised him not to do so, but Zayd refused to
   listen. The Prophet married her when it was revealed in the Qur'an
   (XXXIII:36) that he could do so (Tabari 1961: vol. 2, pp. 562–4).

4 Crecelius 1978: 193–4 maintains that Muhammad 'Abduh failed to combine his Islamic reforms with political action.

5 The corruption of middle-class women can be argued to have been caused
   by the tremendous social upheavals and financial difficulties of the period since the 1960s. One of the contributing factors was again Egypt's
   defeat by Israel in 1967, which brought in its wake the socially unacceptable *zawag 'urfi* (common law marriage). Widows of young officers
   received generous pensions from the government, which were stopped
   in the case of their remarriage. For this reason, they and the widows of
   highly-paid professionals, preferred *common law marriage*. This type of
   marriage followed the main formalities of the Islamic marriage contract
   (an announcement of the intention of marriage and the recital of the
   first sura of the Qur'an in front of two witnesses) but lacked the public
   social announcement prescribed by Islam. Furthermore, the marriage
   formalities are not conducted by a notary appointed by the government
   to register it, and the dissolution of the union is without any formalities. As a result, the descent of the children from this type of union and
   their right to inheritance from their father's estate is problematic. Another result of Egypt's contemporary economic difficulties is the hous-
   ing problem which means that the marriages of a great number of young
   couples cannot be consummated. They wait for years for accommoda-
   tion, and meanwhile they may meet in *felukkas* on the Nile or cuddle on
   the banks of the river. These social problems and upheavals coexist with
   strict traditional outlooks and segregation of the sexes. The women
   caught up in these situations may wear the veil, a sign of virtue, to maintain their status as respectable women who adhere to Islam.

6 This article was also published in *al-Musawwar*, an Egyptian weekly
   magazine, 6th June, 1985.

7 I found in my father's (the late al-Shaykh Muhammad Abu-Zahra) pa-
   pers, his written *fatwas* to some questions, which varied from what seem
   to me simple questions such as the difference between the angels and
   Satan to complicated ones on marriage problems, divorce and the legitimacy of offspring.

5

Mahmud Muhammad Taha's Second Message of Islam and His Modernist Project

MOHAMED MAHMOUD

The work of the Sudanese reformist Mahmud Muhammad Taha has started to draw some attention in academic circles interested in Islamic reform and liberal thought in modern Islam.[1] Taha is scarcely known outside the Sudan, as his career had been exclusively confined to his country, and his publications were not distributed in Arab or Muslim countries—partly because of the ban on them[2] and partly because of the limited capacity of Sudanese distribution channels.

Taha was born in either 1909 or 1911 in the small town of Rufa'a in central Sudan. He studied engineering, graduating in 1936. This was an important period in Sudan's history, as the burgeoning nationalist movement was gathering momentum in its struggle for independence from the Condominium colonization of Great Britain and Egypt. Taha rejected the line taken by the religiously and politically dominant Khatmiya and Ansar forces. Both groups based their tactics on seeking alliances with one or the other co-domini. In 1945 he and other like-minded intellectuals formed the Republican Party, to press for the country's full independence and the establishment of a republic. Taha's activism led to his arrest twice in 1946. His second term of imprisonment lasted two years.[3] These two years, and a subsequent three-year period, proved to be the most crucial in Taha's career, as he withdrew into a *khalwa* (retreat), subjecting himself to the austere regime of the Sufi path. It was during this period of seclusion and contemplation that Taha developed the two theories that were to define and dominate the rest of his career: his theory of Islamic prayer[4] and his theory of a second message of Islam.

After the end of his retreat in October 1951, Taha devoted all his indefatigable energies to the propagation of his ideas. By the late 1970s, he had built a small but highly dynamic and vocal group that not only accepted his ideas and revered him as its *ustadh* (spiritual master) but also tried to live in accordance with his ideals and create its own society. The movement's social composition tended to be of an urban and middle class nature.[5] Taha's disciples were united by a vigorous bond of intellectual unity and a deep sense of spiritual brotherhood. Each disciple saw himself as a *salik* (an aspirant, a follower of a spiritual path) whose goal was his/her spiritual self-realization. A striking feature of the Republican[6] community was the high profile it gave to women, the 'Republican sisters', who played an increasingly visible role in the movement's internal and public activities.[7] Though the Republicans were averse to the *turuq* (pl. of *tariqa*, 'Sufi brotherhood'), they had, to all intents and purposes, created their own *tariqa*; with its distinctive regime, ethos, symbols, and social code.

The fierce hostility of the religious establishment and the Muslim Brothers to Taha's interpretation of Islam led them to stage a trial in absentia in 1968, in which they convicted him of apostasy—passing a death sentence on him and ruling that his wife be divorced from him and his property be confiscated. Neither the country's political situation at the time nor the laws in force allowed for the implementation of such oppressive measures. However, nobody could have speculated at the time that these very measures were to lie dormant for a decade and a half,[8] and were to be carried out by the very regime which was seen by many, including Taha himself, as the country's saviour from religious tyranny.

When Ja'far Numairi's 'Free Officers' seized power in May 1969 all political parties were banned, and those which resisted the ban were forced underground. Taha complied with the political ban, but continued the activities of his movement along educational and religious lines. As he declared his support for the regime, his activities were tolerated. The clash with the regime came in September 1983, when Numairi started implementing *shari'a* laws. The Muslim Brothers—who were at the time staunch allies of the regime—and the religious establishment found in Taha's public opposition of the September 1983 laws their golden opportunity. Working in direct complicity with Numairi, they revived the 1968 apostasy sentence. On January 18, 1985,

and in the presence of a few thousand *shari'a*-cheering citizens, Taha
was executed.[9]

Taha's major works were *al-Risala al-thaniya min'l-Islam* (The Second Message of Islam) (1967) and *Risalat al-salat* (A Treatise on Prayer)
(1966). Though the second work represents the 'esoteric' aspect of
Taha's thought, it is not possible to separate this from the 'exoteric'
aspect of his work as represented by his concept of a second message of
Islam. Here the focus will be on Taha's concept of a 'second message
of Islam' and the extent to which this concept can be grounded within
the context of what has come to be known as Islamic modernism.[10]

It is important to note at the outset that, though Taha is a
universalist and the audience of his ultimate appeal is mankind, his
reasoning is exclusively embedded in a limited body of Islamic texts,
the principal sources of which are the Qur'an and the *hadith* (prophetic
traditions). He takes it for granted that his reader is Muslim and that
the ultimate authority of the Qur'an and the *hadith* is uncontested.
Hence the dispute among believers is of a hermeneutical nature: how
can one reach a 'sound understanding' of the Qur'anic or *hadith* texts?
This goes hand in hand with another key aspect of Taha's thought,
namely ritual: 'sound understanding' leads to 'sound practice' which in
turn opens the door to a higher level of 'sound understanding' and so
continues the process endlessly. This Taha bases on Qur'an II:282
which refers to *taqwa*, the fear of God that induces one to worship
Him. Furthermore, the verse adds that God teaches people. Through
the verse's coordinative conjunction *wa* (and) Taha establishes a causal
link between two categories he sees as inseparable: namely *taqwa* and
'ilm (knowledge). *Taqwa* becomes the source out of which true *'ilm*
flows. As such, Taha does not project himself as a 'thinker' who rationally applies the procedures of a particular hermeneutic method in
supporting his reading of the textual sources. Rather, he sees himself
as an *'arif*, a 'bearer of gnostic knowledge', who has attained his knowledge through an act of direct communion with God. In answering the
vexed question that his opponents often raised, 'who is the messenger
of the second message?' Taha wrote, 'He is one to whom God granted
understanding from the Qur'an and authorized to speak' (Taha 1987:
4). By asserting this, Taha confers upon his thought a transcendent
significance that makes it inextricably intertwined with divine intention, a position not atypical of some of the major Sufis.

In expounding his concept of a second message of Islam, Taha's starting point is a distinction he draws between *madaniyya* (civilization) and *hadara* (material progress/material sophistication).[11] The two categories fall within a hierarchy in which *madaniyya* occupies a higher position. In defining *madaniyya*, Taha introduces a concept central to his thinking: *al-hurriyya al-fardiyya al-mutlaqa* (absolute individual freedom). To be civilized is to be moral, and morality is 'discretion in the exercise of absolute individual freedom' (Taha 51/21). *Hadara*, by contrast, is of an exclusively 'material' nature, corresponding to that level at which man strives to gratify his basic needs and raise his standard of living. Taha's distinction is thus another aspect of the traditional dichotomy Muslim thinkers stress between the 'spiritual' and the 'material'. He is, however, keen to empasize that this distinction is not meant to establish a qualitative difference between the two categories; rather it is one of degree, and the perfect state is one in which both are harmoniously combined. Furthermore, he is equally keen to underline his dissatisfaction with the traditional position:

> Material progress is often disdained as the corrupt work of Satan by those who are unable to see the full picture of social development. [They fail to appreciate that] God is drawing life towards Him, on both two feet of matter and spirit. In fact, from the point of view of monotheism (*tawhid*) matter and spirit are one thing, not differing in kind, but only in degree. (Taha 50/20 [brackets original in English translation]).

On the basis of this distinction, Taha lashes out against Western civilization. He maintains that Western civilization is not in fact a *madaniyya* or 'civilization' in the sense he defines, due to its confusion of values. In as much as he admires the scientific and technological progress of the West, he deplores its failure to pursue and realize peace. Writing before the collapse of communism, he rejected both communistic-totalitarian and capitalistic-liberal models. He discusses what he describes as 'the failure of Western civilization' on both the political and philosophical levels. Politically, the world has become less safe after the Second World War and 'humanity is still in a state of war because of fear of war' (Taha 53/24).

Philosophically, Taha focuses on the two interrelated problems of the individual's relationship to his society and man's relationship to the universe. He accuses social philosophy of having failed to appreciate the relationship between the individual and his society, for its perspective has tended to view the relationship in oppositional terms, dismissing any possibility of reconciliation. In reviewing the problem, he acknowledges the substantial evidence of history demonstrating the conflictual nature of the relationship between the individual and his society. However, he adopts an evolutionary perspective based on an ethical scale according to which man progresses from a savage, animal-like nature to a higher, more refined nature. His method in substantiating this point mixes the use of historical and anthropological material about man's social evolution with his own reading of the Qur'an. Hence, he places the Biblical-based Qur'anic account of the divine command to Abraham to offer his son in sacrifice and the subsequent development in the context of this evolutionary process: of man being elevated from his previous animal-like state and 'becoming worthy of being ransomed by offering an inferior beast in his place' (Taha 58/30). Taha argues that the abundance of violence in human history, which continues into our own times, has misled social thinkers into assuming that the freedom of the individual and the interests of society are necessarily incompatible.

In discussing man's relationship to the universe, Taha dismisses the notion that religion is a phenomenon of humanity's infancy. Man's belief that his scientific knowledge has freed him from ignorance, and that he no longer needs God or religion, is seen by Taha as a serious misconception. In addressing this 'Western' notion, he is particularly scathing about Marxism, which he judges as the epitome of contemporary Western progressive social philosophy. Another aspect to which he turns is what he describes as the failure of Western civilization to come up with a satisfactory social formula that combines socialism and democracy. Once these two values are integrated into a concrete social system, Western civilization will effect its evolution from its current stage of material progress to that of a true civilization.

It is in the light of this criticism of Western civilization that Taha proceeds to offer his concept of an Islamic alternative. His starting-point is that 'in Islam the individual is the end. Everything else, including the Qur'an and the religion of Islam itself, are means to that end ... This means that the human being, whether man or woman, sane or insane, should never be used as a means to another end ... ' (Taha 62/36). He bases this assertion on Islamic eschatology according to which people meet God on the Day of Resurrection individually. He couples this with another assertion—that only Islam is capable of resolving the apparent conflict between the individual's need for absolute individual freedom and society's need for complete social justice. This characteristic is rooted in *tawhid* (God's absolute unity) on the doctrinal level and in *shari'a* on the practical level. *Shari'a* stipulations comprise a system that functions on the two levels of the individual-God relationship and the individual-individual relationship. The absence in this system of a relationship with the universe is compensated for by a concept of *tawhid* that dissolves all boundaries as 'the whole universe has one source, one path, and one destiny. The universe emanates from God, and to God it shall return ...' (Taha 63/37).

This 'return to God' notion firmly situates Taha's position within its broader mystical horizon. For the question of 'return' is a question of acquiring Divine attributes—of the 'limited' striving to unite with the 'absolute'. It is by virtue of this opening up to the horizon of the 'absolute' that Taha propounds the notion of *absolute* individual freedom'. What does absolute individual freedom entail? According to Taha's perspective, freedom is absolute and it is a human right that is enjoyed by individuals irrespective of religion or race. As a right this freedom is however counterbalanced by the duty of properly discharging one's obligations. A failure to undertake this duty results in setting limits on the individual's freedom. This setting of limits should, however, be carried out in accordance with constitutional laws that 'are capable of reconciling the needs of the community for total social justice with the needs of the individual for absolute individual freedom' (Taha 65/39).

Taha maintains that man's failure to live up to the requirements of his freedom lies in his ignorance, which is a function of a certain type of selfishness. For selfishness falls into two categories: the narrow, lowly, and ignorant and the open, sublime, and rational. It is individuals whose selfishness belongs to the first category who are at war with society and it is upon the freedom of such individuals that limitations should be set. People on both levels of selfishness are entitled to think as they wish, express themselves as they think and act in accordance with what they express. The crucial difference is that while the exercise of the freedoms of thought, expression and action at the level of ignorant selfishness is controlled by law, their exercise at the level of sublime self-ishness is free of such constraint.

Dealing with one's selfish, 'lower' self is a key issue which Taha tackles in the light of a specific psychological scheme. It is a scheme that is inseparable from one's act of faith as a Muslim, as its core is an observant fulfilment of the *shari'a*'s injunctions with the view of attaining one's absolute individual freedom. The *shari'a*'s opposite categories of *halal* (lawful) and *haram* (unlawful) are seen as educational means through the agency of which man effects his spiritual progress. Taha does not set much store by the prohibitions of the *shari'a* that fall on specific *a'yan* (plur. of *'ayn*, 'material thing', 'substance') which he sees as of a provisional nature: '… what is really prohibited in the final analysis are behavioural faults and moral deficiencies. Prohibition of material things is only a means of curing the self from behavioural faults and moral deficiencies …' (Taha 71/45–6). He brings into play Qur'an XLI:53: "We shall show them Our signs in the material world, and within themselves, until it becomes manifest to them that He is the Truth",[12] a key verse in Taha's thought to which he often refers. According to his reading, the verse does not contrast man's external, material environment with his internal, psychological environment in a static, discontinuous manner but rather lays emphasis on the dynamic, interactive nature of the relationship between the external and the internal. He maintains that the verse's movement from the outside to the inside reflects the Qur'an's educational method in ridding the self of sin.

An individual intent on self-purification should follow, according to Taha, a reverse method whereby he continually calls himself to account and puts an end to his sin on the levels of action, speech, and thought. Taha's account in this respect is of a mechanistic nature that generally marks his psychological perspective. Once this process of self-purification is complete the locus of one's being shifts to the interior; one is inward-looking and no longer obsessed with the external. When a person attains to this state, where his *sarira* (inner being) is in full agreement with his *sira* (conduct), then *shari'a* undergoes a radical change, as all concrete substances which are prohibited revert to their original state of permission.

Taha's conviction that the *shari'a* will 'wither' at a 'higher' level of mystical attainment overlaps with his profound commitment to the sanctions of the *shari'a*, of which he is highly apologetic. Evoking the notion of *qisas* (retribution—mentioned in Qur'an II:179) he sets out to offer a traditional and psychologically mechanistic defence of the *shari'a*'s penal code. So, the Biblical-Qur'anic principle of 'an eye for an eye' is justified and recommended to present-day Muslims as an effective means of reviving an offender's sensitivity towards their victims and society at large. Taha's logic is based on a plea for the individual to be socially responsible; a failure in this respect results in 'punishment' which is seen in terms of re-education. This logic, however, loses its coherence when he deals with the stipulation of stoning for marital infidelity—the re–education argument no longer holds.[13]

An important aspect of this educational process centres on the significance of modern science. Taha insists that modern science and religion are fully compatible, and that any claim to the contrary shows total ignorance of the nature of both.[14] This is particularly so in the case of Islam. In exploring and determining his position in the universe, man needs the knowledge offered by both science and religion. Science is depicted by him as a modern messenger beckoning man to venture into a world that he cannot experience through sense perception. Taha embraces a kind of 'Islamic animism' by asserting that though our environment is manifestly 'material' its essence is in fact 'spiritual' and adds: 'Early man was wiser than we are now, since he believed, or rather appreciated, that everything in the universe has a spirit' (Taha 79/55). But what, precisely, is the knowledge that religion offers?

In examining this question Taha brings to the fore the intractable problem of *jabr* (determinism) and *ikhtiyar* (free will). This debate goes back to the first centuries of Islam, when the Mu'tazilites argued in favour of free will and their opponents argued in defence of determinism. Taha, like his Sufi predecessors, firmly throws his weight behind the determinist position. He is, however, dissatisfied with the traditional way determinists have argued their case, and proposes to revive the argument in a manner more relevant to present-day thinking and needs. As the Qur'an is ambivalent on the issue, Taha resorts to the *hadith* material for his conclusive evidence. He cites a *hadith* attributed to the Prophet in which he says: 'Anyone who believes has done so according to a predetermined judgment and fate, and anyone who disbelieves has also done so according to a predetermined judgment and fate' (Taha 85/63). Our sense of free will when we act is, therefore, an illusion of which we should be free. This is the established traditional position from which Taha sets out to further argue that man's illusion of free will is in fact made possible through an act of 'divine complicity'. He demonstrates this by two examples of what he describes as crude and subtle illusions. The first example pertains to the earth's shape and the second relates to the formulation of verses LXXXI:28–9. Taha argues that the numerous Qur'anic references to the earth's flatness were designed to serve an 'educational objective'. The Qur'an did not wish to upset the crude illusion of its seventh century Arabian audience and, according to Taha, once Muslims accepted the faith and implemented its injunctions 'they would realize that the earth was not flat, except as perceived by the naked eye' (Taha 88/66). A subtler level of illusion is examined in connection with verses LXXI:28–9 that say: "It is up to each one of you to take the straight path if each so wishes. But you cannot wish except what God, the Lord of the world, wishes". Taha tackles the contradiction between the two verses by placing them within a specific context: an aspirant starts his spiritual journey impelled by the conviction that he acts on his own accord but he eventually reaches a point of spiritual maturity where he realizes that the whole process is, in fact, predetermined by God. Comparing the two examples he gives, one discerns a deficiency in his evidence. Whereas in the case of his second example he can quote the Qur'an in support of the final realization of determinism, he does not adduce Qur'anic support for the claim that one can finally realize *from* the Qur'an that the earth is spherical.[15] Nor can one find such substantiation in the *hadith* or the *akhbar* material of the early Muslim community.

While Taha is a determinist par excellence, he insists at the same time on the crucial significance of 'being sinful'. To clarify his point, he contrasts human beings and 'angels'. Angels are knowledgeable and incapable of committing sin. Despite this, they are less 'perfect' than humans who sin and ask for God's forgiveness. It is by virtue of this process of 'redemption' that man eventually attains to his absolute individual freedom. According to Taha, four ideas interweave in a dynamic relationship leading to man's salvation: *tasyir* (determinism) *khata'* (sin) *maghfira* (forgiveness) and *'ilm* (knowledge). Knowledge is the ultimate means through which man realizes his freedom and regains his pre-Fall paradisaical state. As far as the realization of this knowledge is concerned, Taha adopts a 'humanist' perspective that rejects the traditional Islamic view as regards the eternal torment of hell. He maintains: 'Punishment is not the rule of religion, it is merely a transitional necessity ... Every self is bound to emerge from the suffering of hell and go into paradise' (Taha 107/88). His Sufi vision, however, goes beyond paradise to an ultimate state that cannot be described in terms of language. Man's complete acceptance of God and obedience to Him will lead to his ultimate liberation. Describing the state of such a 'slave of God', Taha writes most elegantly and poetically: 'He has obeyed God until God obeyed him in reciprocity for his deed. He begins to live the Life of God, know His Knowledge, will His Will, enjoy his Ability, and to become God' (Taha 110/90–1).

Taha's concept of Islam is embedded in this Sufi vision. Starting from the familiar confirmation that 'islam' is submission to God, he sets out to stress the 'universal' nature of this act of submission on the one hand and its highly 'particular' nature on the other. On the 'universal' level, all animate and inanimate things are in a state of submission to God. On this level it is God's *irada* (Will) which is at work and it assumes the nature of coercion (what Taha calls *al-qahr al-iradi*). However, human beings are endowed with a unique status in God's scheme for they are capable of making a decisive ascent from this level of unconscious and instinctive submission to a higher level that entails conscious obedience to God, or, in other words, a rise from *irada* (Will) to *rida* (divine 'favour').

On this level of submission, Islam becomes the religion of mankind and of God, i.e. it becomes the only religion that redeems man in the eyes of God. This claim is projected by Taha into the past as well, for he maintains that Islam has always been the religion of man. This view is rooted in the Qur'an, though the difference is that the Qur'an tends to associate the idea with the realization of a Prophetic mission whereas Taha extends it to encompass all religious expression throughout human history. What lies at the bottom of Taha's significant departure from the Qur'anic view is his evolutionary framework, which allows him to assimilate all religious expression in an integrated scale of 'monotheism': 'This [monotheistic] concept of religion appeared first in several pagan beliefs, developed into more advanced beliefs, and finally resulted in the monotheist religions with divinely inspired Books — Judaism, followed by Christianity. The whole process was crowned with the coming of Muhammad and the revelation of the holy Qur'an' (Taha

117/100). His claim that this process culminates in Muhammad's mission reflects the traditional Islamo-centric position which invests Islam with the unique status of being the 'final and complete' expression of what God has intended for man.

The implication of Taha's evolutionary perspective brings him to reconstruct Islam in terms of a living, endless process rather than a body of doctrine with fixed, dogmatic features. He invests the integral relationship between Judaism, Christianity, and Islam with a specific rationale that is expressed in terms of an 'Islamic trinity'. In expounding this Islamic trinity, he adopts a Hegelian triad with Judaism acting as a thesis, Christianity as an antithesis, and Islam as a synthesis. The grounds he offers for such designation are of an ethico-legal nature.

The society to which Moses addressed his message was 'primitive and crude' and its individuals were 'recalcitrant and ill-natured'. Hence, Mosaic law reflected this state of affairs by its emphasis of the legal principle of retribution. It should be noted that Taha's portrayal of Judaism in this respect mixes his evolutionary perspective with the late Qur'anic image of Jews:[16] 'Many scenes in the Qur'an speak of the crudeness and coarseness of the Jews, and how they stayed on the ground every time spiritual advancement was asked of them. This is only natural in that ancient stage in development' (Taha 120/103). In sharp contrast, Christianity was a reaction that 'pulled people to the other extreme', the extreme of a 'spiritual' assertion that made a point of dismissing the principle of retribution, enjoining on people to turn the other cheek. Islam did not identify itself with either the 'material' or the 'spiritual' extreme; rather, it recognized and combined both. The Qur'anic reference of verse II:143 to the Muslims as *ummatan wasatan*, 'an intermediate community', is cited in support of this distinctive status. The verse's reference to the Muslims as being *shuhada'* (witnesses) over the adherents of other religious beliefs, is interpreted by Taha in terms of their being endowed by all the traits that unite people. How this Islamic synthesis works is demonstrated by verse XLII:40: 'The penalty for evil is an equal evil, but he who forgives and reforms, his reward is upon God, He does not love the unfair ones' (Taha 122/106). Whereas the first part of the verse affirms retribution, the second enjoins *'afw* (forgiveness) and *islah* (reconciliation/reform).

This Islamic trinity has a far-reaching implication in Taha's view: it means that the Qur'an contains two messages of Islam, a first message that has more affinity with Judaism, and a second message that is closer to Christianity. The first message was elaborated by the Prophet while the second was expressed in a generalized form. But what do the two messages entail, and in what respects are they different?

For the purpose of identifying the features of the first message, Taha makes a distinction between two categories of Muslims: *al-mu'minun*, (the believers) and *al-muslimun* (those who submit themselves to God). This distinction is informed by his mystical point of departure, according to which there is a 'spiritual spiral' that starts with Islam at a primary level of mere external acceptance—which, historically, included *al-munafiqun* (the hypocrites)—and culminates, after passing through several stages of spiritual development, in Islam as internal and complete submission to God. The internal division of the Qur'anic text into Meccan and Medinan revelations reflects this division of the *umma* (the community) into *al-muslimun* and *al-mu'minun*. In Taha's view, Meccan and Medinan passages are different, 'not because of the time and place of their revelation, but essentially because of the audience to whom they are addressed' (Taha 125/110). In arguing his case, Taha reverses his evolutionary perspective and so, though the Meccan passages precede the Medinan passages, they embody a 'higher level', or the level of the second message. The transition from Meccan to Medinan is hence a descending one from the higher level of the community of Muslims to the lower level of the community of believers. Taha's explanation of this confusing state of affairs is a peculiar implicit contract between God and the audience of the Qur'an: '... people were invited to adopt Islam [in the ultimate sense] first, and when they failed to do so, and it was practically demonstrated that they were below its standard, they were addressed in accordance with their abilities. This offer of the higher standard is the conclusive argument against people' (Taha 130/116). This leads Taha into a further classification that is central to his interpretive and reformist scheme, namely the designation of the Meccan revelation as 'original' and the Medinan revelation as 'subsidiary'. The believers of Arabia whom Muhammad addressed were not mature enough to live up to the standard of the original revelation, and so this had to be abrogated by the subsidiary revelation that was more consistent with historical context. Taha's 'good news' to present-day Muslims is that they have reached a point of maturity that makes them receptive to the higher level of the original revelation and hence the 'subsidiary' revelation is abrogated as far as they are concerned.

Taha sets out to demonstrate that this 'subsidiary' revelation which has traditionally been considered as eternally integral to Islam and ever operative, is in fact no longer relevant and cannot meet the needs of present-day Muslims. In order to drive his point home, he addresses himself to the specific issues of *jihad*, slavery, capitalism, gender inequality, polygyny, divorce, the veil, and gender segregation. He maintains that though all these are integral aspects of the subsidiary, first message of Islam they are, in fact, incompatible with its original, second message.

Taha's treatment of *jihad* is a good example of his method, for he disregards the historical dynamics leading to the violent conflict between Muhammad and his opponents in favour of a theory of moral guardianship. Thus, Taha repeats the stereotypical Islamic image projecting Arab polytheists as having 'persisted in worshipping the stone they carved, severing relations with the next of kin, destroying life, and burying girls alive' (Taha 132/120). This 'state of ignorance' was an abuse of freedom that had to be combated, and hence *jihad* was instituted. The polytheists are thereby seen by Taha as legal minors and moral degenerates who had either to be killed or placed under Muhammad's guardianship.

In his treatment of slavery, Taha likewise reconstructs the context within Islam and, in particular, during the Prophet's life. His position is identical with that of modern Muslims who justify slavery under Islam in terms of the institution's economic and social necessity while insisting, at the same time, that Islam's real target was to abolish it.[17] Besides adopting this common line of defence, Taha redeploys anew his notion of guardianship. Reducing defeated polytheists to slavery is justified in terms of a peculiar kind of retribution: 'If an individual is invited to become the slave of God but refuses, such refusal is symptomatic of ignorance that calls for a period of training. The individual prepares to submit voluntarily to the servitude of God by becoming the slave of another person, thereby learning obedience and humility, which are becoming of a slave' (Taha 137/124).

Islam's original message, in Taha's view, is antagonistic to capitalism. In summing up Islam's socioeconomic ethos Taha uses a common mystical image, that of a traveller: man's life on earth is a journey from a state of transience to one of everlastingness. On the basis of this belief he rejects private property in favour of a common or joint possession of property, which he sees as the natural order of things.

The issue of women and their status is central to Taha's reform. The cornerstone upon which he establishes his position is that the original principle in Islam is complete gender equality. This, in common with other modern Muslim thinkers who espouse a similar position, he deduces from eschatological scenes in the Qur'an where men and women are individually accountable before God on the Day of Judgment. Aspects of the *shari'a*'s discrimination against women are seen as inevitable transitional measures, meant for a time when 'neither society as a whole, nor women in particular, were ready for the ultimate good Islam had for women' (Taha 140/127). One such measure the *shari'a* had to tolerate was polygyny. Taha points out the socioeconomic context which reinforced the institution in the past, and to a change of context in the present time. However, his reading of Qur'an IV:3, 'Marry of women as many as may be agreeable to you, two or three or four; and if you fear you will not be able to do justice [among your wives] then [marry only] one' (Taha 141/128), goes on to stipulate monogamy as Islam's ultimate objective.

Taha's anti-polygyny position should be situated within the broader context of the social changes sweeping the Muslim world, particularly in its post-colonial era. When he proceeds to discuss divorce, however, he relates to an altogether different context. He reduces the problem of divorce to a problem of poor choice. Once this problem is resolved, when 'God completes His light and the sun of Islam arises' (Taha 142/131), then divorce as a corrective measure for the individual's error of judgment will end, and marriage will become 'an eternal relationship' as Islam had originally intended it to be. As we can see, the context within which Taha raises the problem and the solution he proposes are chiefly informed by his mystical perspective. In dealing with the veil, Taha argues that Islam originally enjoins *sufur* (unveiling) and that veiling was meant as a temporary and educational measure. Likewise, Islam is in favour of a desegregated society where men and women are able to mix. This Islamically desegregated society is, however, 'free from the permissiveness that afflicts present-day desegregated societies' (Taha 145/133).

The point of departure in Taha's defence of his concept of a second message of Islam is a commonly asserted belief that modern Muslim thinkers declare time after time: present-day Western civilization is spiritually and socially bankrupt, and mankind needs to turn to Islam to break out of its predicament. However, Taha's position is characterized by a greater degree of receptivity as regards Western civilization, which he seeks to 'cross-fertilize' with the second message of Islam. He does not offer this as an answer to the predicament of present-day Muslims, but rather as a 'universal' answer to all the woes of mankind. In this respect, Taha is Islamo- and Euro-centric, for he completely disregards other civilizations and traditions.

The locus of Taha's vision is the individual, as we have seen in his notion of absolute individual freedom. Ultimate *islam* (submission) is a state of internal unity or peace, 'when the conscious mind is no longer in conflict with the subconscious', and man has fully realized his individuality. For this to be attained, humankind needs to bring about 'the good society' which is based on three equalities: economic, political, and social.

Taha's positions of egalitarianism and anti-despotism led him to reinterpret Islam along a socialist-democratic line. However, he does not call his brand of socialism 'Islamic' but rather appropriates Marxist terminology and calls it 'scientific socialism'.[18] This appropriation goes further, for Taha claims that Islam is not only socialistic but ultimately communistic. He maintains that property is intrinsically owned by God and society at large. Individuals own the 'benefits derived from property' (Taha 156/147). Socialism involves the generation of wealth on the one hand and the equitable distribution of resources on the other. Under socialism differences between incomes exist, and it is when these disparities disappear and absolute equality is achieved that communism is realized. Interestingly enough, the model of this communism, according to Taha, is the Prophet himself, for the Prophet carried out his *zakat* (alms giving) at the level of *'afw*, i.e. expending whatever exceeded his immediate personal needs. What is realized under communism is a miniature earthly paradise of the ultimate paradise to which the Qur'an refers.

For Taha, democracy is not 'merely a way of government; it is also a way of life' (Taha 159/152). He defines democracy as 'the right to make mistakes' and underpins his definition by a Prophetic tradition saying: 'If you do not make mistakes, and then ask for forgiveness, God shall replace you by people who make mistakes, ask for forgiveness, and are forgiven' (Taha 160/153). A key point in which Taha differs from most Islamist thinkers who theorize about democracy in Islam is that he does not subscribe to the view that equates democracy with *shura*, 'consultation'. Democracy was a condition for which the Prophet's contemporaries were not ready and hence Islam had in this respect (as in other respects) to descend from its original (Meccan) level to its subsidiary (Medinan) level. In dealing with democracy, Taha does not project the Prophet as a model democrat (as in the case of projecting him as a model communist); he is rather a 'righteous guardian'.

The culmination of both economic and political equalities is social equality. The central place accorded to the individual in Taha's scheme is re-emphasized —no discrimination against the individual on grounds of birth, race, colour, faith, or sex is allowed. The criterion for a truly civilized society is the way it treats its weaker members, in particular women and children. Social equality is the most difficult of equalities for it requires a slow and arduous process of re-education, whereby man rids himself of fear and prejudice and releases his full human potential. Taha's ultimate goal is human perfection, which he believes to be realizable through man's conscious shaping of his history. Despite his philosophical commitment to determinism, he effectively suspends Divine contingency and is quite willing to allow man's free will the space it needs to work on its past and refashion its present and future.

To understand Taha's concept and formulation of a second message of Islam one has to situate him within the larger context of Islam and the challenge of modernity. Though he tends to confine his references almost exclusively to the Qur'an and prophetic traditions, his project unmistakably falls within the horizon of former modernists such as Sayyid Ahmad Khan (1817–1898), Muhammad 'Abduh (1849–1905), and Qasim Amin (1863–1908). Taha is fully aware of the crisis of Islam in the context of modern times, particularly since the colonial encounter and the imposition of a global hegemonic European economic and cultural structure.[19] Like the modernists who preceded him, he does not see his project in terms of grafting 'Western' elements onto Islam, but rather of reinvigorating 'dormant' elements that are intrinsically Islamic. However, whereas other modernists ascribe the failure of Muslims to appreciate these suppressed elements to their intellectual and spiritual degeneration, Taha sees this as part of God's design.

In common with the Islamic modernist impulse, Taha is keen to expand Islam's interpretive horizon. At the heart of this procedure lies the contentious problem of the relationship between reason and revelation. For Taha, as for other modernists, the tension between reason and revelation posited by the scholastic theologians and by Ibn Rushd is a false problem that cannot conceivably arise. According to Taha's Sufi outlook, any conflict between the two categories is a function of 'ignorance' that can be resolved through the application of *taqwa*, 'the fear of God that heads to true worship'. Worship leads to true knowledge, the acquisition of which is contingent upon an initial act of proactive assent to the authority of revelation. According to Taha there is no place for individual reason in understanding the intentions of God, and consequently knowledge has to come direct from God and be certified in the light of revelation. This restrictive assertion notwithstanding, Taha's reinterpretations display remarkable freedom and creativity. The departure from Medinan revelation that he institutes does effectively render a large portion of the Qur'an inoperative and irrelevant. As such, modernizing Islam, according to Taha, involves a dialectical process of negation and affirmation to which the Qur'anic text has to be subjected.[20] His method is one of establishing direct hermeneutic contact with the Qur'anic text, and hence the modernist propensity to dismiss received tradition takes an extreme form in Taha, who scarcely refers to the post-Qur'anic/post-Prophetic legacy. This exclusion of received tradition contrasts with the inclusion of another tradition, namely modern science and modern social, political, and economic values. The horizon of the Qur'an is expanded to fuse into the epistemological and social horizon of the modern age.

The outcome of this contact is knowledge that claims to be 'true' and 'authentic' in the light of the Qur'anic text's ultimate intentions. The nature of the epistemic context within which this knowledge generates itself and operates makes it necessary that it projects itself in non-relativistic terms. Thus, while Taha's perspective rejects the authority of tradition it ends up instituting its own tradition and authority. And it is by recourse to this tradition and authority that he 'negotiates' modernity and engages in making specific choices. Some of these choices are based on a commitment to modern principles and others are determined by a commitment to tradition. Hence, Taha is quite willing to do away with the *shari'a*'s discriminatory stipulations concerning women and non-Muslims, but when it comes to the *hudud* sanctions of the penal code he considers them as immutable features of revelation that are not subject to historical context.

Taha's brand of Islamic modernism synthesizes many strands of thought: Sufism, evolutionism, liberalism, Marxism, and psychoanalysis. Among these it is evolutionism which permeates all the levels of his thought, and stamps it with a characteristic openness. Unlike Jamal al-Din al-Afghani (1838–1897)[21] and other modernists who rejected Charles Darwin's theory of evolution and the concept of evolution, Taha was willing to incorporate evolution into his thought. He does not see evolution in linear, but rather cyclical and spiral terms—while he insists on the ultimate unity of all phenomena which in the end are destined to dissolve in God. Hence his constant reminder that differences between things are intrinsically of degree and not of kind. With this evolutionism goes a commitment to the idea of progress and a pronounced meliorism. Taha sees human history in Hegelian, progressive, optimistic terms. The Hegelian Idea is replaced by a Sufi concept of God as an active agent of change on one hand, and as the ultimate end of history on the other hand. Man's history is described in terms of a perpetual ascent from lowlier to higher states in an infinite process of self-realization.

A significant aspect through which we can further examine Taha's modernism is his insistence on combining democracy and socialism in one system as the only formula that can address the politico-social plight of modern man. In a typically modernist fashion that affirms the primacy of the individual, Taha maintains that both democracy and socialism should serve as means for the realization of the individual's potential rather than as ends in themselves. Despite Taha's deterministic starting-point, his discussion of democracy and socialism postulates man's freedom—his ability and responsibility to take an active part in shaping his history. His concept of 'absolute individual freedom' is so central that he uses it as a touchstone against which the ultimate value of any concept or institution can be measured. However, he never loses sight of the social context within which individual freedom operates. As we have seen, he insists that what makes Islam uniquely suited to meet the needs of modern man is precisely its ability to harmonize the two seemingly contradictory aspects of absolute individual freedom and social justice.

Taha's belief in absolute individual freedom informs his view on ritual, an aspect that is incorporated into a psychological theory drawing on the insights of psychoanalysis. Ritual is seen as operating on both the conscious mind and the unconscious, freeing man of the inherited fears of the species and fears acquired during the individual's life span. Using verse XLI:53 as a key passage, he argues that the tackling of man's psychological problems should follow a path proceeding from the 'external' to the 'internal'. Ritual is seen as the methodological process through which such a movement is effected. On the basis of this theory, Taha is evidently trying to 'rationalize' ritual and make it more relevant in terms of what he sees as the psychological plight of modern man.

The feminism Taha espouses blends modern and traditional elements. Though he rejects the glaring forms of discrimination against women as enshrined in the *shari'a*, he nevertheless operates within a doctrinal horizon that constructs a hierarchy within which women occupy an ontological status below that of men, Eve being 'an outside projection of Adam's lower self' (Taha 1971: 125). On the practical level of socio-political change he attaches great importance to 'motherhood' and in his blueprint for a socialist society he wants to see women's work as housewives remunerated. What should be stressed here is that Taha's feminism does not invest women with their own autonomy, but rather aspires to entrench them within their traditional 'maternal' role: '... women and men are recognized as equal even though they may be given different roles in society. Thus, when a woman is being trained to become a mother, her service to the community is not considered less valuable than the service rendered by her brother who is trained to become an engineer, physician, or legislator. There is no limit to training for good motherhood. The more a girl learns, the more valuable she becomes as a mother' (Taha 163/158).[22]

Besides placing Taha's modernism within the overall context of the modernist movement in the Muslim World, one should also take into account the specific influences of his Sudanese context. The two direct influences that shaped his intellectual formation were the mystical milieu of central Sudan where he grew up and his active involvement in the political and intellectual debates of the 1930s and 1940s—which set the ground for the struggle for independence. Taha's own commitment to the trials and tribulations of the Sufi path did not follow the traditional path of noviceship, and the subsoil in which his roots are grounded is the philosophical-esoteric tradition of Muhyi al-Din Ibn al-'Arabi (1165–1240). The movement Taha created internalized the Sufi tradition at large, and the Sufi tradition of central Sudan in particular, though it consciously distanced itself from institutionalized Sufism and stressed that the only path open for spiritual invigoration was the imitation of the Prophet.

Parallel to the deterioration of Sufism into uninspiring ritualism was another aspect which Taha found particularly alarming, namely, *ta'ifiyya* (sectarianism). In the context of post-colonial Sudan, sectarianism has come to denote the politico-religious polarization of the Khatmiyya and the Ansar, the two major forces that have dominated the country's political history during the periods of multi-party democracy. The debates of the nascent intelligentsia of the 1930s and 1940s agonized about the relationship with the two major sects and their traditionalism. Taha's hostility to sectarianism was so profound and relentless that, unlike many colleagues of his generation who went into politics, he was adamantly and consistently opposed to their politics throughout his life; so much so that he was willing to endorse military governments on the grounds that they undermined the influence of the two major sects. Taha was also bitterly and consistently antagonistic to another important group, namely the *'ulama'*. Both forms of antipathy and active opposition are ingrained in the modernist discourse of the post-colonial intelligentsia, and, in particular, in the discourse of the Sudanese Left.

An Islam that is close to the Islam of the *'ulama'*, though more dynamic than it and in some respects more radical, is that of the Muslim Brothers or the Islamists. Here, again, Taha showed his unrelentling opposition. This can be traced to the historical conflict between Sufism and orthodoxy on one hand and the political competition between schools of thought that appeal more or less to the same constituency of urban, literate, middle-class people. Like the *'ulama'*, the Muslim Brothers were seen by Taha as representatives of a legalistic Islam that does not touch the more vital problems of social and political change.

In opposing the political involvement of religious sects and the traditionalism of the *'ulama'*, Taha went along with some aspects of the secularization process in Sudan. This went further, as we have seen in the case of his espousal of democracy, socialism, and social equality. This, however, should not be unduly stressed, as he was profoundly committed to his version of an Islamic revival, that firmly places Islam in its second message version at the heart of man's transformation.[23] The forms of secularization and modernism that Taha accepts are subsumed under a broader principle that sees the 'hand of God' in the workings of human history. Coming from a mystical background that emphasizes the unity of being—and with his eclectic intellectual disposition—it is no wonder that Taha was capable of producing one of the outstanding projects of Islamic modernism.

Notes

1   See, for instance, 'Ali 1992, and Oevermann 1993. For overview articles see Khayati 1991, Duràn 1992, and Rogalski 1996. For a recent dissertation giving a lucid exposition of Taha's thought see El-Tayeb 1995.

2   On 5 May 1972, the Islamic Research Academy at the Egyptian university of al-Azhar issued an apostasy *fatwa* against Taha based on its reading of *The Second Message of Islam*. A similar *fatwa* was issued on 18 March 1975 by the Islamic World League Organization of Mecca, calling for the treatment of Taha as an apostate and for the banning of his publications.

3   For more details about the circumstances leading to Taha's second arrest and other biographical details, see Abdullahi A. An-Na'im's introduction to Taha 1987. Throughout this paper I will be using An-Na'im's translation (Taha 1987) and the Arabic original, *al-Risala al-thaniyya min al-Islam* (Taha1986). The first page citation refers to the translation.

4   Taha's theory of Islamic prayer rests on the concept of *asala* (authenticity). He maintains that the stipulated prayers of Islam are meant to set the worshipper on the path of imitating the Prophet (*taqlid*). This act of conscious imitation leads, in the end, to the realization of a mystical union with God at the point of which one is authentic and imitation comes to an end. See Taha 1966.

5   In his well-documented unpublished dissertation on the Republicans, Haydar Badawi Sadig 1988, 17–20, gives valuable information about the members' socio-economic background. The movement is dominated by the lower middle class and middle middle class, with officials comprising about 48%, teachers about 26%, students about 14%, petty traders about 8% and workers about 4%. Literacy is extremely high with

only 8% illiterate, and 38% are university graduates. The vast majority, about 75%, come from central Sudan, the most highly developed region of the country. In terms of age structure, about 85% belong to the young age group of 15–40.

6   The name 'Republicans' (*Jumhuriyyun*) has prevailed in the way Taha and his disciples described themselves and in the way they have been described by others (Some of their opponents called them *'Mahmudiyyun'*, i.e. the followers of Mahmud [Muhammad Taha], but this name never gained currency). The name has survived as a vestige of the movement's history, but it is important to note that it does not do justice to the complexity and depth of Taha's message. In a pamphlet entitled *Ma'alim 'ala tariq tatawwur al-fikr al-jumhuri* (1976), the Republicans stated that they had opted for the retention of their name without indicating the Islamic nature of their organization in order to distinguish themselves from other Islamic organizations, which were keen to parade their 'Islamic' labels without being Islamic in 'essence'. This reads like a polemical point that the Republicans wanted to score against their opponents. It is more likely that the Republicans carried on using the name as a matter of practical convenience, rather than going to the trouble of introducing and establishing a more relevant name that indicated the distinctive nature of their thought.

7   Sadig 1988: 17, points out that the number of women reached about 30. For comments on the role of women in the Republican movement see Duràn 1985, and Hale 1996, 85–7.

8   For a discussion of Taha's apostasy case see an-Na'im 1986.

9   For a graphic description of Taha's execution see Miller 1997: 11–18.

10   For a concise discussion of the main features of Islamic modernism see Dessouki 1987. See also Rahman 1982, Watt 1988, al-Azmeh 1993, and Safi 1994. A recent book that touches on some problems of modernism in the context of postmodernism is Ahmed 1992.

11   This is a distinction made in modern Arabic. Classical Arabic uses *hadara* (or *hidara*) in the sense of taking an abode in an urban centre and does not use *madaniyya*. In modern Arabic both *hadara* and *madaniyya* assume sophistication and progress, and the two words tend to be used interchangeably. See for instance The Cairo Academy's *al-Mu'jam al-wasit* (1960) and Hans Wehr's *A Dictionary of Modern Written Arabic*, which renders both as 'civilization' and adds 'culture' under *hadara*.

12   I am quoting here an-Na'im's translation which is closely based on Taha's interpretation

13 In justifying stoning and capital punishment, Taha invokes the notion of 'atonement': the punishment in this world would 'purify' the wrong-doer.

14 Taha refers to two levels of Islam: *'aqida* (belief) and *'ilm* (knowledge). Modern Arabic uses the word *'ilm* for both knowledge and (modern) science. In translating Taha's reference on p. 50 to Islam as *'ilm'*, an-Na'im opts for the rendering 'science'. This limits Taha's sense for he sees Islam as a belief system that incorporates science but cannot be reduced to it.

15 Some modern Muslims have argued that the Qur'an confirms that the earth is round. To substantiate their claim they cite verse LXXIX:30. The verse uses the verb *daha* (which means 'to spread out, to flatten') in describing God's act on the earth. Modern Muslims who were dissatis-fied with the verb's given meaning extended its semantic field to mean, 'to make in the shape of an egg', therefore establishing a Qur'anic basis for the earth's roundness. For such a reading, see Nawfal 1966: 166–7.

16 The Qur'anic image of Jews developed through an early phase of 'recon-ciliation' into a later phase of 'rupture'. During the early phase the Jews were called upon to join in a 'monotheistic alliance' against the Arab 'polytheists'. The failure of this led to a break in the relationship be-tween the budding Muslim community and the Jewish community of Yathrib (Medina) and the Qur'anic image of Jews developed into a con-sistently negative one. The Qur'an did, however, draw a very firm dis-tinction between the Jews and their religion. In Taha, this boundary is blurred.

17 This apologetic line was particularly popularized by Ameer Ali 1922. Middle Eastern reformers such as Muhammad 'Abduh and his disciples expressed a similar position.

18 This in fact reflects the power and tremendous prestige the Left, and in particular the communist Left, enjoyed in the 1960s in the Sudan and some other Middle Eastern countries. A striking example of this is that Nasser's Arab Socialist Union opted in its charter for 'scientific social-ism' despite the stream of writings on 'Arab socialism' and 'Islamic so-cialism' as competing labels at the time. For the rise of the communist Left in the Sudan see Warburg 1978.

19 For a perceptive treatment and problematization of this crisis aspect see Tibi 1981 (Engl. transl. Tibi 1988).

20 The concept of dialectic is central in Taha's thinking. In his treatise *La illaha ila 'llah* (1969), he argues that Islam's doctrinal formula entails ne-gation and affirmation, and, as such, is meant to lead man to God through a dialectical process.

21 For al-Afghani's position on Darwin see a translation of his *Refutation of the Materialists* in Keddie 1968: 130–74.

22 The argument in Muslim countries linking women's education to motherhood and better housewifely conduct goes back to the nineteenth century. In 1873, Rifa'a Rafi al-Tahtawi wrote his *al-Murshid al-amin li-'l-banat wa-'l-banin* (The Good Guide for Girls and Boys) in which he argued that the education of girls makes them better housewives for their educated young husbands. In his *Tahrir al-mar'a* (1900), Qasim Amin argued in the same vein. This emphasis on motherhood and 'functional education' was, however, seized upon by the traditionalists who were against the liberation of women, but who could not at the same time publicly oppose the very idea of women's education. Such traditionalists therefore direct their energies towards dictating the curricular content of what should be taught to women. In his *Ustadh al-mar'a* (Cairo: 1973), Muhammad al-Bayhani writes: 'If a woman is to be educated, what is suitable would be to learn the principles of religion, homemaking, child rearing and what is necessary concerning health, worship and human relations.' Cited in Haddad 1982: 58.

23 In his introduction, Abdullahi an-Na'im is willing to describe Taha's thought as 'fundamentalist' and maintains that, '... the Republicans would claim to be fundamentalist in the sense of advocating a return to the fundamental sources of Islam to develop a modern version of Islamic law' (Taha 1987: 8, n. 11).

6

Mohamed Talbi's Ideas on Islam and Politics
A Conception of Islam for the Modern World

RONALD L. NETTLER

Mohamed Talbi is a contemporary North African Muslim intellectual. Born in Tunis in 1921, Talbi was raised and received his education through to university in his own country. He then travelled to Paris to pursue post-graduate studies in the history of North Africa. Upon completion of his work in Paris, Talbi returned home to embark upon a most remarkable intellectual career. Becoming eminent as a scholar of North African history in the Middle Ages, Talbi also developed another line in the field of modern Islamic religious thought and interreligious relations in the modern period (two subjects which for him are intimately related). Talbi's career has thus been 'two-pronged', and it is the side of modern thought and religious and interreligious relations which shall be our main concern here.[1]

Talbi has been a prolific writer on modern Islam and on interreligious affairs, as well as participating in various events of interreligious dialogue. His writings in Arabic, French and English vary in level of specialization and technical detail, thus collectively appealing to a wide readership. In Arabic, and amongst Talbi's intellectually most challenging works, are two books which represent his main ideas and methods in these modern subjects: 'Iyal Allah (Families of God) and Ummat al-wasat (Community of Moderation). The former is in the format of questions put to Talbi and his answers, and the latter is a collection of some of Talbi's essays on a variety of issues of contemporary concern. Both books are, in my opinion, significant contributions to 'modernist' Islamic religious thought in the latter half of the twentieth century.[2] Families of God spe-

129

cifically addresses a wide range of modern Islamic and more general religious issues in the context of intra-Islamic relations and relations between Islam and other religions. *Community of Moderation*, as a collection of essays on specific issues, is perhaps even more wide-ranging, but always with relevance to Talbi's basic concerns.

In both these books—as well as in many of his other writings—Talbi addresses various aspects of the relation between religion and politics in Islam, both directly and implicitly in discussion of other issues. This problem of religion and politics is, for him, one of four basic subjects of Islamic concern in our age. The others are: interpretation of Qur'an and tradition, religious epistemology, religious polemics and religious dialogue.[3] Though one would be very hard-pressed to say, unequivocally, which of these subjects is most important in Talbi's view, my impression is that religious polemics and dialogue (internal to Islam and between Islam and other religions) is perhaps the most *prominent* theme in Talbi's writings. However, it is also true that these subjects, for Talbi, form an interlocking set of modern Islamic concerns throughwhich he develops he main ideas (which he then is able to apply to other 'subsidiary' issues of societal importance). In isolating and examining Talbi's approach to any one of these subjects, then, one inevitably discovers the presence of some or all of the others. Each might be understood as a 'microcosm' of Talbi's whole thought, whilst retaining its uniqueness and individuality. Talbi's ideas on Islam and politics must also be seen in this way. I shall, consequently, first offer a general profile of Talbi's thought, arising as it does from his consideration of the three other main subjects, and then discuss specifically his ideas on Islam and politics. Seen in this context, Talbi's ideas on Islam and politics truly constitute a comprehensive conception of Islam for the modern world.

Talbi's intellectual method and attitude may be characterized as a cautious empriricism, couple with a firm belief in certain axiomatic truths of the human condition. These truths derive either from sacred sources (the Qur'an and *hadith* literature) or some other—often undefined—source of knowledge. There is, then, a tension in Talbi's method and attitude between the tentativeness of empiricism and the absolute certainty of the 'revealed' truths. Talbi's empiricism is that of the working historian who sifts and weighs evidence, arriving at conclusions which he assumes, even in the best of cases, to be provsional. Human history is enormously complex and ever-changing: securely fixed points in this panorama are few. Religious phenomena, like all other aspects of human life, follow this pattern and must, therefore, be understood and analysed according to patterns of historical causation. For Talbi, this does not militate against, or in any way relativize, religious belief. On the contrary. Religion can only be strengthened in being constantly measured and interpreted against the empirical standard of history. But this intellectual approach does contain the inner tension mentioned above, which is manifest and influential in Talbi's various discussions of these four main subjects.

Talbi's approach to the Qur'an (and the literature of *hadith*)—his 'exegetical method'—is based on an understanding of the text through its historical context. Talbi sometimes refers to his method as an 'historical methodology' or 'historical reading' (*qira'a ta'rikhiyya*): Qur'anic verses should be interpreted within the contexts in which they were revealed, and not in abstract isolation from those contexts (Talbi 1992: 70). Such removal from their historical moorings renders the verses grist for the mills of all sorts of special causes, and particularly, in our time, those of the political Islamists. The proper understanding of the Qur'an in historical context, then, prevents such deleterious 'universalization' of historically-conditioned material, whilst enabling us to interpret God's word in its originally-intended significance. On the other hand, Talbi still sees in the Qur'an certain universal, axiomatic truths. These are, for the most part, social and ethical truths which, in Talbi's view, transcend time and place and thus provide an absolute universal moral guidance for humanity, everywhere and at any time.[4]

Talbi gives several examples of the use of his exegetical method. Thus he argues that many of the details of human life and behaviour—such as the length of one's beard or the mode of one's dress—have been standardized for all ages in many Islamic codes, when, in fact, such customs and behavioural details are historically determined and may reasonably be expected to change through history. Why, for example, should a Muslim man in our time be required to wear a beard in the way the Prophet is reported to have worn his? (Talbi 1992: 76–7.)[5] Or, in another context, how can we today understand the seeming Qur'anic approval for the corporal punishment of women? In an article which later became a chapter of his book *Umma al-wasat*, titled 'The Issue of Disciplining Women Through Corporal Punishment', Talbi applies his historical exegesis to verses 34 and 35 of sura four, *al-Nisa'* (the chapter 'Women' in the Qur'an) (Talbi 1996: 115–41). In verse 34, in the context of a discussion of the reciprocal roles of men and women, three suggestions are made for dealing with women whose 'recalcitrance' men fear: 'admonish them; refrain from sharing beds with them; *strike them*'. Talbi says this verse '… has been used often and repeatedly to prove that Islam degrades woman and puts her legally in a position lower than that of man' (Talbi 1996: 115). Other Qur'anic verses (e.g. Qur'an II:222, 282) as well as numerous *hadiths*, are similarly used, says Talbi, to make this same point. The issue itself—the treatment of women—has only now in our time been thought to be a problem everywhere. In Talbi's view, for Muslims the answer lies in understanding such verses historically, and thereby ruling out their literal general interpretation and application. Talbi does this with respect to IV:34, with some consideration to tangential material in IV:35. His argument is long and detailed, not for full reproduction here; but its essence is that, in fact, the history of early Islam proves that there was a 'feminist movement' which accompanied the Islamic revolution. And this movement was 'strong and tough'. Indeed, Talbi even claims Muhammad was a 'feminist' (*nasawi*), something for which he believes '… there are many indications' (Talbi 1996: 121). The reason for verse 34, the literal words of which would seem to contradict his thesis, are to be found, Talbi asserts, in a complex social and political situation in Medina during the first three years of the Muslims' authority there. Talbi claims that at first the Prophet enacted progressive legislation for women, in keeping with God's will and women's demands. But God revealed verse 34 (in the year 3AH) in response to a growing internal conflict between feminist and anti-feminist forces, in a context which involved an array of intertwined political factors. The verse represents God's decision to avert an impending intra-Muslim catastrophe through the 'lesser evil' of a somewhat 'retrogressive' revelation. But this verse must be seen, according to Talbi, in the historical context he has reconstructed on the basis of his reading of sources. With this, one then knows the 'anti-feminist' content of the verse reflects a local temporary situation in Medina and not God's universal teaching (Talbi 1996: 121–4). For Talbi, Muhammad's early 'feminism' represents God's true will for the longer term, as a general ethical standard.[6]

As contrasted with this sort of historical-contextual exegesis of the sacred sources, and often deriving from it, Talbi discerns in the sources universal ethical truths as well. These are large ethical principles such as loving good and justice and hating the bad. The common Qur'anic injunction to uphold the good and reject the bad (*al-amr bi-'l-ma'ruf wa-'l-nahy 'an al-munkar*) is, for Talbi, one of these principles and a way of enjoining the others. But, one must ask, how does Talbi *know* what the Qur'an's meaning is in this case? There is no historical and social context for him to appeal to here, for these are universal values. Talbi's answer is that he and all human beings *know* these values and principles through a special innate human nature (*fitra*) which seems to precede and to be more basic than revelation itself. The Qur'an, then, is '... reaffirming this fundamental spiritual value which is innate in every man' (Talbi 1992: 77), when it admonishes God's servants to do good and reject evil. Through this special nature, human beings love good and justice and reject evil. This obviously implies also that they innately *know* what is good and what is bad, and this knowledge is applied in making ethical choices. Thus, '... whenever one does wrong, one knows it is evil' (Talbi 1992: 77).

For Talbi, then, one knows the meaning of much of the Qur'an through the historical contexts and circumstances of revelation, whilst elsewhere in the text large universal principles are revealed, evoking receptive responses of recognition from us based on our natural understanding (*fitra*). Much of the Qur'an, in this view, is relative and context-bound in its significance. It would seem to be most informative as a record of its own historical circumstances. The religious value in this for the Muslim community is great, but it cannot easily yield atemporal universal principles. These we 'know' already through our inborn human nature; the Qur'an simply evokes these principles from us. The implication here—Talbi does not make it explicit—is that the 'most important' part of the Qur'an is these universal truths which all people possess through their natural faculty (*fitra*).[7]

Intimately related to Talbi's conception and practice of exegesis is his theory of knowledge ('*ilm*). Here Talbi again speaks from within his experience as a historian, and derives an epistemology very much in this mould. Knowledge, for Talbi, is usually provisional—more certain or less certain to be sure, but even when more, still tentative. One must always be prepared to reconsider what one 'knows', for new evidence or a different perspective will often change one's view of what one 'knows'. Talbi thus rejects the notion that any person can be learned (*'alim*) in a totally authoritative way. For if all knowledge is provisional, then all knowers must live with some degree of uncertainty with respect to their knowledge. This is Talbi's conception of himself as an historian, a role which is based upon this view of knowledge. Also involved here is the moral value of intellectual humility, associated as it is with the provisional knowledge of the historian. We are all 'seekers after knowledge' (*tullab ma'rifa*), even the most illustrious of intellectual workers whose knowledge is still provisional (Talbi 1992: 45). Intellectual progress, in Talbi's view, is just '... the sum of a series of ups and downs' (Talbi 1992: 46), and the great figures have contributed to the declines—when they were in error—as well as to the high points.

Talbi derives a general intellectual principle from this notion of human knowledge as a process of gradual (and rocky) piecemeal progress: Every individual must be a *mujtahid* (Talbi 1992: 46). By this he means, it seems, not just the implied rejection of *taqlid*—which is certainly present—or *ijtihad* in its classical legal sense of the independent judgement of the legal scholar (*mujtahid*), but rather that every individual Muslim must employ critical reason in all matters, and thereby make an independent judgement.[8] And critical reason here has connotations of a modern type of intellectual process. Talbi's logic seems to be as follows: We know empirically that knowledge for individuals is always provisional and ever-changing according to new discoveries; for humanity in general—the sum total of all individuals—progress in knowledge is, consequently, a gradual and long process of development through trial-and-error. In light of all this, individuals ought then to relinquish the notion of intellectual certainty—it is illusory—with its attendant risk of breeding fanaticism, and acknowledge in their intellectual life the empirical and tentative nature of the process. Talbi has, in effect, discovered empirically the empirical process of knowledge which he universalizes as an epistemological principle for all. This principle is critical in Talbi's discussion of intra-Islamic and interreligious relations and dialogue.

Talbi locates the crux of the problem regarding such relations in the absolute certainty of individuals and collectivities that their particular positions, on whatever issue, are true and final, to the exclusion of all other views and opinions.[9] It is the negation of the other which for Talbi is so detrimental and dangerous. One may even consider one's own truth to be the only one—though this is not advised—if one gives others the right to voice their views and takes those views as legitimate. Humanity is naturally, and rightly for Talbi, fragmented and varied in its outlooks. This quality—*ikhtilaf*[10]—is part of human nature, God-given. Within Islam and between Islam and other religions this is expressed in different schools and trends and different religions, all of it God's tapestry. The problem arises when individuals, groups or religions deny the right of others to express their views, and when they refuse to see those views as being of equal value to their own. From this comes conflict and, even, war. Within Islam, Muslims have for centuries denied other Muslims this right and status; and for centuries Muslims have often thought of other religions as inferior, and engaged in conflict with them. And others have, of course, from similarly distorted perspectives, seen and behaved towards Islam in this way. This is all very sad for Talbi, for in his view, '... man is by nature a pluralist (*ta'addudi*)' (Talbi 1992: 65), and these observed tendencies towards solipsistic antagonism regarding others actually run counter to human nature. In an analysis of what happened within Islam, Talbi tries to show historically how the insularity of opinion often overrode the natural tendency toward pluralism:

> Thus did sectarian trends—often with political overtones—take hold and develop in the wake of Islam's early civil conflicts (*fitan*). And this happened essentially from the felt certainty of knowledge on the part of those who founded and perpetuated these trends. Rather than understand the provisional nature of their knowledge, which would have induced in them a properly (and naturally) pluralistic approach toward others, these groups took the absolutist approach that their Islam was the only "true" Islam. And from there the path to strife (sometimes bloody) was indeed short. The situation between the great religions was similar, leading to international conflict (Talbi 1992: 66).

Talbi's solution to all this is for Muslims, within their own religion and between their religion and others, to invoke the instinctive value of pluralism (*ta'addudiyya*) and use this as the foundation for the inculcation of mutual respect (*al-ihtiram al-mutabadil*). This, in his view, would ensure that the natural (and divinely-sanctioned) diversity of religious opinion (*ikhtilaf*) became the mutual respect so needed by today's world. All religions would need to undergo this process, but Talbi is most concerned with Islamic internal religious-political strife and relations between the three 'Abrahamic faiths'. In his view, amongst these faiths Islam most naturally exemplifies the ethos of toleration and respect. Talbi's logic here is as follows: differences of religious views (*ikhtilaf*) are a natural human trait in Islam (indeed universally). This we know empirically and from textual sources. This trait reflects the general human propensity to pluralism (*ta'addudiyya*) which can be transformed into mutual respect. And this, finally, will be expressed in dialogue (*al-hiwar*) (Talbi 1992: 67–72). Talbi has thus discovered an immutable general moral principle within the empirical flux of history. And again his thought here is developed in the creative tension between the empiricism and the large axiomatic principle.[11]

The above is a survey, however brief, of Talbi's ideas on three of the four subjects which I consider to be central concerns in his thought. The fourth, Islam and politics—as our main interest here—will be considered in greater detail. My exposition of this is based mainly on part two, 'Knowledge and Politics in Islam', of chapter two, 'Islam and (Some) Difficult Questions', in Talbi's book, *Families of God* (Talbi 1992: 86–121). Here Talbi presents a thoughtful and detailed explication of his ideas on the subject of Islam and politics, in answer to a number of proffered issues and questions (thirteen in all) requiring his response. I shall generally follow the flow of this discussion in my exposition, although for reasons of concision and clarity I shall not treat all points or all questions in the text.

The first two remarks and questions put to Talbi (the second being an extension of the first, for clarification) ask his view '... as a Muslim and an intellectual' on particular attempts in modern Islamic thought to see modern Islamic institutions as 'newer versions' of ancient and medieval precedents. These attempts to 'read Islamic history' in a new way and to approach textual exegesis from such 'a new perspective of discourse' have been numerous and influential. Some examples given are modern monetary policy as a newer version of the medieval Islamic institution of *hisba* and parliamentary trust as a modern form of the medieval *mubaya'a*, loyalty to a ruler or king (Talbi 1992: 86–8). The modern Muslim thinker mentioned specifically for Talbi's response here is the Moroccan activist and founder of the *Istiqlal* party, 'Allal al-Fasi, with his notion of democracy as a newer version of the ancient Islamic institution of *shura*. In this view, *shura* was democracy. Talbi expresses general respect for al-Fasi as one who has had interesting and challenging ideas and has not been an 'intellectual terrorist', but he says he cannot agree with all of al-Fasi's ideas: 'I accept some things from him but not others' (Talbi 1992: 87).

On the general issue of seeing modern institutions in the image of their putative forebears, Talbi takes a decidedly cautious, even sceptical, position, agreeing that there may be something there but withholding his full approval. He says all people are influenced by their own historical civilization in general, as well as by more specific and immediate local factors. And many are influenced by foreign cultures. For example, one finds people in the Arab world who, by virtue of Russian influences on them, appear to all intents and purposes to be Russian. But this for Talbi is neither here nor there; he is much more concerned to treat contemporary issues with a direct approach, playing down the influence of early 'precedent': 'I think the most useful thing is that we address our problems according to the way they present themselves, and that we do our best in resolving them, and try to find for them successful solutions which would enable us truly to overcome the difficulties and to move forward, and preserve for ourselves, as much as possible, successful means, by not looking for precedents' (Talbi 1992: 88–9).

The third set of remarks and questions put to Talbi continues with the subject of the first and second, but in a more specific way, focusing on the issues of *shura* and democracy. Here Talbi will apply the general principles outlined above, but in a more nuanced and detailed fashion. The questions and issues are put in two ways: (a) The point is not so much to compare the terms *shura* and democracy, seeking historical precedents and phenomenological similarities, but rather to explore the internal meanings and different historical manifestations of each term and institution. We then find, for example, that democracy as idea and reality has not always been a perfect and happy thing—indeed, it can, and has, been expressed as tyranny, *e.g.* 'democracy of the proletariat.' (b) The real question has to do with '... attempting to make a conception (of government) in the Arab Islamic realm which would realize the highest ideal, whether we call it democracy or *shura*' (Talbi 1992: 89). But the situation now is that we have 'the Islamic conservatives' holding fast to the concept of *shura* and the proponents of Western culture adhering to their idea of democracy, '... without there being an historical-critical position and without arriving at a crystal clear conception of this highest ideal, appropriate to the historical framework, consonant with our cultural ambience and supporting the principle of freedom' (Talbi 1992: 89).

Talbi more or less agrees with these ideas and sentiments, although in his responses he develops the ideas along his own lines. To begin, Talbi concurs with the notion that 'democracy' or 'shura' needs to be precisely defined in its internal conceptual and historical dimensions, rather than worrying about whether one influenced or was the 'forerunner' of the other. 'Democracy' itself from this angle might then prove to have taken many conceptual and practical forms, not all of them as positive as the usual connotation of the term in the popular mind: 'I shall not forget that Western democracy said to me in the year 1960 that Algeria is an inseparable part of France and that it is French territory. And I shall not forget that French democracy killed millions of Algerians, claiming that they had contravened international law. So whom do we fool by this word democracy?' (Talbi 1992: 89–90.) But for Talbi this political veneer of 'democracy', behind which some real evil may lurk, is, unfortunately, indicative of a common human trait: 'The life of peoples has always been and will forever be based on many examples of dissimulation, whether wittingly or unwittingly' (Talbi 1992: 89–90). Facile judgements and assertions—such as the shura-democracy equation—would for Talbi, it seems, derive from this 'normal' human dissimulation and simplification in discussions of very complex historical and intellectual issues. The proper antidote for this malady, particularly for intellectuals and scholars, is caution (intibah): 'Personally, as an historian, I am extremely cautious, always, with respect to these issues, because fraud in history is a limitless sea. All this, therefore, calls us to strive for balance and the absence of exaggeration' (Talbi 1992: 90). And the shura-democracy equation is, for Talbi, that sort of unfounded exaggeration: 'Thus we do not say that shura is democracy, because this is a pure falsehood' (Talbi 1992: 90). If people exercised historical and intellectual caution in investigating such matters they would know this to be the case: 'Shura was never democracy, for many reasons; amongst them: Democracy did not exist in a real way in Islamic civilization. There were no voting cards, ballot boxes, voting, sorting of votes, and so on. None of this ever existed (in Islam)' (Talbi 1992: 90). Here the empirical caution of sound history must take priority over the misleading imaginings of those who—whatever their views—are driven by a powerful need to connect past and present in such a way that the present is modelled on the past and the past is uncritically invoked as precedent for current issues. For Talbi the past is just that: over and done with. History cannot repeat itself, nor should we practice the (inevitable) distortion and fraud which are attached to such an endeavour. Indeed, Talbi thinks this is illogical and irrational: 'But is it possible for us to think that life today must conform to some principle of a life which preceded life today by almost fifteen hundred years? That is something impossible, and this issue has now been exhausted' (Talbi 1992: 90).

If the nitty-gritty of empirical history, then, provides only a record of what happened, and if the recorded past is, therefore, no early version of something which can, and ought to be, recapitulated now in order to achieve a divinely-directed millennium, then can the Islamic past provide any guidance (in this case political) for the present and future? For Talbi, the answer is that, if we approach history through a simplistic comparison of practices and institutions, without regard for the very different contexts that have shaped them, history cannot teach us anything. But is the past of absolutely no value in guiding us to a better present and future? Is history simply a record of what happened and what was thought in the past? Even if Islamic history contains no early forms of 'true democracy' to be resurrected in the present, does it not at least contain some principles or useful models for later ages? Talbi would answer affirmatively here, extracting general principles from the historians' record and universalizing them.

Deep within the empirical flux of early Islamic history, in the institution of *shura*, Talbi discerns not 'early democracy' awaiting contemporary resurrection but rather some general human truths: 'But there remains here some fundamental concept in human thought such as the notion of justice. So is it by way of historical precedent that we say that Islam invites us to justice? And is justice today in its modes, methods and mechanisms the same justice which always has been? This is not historical precedent, because the concept of justice is an external spiritual value, divorced from any consideration of formation, genesis, or milieu from which justice (may have) come forward to people ...' (Talbi 1992: 90). If justice is an Islamic value—and for Talbi it seems to be—this is because justice is, first and foremost, an eternal *universal* human value. We need not see the origin of justice in history, as it is not there; rather its *tracings* through the ages are there. Justice (and other basic spiritual values) originate *in the human mind* where it is within the basic structures. Thus social justice, which Talbi says is today widely discussed, must also be subsumed under general justice as a kind of sub-category, for it comes under justice '… as a spiritual and ethical value, since here are basic ethical values *deep-rooted in our minds*' (Talbi 1992: 90). These principles, or values, Talbi now also terms 'ethical' as well as 'spiritual', but the meaning is the same and remains clear: Human beings are born with these values as a kind of internal spiritual-ethical system. The role of religion in all this must still be clarified.

Islam—or any other religion or philosophy—may enjoin us to be just, but in doing so it evokes this value from our minds where it is implicit. Revealed religion is not the ultimate *source* of such values; it simply elicits these responses from us. This is the same argument we saw above, where Talbi asserted that human beings know and want to do the good 'instinctively' (knowing it axiomatically), whilst at the same time knowing and rejecting the bad. With respect to *shura* and democracy, Talbi develops this line of thought more precisely.

'*Shura*', says Talbi, 'is therefore essentially one of these ethical values, because of its concern for the exercise of power in a way which makes possible consultation as the goal of arriving at a collective opinion which would serve society, whether that be at the pinnacle of political power, in the tribe, in the clan, or even in the family, where *shura* exists between husband and wife …' (Talbi 1992: 90). Human beings, he says, need at least a certain '… minimal quantity of consultation, in order that we might attain an orientation which would include the cooperation of all the people, or the majority of them, in that orientation' (Talbi 1992: 90). *Shura* is, then, 'an ethical value' because of the qualities it possesses. And it may well have practical application today, for reasons which Talbi will shortly state. But *shura*'s meaning and qualities may be discussed only through a phenomenological investigation of the concept and the institution as Talbi has done, and not by a (spurious) comparison with 'democracy' and a (false) assertion that *shura* is really democracy. And likewise with respect to democracy, whose own meanings must be discovered in the same way. Thus: 'It is impossible for us under any conditions to make *shura* identical to the concept of democracy' (Talbi 1992: 90–1). The reason is

'... that democracy is the rule of the many, whilst when we analyse *shura* we do not find in it the idea of the many; rather we find in it consultation' (Talbi 1992: 91). Therefore, '... Islam urges consultation, and it is generally agreed that consultation may be conceived as one wishes, and there have been many conceptions of *shura* throughout Islamic history' (Talbi 1992: 91).

In an attempt at conceptual clarification, Talbi has provided basic core meanings of *shura* and democracy. These meanings are, it seems, drawn from a combination of internal semantic components as well as original historical contexts. Thus Talbi tells us, with respect to *shura*, that '... the Prophet would consult with his companions. There is no doubt about it. Indeed, he would sometimes take their opinion, even when that opinion led to defeats, as for example in [the battle of] Uhud' (Talbi 1992: 91). But these ethical concepts, when viewed historically are seen to undergo vast transformations, often being expressed in forms far from, or even contrary to, these essential qualities.

Here again, the continued creative tension in Talbi's thought between universal values and the empirical history in which they are carried and expressed looms large. The universal values by definition— although perhaps historically identified with certain cultures more than with others—are 'universal' and thus potentially (if not actually) are present everywhere. *Shura* is a case in point for Talbi. For it actually '... also existed before the Prophet, because there was then (in Mecca) a house in which the tribal chiefs would need to confer on their affairs and to consult with one another in their issues [of mutual concern]' (Talbi 1992: 91). For Talbi, it is this omnipresence (or what he perceives as such) of the ethical values which, empirically discovered by the historian, points towards an independent, universal substratum, underlying the historical: 'Therefore *shura* is, then, a value embedded in humanity, in every land on the earth' (Talbi 1992: 91). It was, for example, a feature of Berber society in Tunisia before Islam, just as it was in Jahili Arabia, and no doubt everywhere else. Rejection of this 'ethical value' results in tyranny.[12]

Returning to the issue of *shura* and democracy, Talbi now connects this issue with his discussion of the natures of both *shura* and democracy. The Qur'an, says Talbi, '... calls clearly and indisputably for consultation in the affairs of the *umma*. [The Qur'an] thus rejects tyranny conceptually and, by extension, tyrannical rule'

142

RONALD L. NETTLER

(Talbi 1992: 91). Talbi seems by implication here—as above—to mean that the consultation and related rejection of tyranny which for him form the core concept of the Qur'anic *shura* do overlap to some extent with the core meaning of democracy as 'rule of the majority'—at least when democracy is defined in a positive way that includes rejection of tyranny. But Talbi reminds us '… the Qur'an is not a constitution, and even if it were a constitution it would have become outmoded and left behind by time, just as many constitutions and political systems became outmoded, and just as time will in turn no doubt leave political systems behind' (Talbi 1992: 91). The empirical details of history (including, it seems, even the social, legal and institutional aspects of the Qur'an itself) are, again, transient with no *permanent* value or utility. It is only the universal and fixed moral principle of *shura* which is relevant for Talbi. Thus concerning the details of political institutions and systems, '… the Qur'an leaves for the *umma* the freedom and responsibility to organize consultation in the institutions which the *umma* chooses. For the principle of consultation is ethical, and is part of man *qua* man, as possessor of reason, as we have explained …' (Talbi 1992: 91). The main—and presumably sole—guideline for any community in organizing its affairs is that it chooses the 'best means', and this always involves rejecting tyranny. Today, says Talbi, we seem to think the best means is 'Western democracy'. This is fine, so long as we do not adopt some false notion of tyrannical democracy (e.g. the Soviet Gulag), as was said above. 'The Qur'an', again, 'enjoins true *shura* whose form is historically conditioned and whose implementation is consonant with conditions of time and place, without rigidity, and which promotes justice, harmony and equality for all people' (Talbi 1992: 92). If Muslims want to institute Western democracy today and their condition is suitable, then let them do it. But one must remember that '… if we do not find this institution anywhere in Islamic history, then we also cannot find it in Western history either, where the ruling political conception was the divine right of kings' (Talbi 1992: 92).

Modern democracy of the best kind is, for Talbi, a desirable form of government, and *shura* does overlap with it in some essential respects, most notably in the rejection of tyranny. But, again, for Talbi this does not mean that modern liberal democracy had historical precursors which were in all institutional details perfect 'early democratic versions', divinely sanctioned (even enjoined): 'Let us leave history to history.

The main thing is that we do not find in the Qur'an or *umma* anything which opposes democracy, and this is sufficient for us. Indeed we may even find something which enjoins and justifies democracy' (Talbi 1992: 92). Although Talbi does not explicitly define this 'something', it seems it is the anti-tyranny ethos which he sees as being the core ethical value in *shura*. This for Talbi is the point of many modern reformist Muslim leaders (*zu'ama' al-islah*), particularly in North Africa, the area Talbi knows best. He points out, in this respect, that the first modern constitution in the Arab and Islamic world was the Tunisian constitution of 1861 (Talbi 1992: 92). But neither *shura* nor any other traditional Islamic institution may be seen here as the 'precursor' or 'model' for this constitution, except in the most general sense of the anti-tyranny ethos.[13]

In his responses to these first issues and questions—around *shura* and modern democracy—Talbi has begun to draw the lines of his general theory concerning Islam and politics. Prominent thus far are his historical-contextual approach and his related designation of large universal principles embedded in the historical details. Thus, the Islamic politics of a particular time and place may not in his view be regarded as a divinely-sanctioned model to be instituted everywhere at all times. All that may be extracted for future reference is the large ethical principle implicit in the particular situation or text (sometimes explicit in a text). But such principles are, it seems, in any case universally present in humanity.

In his responses to subsequent issues and questions, Talbi extends and adds detail to the theory delineated above. The focus is in particular on the issue of the mixing of religion and politics in Islam, especially as this conception has been promoted amongst 'Islamic movements' and by 'Islamist' ideologues.

In a discussion titled '*Shari'a* and Politics', Talbi is asked for his views on certain issues: 'Whilst we continue talking about justice, we (must) refer to an issue which the Islamic political movements have continuously put forth, ... the total synthesis of religion and politics' (Talbi 1992: 92–3). Talbi's interlocutors say that of course we know how the connection between the *faqih* and the politician often went in the past, as, for example, its theory was elucidated by the great mediaeval thinker 'Ali b. Muhammad al-Mawardi (974–1058). But today 'political Islam', as represented intellectually by Mawdudi and Sayyid

Qutb, '... speaks about the *Jahiliyya* of the twentieth century, claiming Islam as religion is mainly law and calling for the application of that law. The Islamic movements seem to be propounding this idea ... which is a mixing of religion and politics. How does Professor Talbi see this question, beginning from his reading of Islam?' (Talbi 1992: 93.)

Talbi's general answer to these questions is, first and foremost, that of the cautious historian, and does not initially clearly indicate his own position. Thus he says al-Mawardi's theory was by way of justifying religiously the legal and political activities of the 'Abbasid caliphs to whom he was attached (and beholden). As such, al-Mawardi's theory may be seen as a legal ruse (*hila*) of a well-known type. And in our own century, says Talbi, the very different (opposite) sort of theory propounded by 'Ali 'Abd al-Raziq, *viz*, the total separation of religion from politics, was itself in the same category. For although Raziq's theory was not successful in achieving implementation—the Muslim world was then unprepared for this—Raziq did (and still does) have many supporters; and his ideas have found their way quietly into Islamic political thought and practice (Talbi 1992: 93-4). And this quiet success was a result of Raziq's theory being generally an expression of the *zeitgeist*. In both cases, then, al-Mawardi and Raziq, a scholar created a 'justification' for the conditions of his time and place in a theory which, in essence, affirmed and supported that reality.[14] This is not dishonest or illegitimate, says Talbi; it is, rather, normal for human beings: '... This act of justification derives from the depths of man, since man is always and ever justifying [his behaviour and institutions]. And if he does not do that, he is mad, in the sense that he would then act without justification. [Justification of this kind] is, then, a natural inclination in every person and in all societies' (Talbi 1992: 94).

Talbi, as the objective, analytical historian, has not given us his own opinion on the mixing of religion with politics. He has simply, it seems, provided an analytical tool in the form of a principle: We may understand any Muslim approach to this issue—pro or contra—as a response to the historical conditions of a certain time and place. And man, *qua* man, must for his very sanity practice this sort of justification (*tabrir*). But this is not all Talbi has to say on the matter.

Further issues and questions posed to Talbi are designed to elicit, from a somewhat different perspective, clear and unequivocal positions on the problem of politics and religion in Islam. Thus: 'Political Islam is amongst those contemporary phenomena which are difficult to trace back to a clear and defined textual source. What is the connection of these phenomena with Islam, in letter and in spirit?' (Talbi 1992: 95.)

Talbi's general argument in response is that contemporary Islamic movements and 'political Islam' promote a principle which imposes itself on others by virtue of its thoroughgoing and unyielding nature. Political Islam—in its most prominent manifestations—makes a claim about the 'essence' of Islam, *viz* that Islam is divinely ordained to express itself in political forms and that this is its basic nature. Such a doctrine, in Talbi's view, is extremely dangerous, in two related ways: First, in itself it is intolerant of other views of Islam. Since it says (or implies) that Islam is *essentially* political, any other view of it must be wrong; secondly, if implemented, this doctrine of political Islam would, by virtue of that implementation, create a societal or collective religious orthodoxy which would inevitably place heavy strictures on those who proclaimed other views of Islam (Talbi 1992: 95). Individual freedom and mutual respect between those holding opposing religious views—two of Talbi's personal higher Islamic values—would become impossible. Nobody, says Talbi, after denying any particular personal authority or expertise in religious-legal affairs, has the right to speak 'in the name of Islam' (Talbi 1992: 95), and thereby to dictate for others the nature of the faith.[15] Indeed, in a statement which implies an antipathy towards any collective religious orthodoxy, Talbi says '… concerning knowledge, the religious organizations are numerous, and they promote different interpretations. Each thinks it is the foundation of Islam, its basis, and its source, and that anyone who disagrees with it is in error. I do not subscribe to any trend which speaks in the name of Islam, establishing itself as an ultimate authority and authoritative source' (Talbi 1992: 95). He calls, rather, for each individual to be '… equipped with modesty and respect for the other' (Talbi 1992: 95). This is presumably not compatible with political religion or any collective orthodoxy. Even the tolerance (*tasamuh, samh, samaha*) of one person for the other's views, which in the Islamic Middle Ages was, in Talbi's opinion, a progressive step, was still imbued with condescension. And, he argues : 'For now, in the twentieth century, that will not suffice. Rather, it is necessary that we move to another stage, the stage of respect for the other; and respect is not graceful condescension—it is a right of the other. All people are equal in this right:

the right of mutual respect' (Talbi 1992: 95). In this regard, Talbi says he could never do what the adherents of political Islam are so prone to do: pronounce others to be *kafirs*, call on like-minded souls to emigrate from the presumably impure modern secular society (*hijra*), institute a regime of fundamental Qur'anic legislation (*hakimiyya*), or follow any of the other Islamist or ideological trends (Talbi 1992: 95).

Talbi prefers for himself (and all others) the way of the philosopher who thinks freely, for himself, and may or may not belong to a school: '... And he does not speak in the name of all of philosophy' (Talbi 1992: 96). He may belong to one or another school and may change his affiliation. This bespeaks total intellectual freedom, and for Talbi, '... freedom is the basis of everything' (Talbi 1992: 96). Thus, he has chosen history—since he is a historian—as his way of considering these issues. In his own freedom of thought and historical investigation he can come to terms with these modern problems and seek their histori-cal causes and origins. This is Talbi's approach to understanding the contemporary Islamic movements. He can thereby be '... a historian and a Muslim at the same time' (Talbi 1992: 96) and make his princi-ple of intellectual freedom and mutual respect the foundation of his personal Islam. In this way Talbi sees the Islamic movements as being phenomena which have precedents in Islamic history, in the general pattern of the schisms and fragmentation which the sources describe, as well as being contemporary developments arising from local eco-nomic and other causes. And in this way Talbi upholds his principle of intellectual freedom in his rejection of the movements and their fa-naticism (*'unf*). In a further personal statement, Talbi focuses his position and comes very close to defining what Islam is for him—despite his prior claim that he does not feel authorized to define Islam: 'As for me personally, as a Muslim—and I emphasise this, just as I emphasise that I am a Muslim who does not adhere to any school, for reasons which I have already clarified—I understand that the Muslim com-munity is one in its stance towards God, with prayer and in its religious observance. But as bad luck would have it, the Muslim community has always been torn apart in areas other than worship' (Talbi 1992: 97).

The solution for Talbi is, once again, his dream of mutual respect (*al-ihtiram al-mutabadil*): 'Perhaps it is possible that the disagreement in the community might lead to good results, if it were based on mutual respect and the absence of mutual recrimination. Then everyone would say, this is my view and this is my belief, which I shall explain without forcing it on anyone in any form' (Talbi 1992: 97). Talbi believes '... this position dispels the tensions and all types of fanaticism which lead to the perpetuation of the great civil strife' (Talbi 1992: 97). This 'great civil strife' (*al-fitna al-kubra*) is, of course, the early fissiparous event in the Muslim community over the succession to Muhammad, and related subsequent conflict, all of which signalled the breakdown of whatever unity had existed in the early *umma*. In Talbi's view, '... all the Islamic movements which call for fanaticism are in some form connected to this great civil strife' (Talbi 1992: 97)—presumably also (especially) those movements in our time.[16]

Thus, reiterating from a different perspective some of the ideas stated earlier, Talbi also gives us here, I believe, his view of the true or essential Islam, a view which has been lurking implicit in his exposition. Islam is basic religious observance, prayer and worship of God, and, to extrapolate in what I hope is not an unreasonable way, the universal ethical principles Talbi adduces above. Perhaps also to be added here are the intellectual freedom and mutual respect which Talbi holds to be the essence of the good society. Talbi's Islam is, then, basically a sort of pietism and humanistic ethical system. It is most definitely not political. Although earlier demurring from defining Islam, for fear of being one of those who 'speak in its name', and thereby creating an attitude of intellectual coercion, Talbi has now said what he believes true Islam is.

Continuing in the same vein, but now from the perspective of the *umma* and its history as seen in the modern context, Talbi answers a question about attempts that have been made to fill the gap left by the defunct caliphate. Talbi first summarizes what he sees as the general situation in today's post-caliphate world: 'There are two fiercely competing trends: the secularists whose influences are predominantly Western, and the counter-trend, which has already been mentioned' (Talbi 1992: 97). By this 'counter-trend' Talbi means the Islamist ideologues and movements who wish to resurrect a presumed political unity of the *umma*. It is these arguments which Talbi wishes to focus on, rather than those of the secularists. Here he will treat the claims of political Islam from a different angle than that used above.

Talbi goes on the offensive, first as the historian, attempting to undermine Islamist arguments through historical claims. Thus: '... This presumed political unity of the Islamic *umma* is only fantasy and imagining fixed in (people's) minds to the extent that it replaces reality. We all know that political unity for Muslims, from the time of the great civil strife until today, has been finished' (Talbi 1992: 97). Talbi presents a number of historical examples of this disunity to support his point. These range from the Umayyad period to the present when, he says, it is sufficient to recall the divergent positions taken by the Arab states over the Gulf crisis. 'All this', he says, 'confirms that the *umma* is the focus of conflicts and schisms. Is it possible, in light of this aspect of the *umma*'s history, that it could be a basis for a political unity which had not been realized during more than a thousand years?! I do not believe that political unity will be realized in the coming era ... ' (Talbi 1992: 98–9). Talbi adds, as a relevant aside here, a reference to the fact that today 40 per cent of the world's Muslims live as minorities in non-Muslim societies, and that even 'Muslim societies' are more mixed than ever (for example, Lebanon, Syria, Iraq, Egypt).

Considering the history of the *umma*, then, as well as present-day realities, for Talbi Islamic political unity and an Islamic state are chimerical in the one instance and, consequently, unnecessary in the other. Talbi then can address the great reigning conception of most of modern political Islam, the notion that Islam is religion and state, *din wa-dawla*. This notion, he says, is not consonant with reality, for all the historical reasons already given. And being in harmony with past and present historical and political reality is for Talbi crucial: 'We must in our thoughts always and ever be cognisant of reality, taking reality as our starting point' (Talbi 1992: 99). Here again Talbi as historian invokes that principle of historical truth in all its detail as one important standard against which religious doctrine may be measured. And the 'Islamic movements', with their totally unhistorical claim of the traditional Islamic *umma* as a political unity, provide an egregious case of a false religious doctrine: 'The Islamic movements in our view, then, constitute (an instance of) employing *shari'a* in a way not cognisant of reality or history, as an edifice characterized by 'retrospectiveness', imaginary and chimerical, incompatible with reality' (Talbi 1992: 100). The practical consequence of the aggressive propagation of such a historically unfounded and practically impossible doctrine is, says Talbi, '... the tensions which we live today on the political plane, tensions in which a fanatical extreme has been reached' (Talbi 1992: 100).

Talbi's solution for this sorry situation is the same as that given above for other problematic dimensions of religion and politics in Islam: the cessation of attempts to argue and implement a 'necessary' monolithic political structure in Islam and the introduction and implementation of an attitude of mutual respect which is so central to Talbi's world view. This would provide for the dialogue (*al-hiwar*) which he views as the necessary mechanism for a cohesive Muslim society: 'For dialogue will make it possible for us to be extricated from our problems, thing after thing, day after day, and it will put us at the heart of the pluralism which is fundamental to our destiny and our future' (Talbi 1992: 100–1). Talbi explores this further in such a way as to elaborate also on his own conception of Islam.

Thus in response to his interlocutor's assertion that he (Talbi) seems to detach Islam from any political function, Talbi begins with his characteristic claim that he, as historian, '… does not speak in the name of Islam' (Talbi 1992: 101); but he also claims that his very status as historian and his consequent knowledge of Islamic history 'authorizes' him 'to affirm' that '… there does not exist a sole Islamic governmental form' (Talbi 1992: 101). This is so far reiteration of Talbi's historical argument against political Islam: that this political form never existed, so they have no right now to seek to reinstate it. However, Talbi now leaps far beyond this premise, extending his argument in elaboration of his personal view mooted above: '… And even if we should assume in the end, for the sake of argument, the existence of a sole governmental form, it would not interest me, because it is possible for a Muslim to live content in his Islam and to live a full Islamic life in London, for example, where the government is in the hands of Mrs Thatcher. This government would never prevent the Muslim living an excellent and satisfying Islamic life, while the Muslim in another system, which claimed to be an Islamic order, might be suppressed and subjugated' (Talbi 1992: 101). Talbi is not concerned, he says, with respect to the life of the Muslim, about the outward form of a particular political system, that is, whether Islamic or non-Islamic, but rather with the freedoms the system gives to people. The best political system, he says, is the one which respects people and, in his view '… Islam must of necessity be that system' (Talbi 1992: 101).

Talbi has here clarified his position and made explicit certain underlying assumptions. First, not only was Islam never historically a political unity for him, but this 'fact'—though earlier the first line in his polemic against political Islam—now recedes as a polemical point, in favour of a further stage in the argument: even if Islam had historically been such a unified polity, Talbi does not care. For him the important issue, it seems, is not whether a government is properly 'Islamic', but whether it gives full freedoms to its people and 'respects' them. Indeed, Talbi has turned the issue fully on its head by erecting this principle of freedom and respect as the proper basis of government *to which Islam must conform*.

But for Talbi Islam's conforming to this principle should not be so difficult, as '… I have always been convinced, and I try to convince (others) that Islam is peace in its essence and in its mission, though it has not been spared from the morass of history, like the other religions and sects' (Talbi 1992: 102). Despite his own frequent protestation to the contrary, Talbi has now explicitly defined the *basic nature* of Islam, as he sees it. And he arrived at this conclusion from an 'historical perspective'. The meaning here seems to be clear: history tells us that there was no monolithic Islamic polity of the sort that political Islam wants to reinstate on the grounds it was the original essential Islam. Thus, by exclusion, as it were, history has left a non-historical ethical and spiritual essence of Islam as the true nature of the faith.

The arch historian Talbi has, again, discovered an ahistorical value *by way of history itself*. The (creative) tension between historical facts and universal values appears yet again as a basic feature of Talbi's thought. Islam clearly represents eternal ethical values at its core, though these have understandably been mixed in 'the morass of history'. This mixing helps to explain the various attempts, past and present, of political Islamic movements to impose an 'Islamic government' which they, in their acute misreading of history, take to be the eternal nature of Islam. As for Talbi, the nature of Islam has now been shown to be decidedly apolitical and ethical; his answer to the questions concerning Islam and politics may certainly be understood as affirming a separation between these two realms. Indeed, for Talbi the various contemporary attempts to politicize Islamic religion are 'an exploitation of religion': 'And I am against the exploitation of religion under whatever guise' (Talbi 1992: 103). But though religion and politics may in Talbi's view not mix in the ways thus far discussed—i.e. the imposition of some idealized (arbitrary) 'true Islamic' political form on the individual and society—is there absolutely no intersection or overlap between them? After all, even pure spiritual and ethical systems—Talbi's view of Islam—exist in communal/political settings and must, one would assume, in some way be related to that larger milieu. Talbi has an answer to this which is in itself interesting, and also helps to further to clarify his thesis concerning religion and politics.

After a lengthy discussion of attempts to impose a (false) political Islam on society—particularly in Iran—Talbi asks '... What is the spiritual value to a religious way of life not derived from self-discipline, belief and conviction? Do we want in our modern societies, which have witnessed radical changes crystallized in the rights of man, to encourage hypocrisy, dissimulation and duplicity, when God disdains that and punishes those who lie?' (Talbi 1992: 112.) With fidelity to his basic conception of religion as ethical and spiritual, Talbi strongly implies here that religious observance, even (especially) the 'legal' kind which political Islam emphasizes, is a worthless sham unless it derives from the proper internal spiritual and ethical state. More explicitly: 'The nature of religious belief and the way of life which follows it and springs from it is that belief is either spontaneous and free or it does not exist. Thus without freedom of choice, self-discipline and responsibility religious belief is not properly established' (Talbi 1992: 112). Nor is the sinner able properly to 'return to God', says Talbi, '... except through a free inner movement which renders him able to renounce sin' (Talbi 1992: 112–13). This 'return to God', for Talbi, using the pietistic, mystically-tinged term *'tawba'*, is an internal spiritual process occurring after 'the separation [from God, caused by] disobedience' (*mufaraqa al-'isyan*) (Talbi 1992: 113). If successful, this return (or repentance) restores the shattered harmony between the Creator and the created, enabling both sides, once again, to be close to one another. 'This is not achieved through pressure and compulsion, for repentance does not thereby occur ...' (Talbi 1992: 113). Such spiritual processes—whether repentance of the sinner or some more ordinary internal religious evolution—are for Talbi the stuff of true religion. And such processes may indeed even be thwarted especially in those very societies which publicly promote (and impose) a 'religious' way of life through the political apparatus.

The only true connection between religion and politics for Talbi, then, would seem to be in the existence of a liberal, pluralistic and secular society which enables and encourages true (ethical and spiritual) religion to develop. Thus: 'So pluralism today and the right of people to choose their way of life and their path oblige us to deepen religious belief and to render it more profound. That is the meaning of piety (*ikhlas*), and that is not accomplished by force and the scourge of the executioner. The Islamic way of life which enriches the spirit and satisfies God comes only from conviction and self-discipline, which are attained solely through an appropriate Islamic culture, other than coercive' (Talbi 1992: 113). Politics and religion are, again, properly related through the liberal society which enables individual Muslims to perfect themselves spiritually. This society is Islamic by being benignly apolitical, allowing individuals free choice of their way of life, '... without being pressured in any way except by the discipline which conscience dictates' (Talbi 1992: 113). 'Freedom of belief, self-discipline and freedom of conscience' are the foundations of such a society.

Mohamed Talbi's conception of Islam for the modern world is here derived from, and entwined with, his ideas on Islam and politics. And his ideas on Islam and politics must be understood within the context of his general intellectual outlook and method: a thoroughgoing historical empiricism in exegesis juxtaposed with the assertion of certain fixed, axiomatic principles, ethical and religious, which were often 'discovered' in the very nitty-gritty of history. But this 'discovery' is for Talbi merely an evocation of human nature (*fitra*). Thus the Islamic (or indeed, any other) revelation and the subsequent textual and communal history emerging from that revelation yield the universal human principles of goodness, mutual respect, equality of views and doctrines, and peace. Associated 'subsidiary' principles may also be revealed, such as feminism. Much of the detail, political, legal and other, which historians use in their work serves to inform us about the nature and persona of Islam as an historical and social phenomenon. The information thus obtained may be important and useful, but it cannot be 'imposed on the present' in the way attempted by the Islamic movements and ideologues. Indeed, Talbi argues that the political model claimed by the Islamists to have been the erstwhile structure of Islamic political unity, and divinely-ordained to become the only pattern for Islamic politics in the future, never existed. This conclusion arises from a careful scrutiny of history; and this may be the historian's contribution to the contemporary debate. History serves this purpose. But even if the political Islamic historical claim would be true by the historian's own highest standards, it would not thereby represent a principle to be implemented in all times and places. For human institutions and organizational forms are always time-bound and limited. And when such things die a natural historical death they cannot be revived. Nor ought they to be. Talbi's views consider such attempts a sort of 'ideological necrophilia'. Only the universal ethical principles revealed (and evoked) by Islam's (and others') revelation may have such a perpetual life, as religious and general history exemplify these principles which are part of human nature.

Talbi's conception of Islam for the modern world is, then, the spirituality and ethics which are the abiding universal heritage of revealed religion, in a framework of individual Islamic piety. The best political order is that which evinces the universal values which make possible the individual's free and spontaneous choice of this pious Islamic path. The imposed *shari'a* of the 'Islamic state' proposed in various formats by the ideologues of the Islamic movements is itself, to a great extent, history-bound, contextual and ephemeral. The best 'political' format for Islam is, consequently, the great universal values rather than any system of 'Islamic' law or government. These great values are, for Talbi, themselves the essence of true Islam. And they will need to be evoked again and implemented in order for Islam to remain viable and to take a constructive role in modernity.

It remains, finally, to discuss, however briefly, certain of Talbi's ideas in their traditional Islamic and modern intellectual contexts. In the traditional context, Talbi may be seen as reflecting certain trends of contextual Qur'anic exegesis, pietistic and theoretical Sufism and Mu'tazili ethical theories. In exegesis, the classical approach using the *asbab al-nuzul*, or historical causes of discrete revelations, certainly provides some foundation for Talbi's method. Talbi's conception of Islam as a kind of pietistic personal faith has resonances of, for example, a Sufi such as al-Muhasibi; and his conception of the spiritual equality of all religions may well reflect the ideas of Ibn 'Arabi (Talbi 1992: 80). In ethics, Talbi's notion of an innate human understanding (*fitra*) of what is good and bad, unrelated to revelation, is perhaps an echo of the thinking of the Qadi 'Abd al-Jabbar, the Mu'tazili, and others in that movement (see Hourani 1971: *passim*, and Hourani 1985: *passim*.). But even if these classical influences (or some of them) are operative in the background to Talbi's thought, they do not 'explain' it. Further understanding might be gained by placing Talbi in the modern context, Islamic and Western. Here he would seem on the Islamic side to fit in that great 'Sunni mainstream' of modern thinkers who have sought some 'quintessential Islam' in earlier tradition, which would, in their view, render Islam viable in a modern world of critical thought, changing values, shattered institutions and the new international 'global village'. Though very diverse in their views—from 'Islamist' to 'modern, liberal'—these thinkers share this common practice of designating some quintessential Islam upon which they build their thought. Among Talbi's main intellectual sources here may, for example, have been Muhammad 'Abduh, with his appeal to (critical) reason as typifying Islam and 'Ali 'Abd al-Raziq in his separation of Islamic religion from politics. From the Western side, Talbi himself acknowledges an intellectual debt to the German theologian Hans Kung in his writing on the theology of inter-religious relations (Talbi 1992: 152–3).

Many other (mainly putative) influences might be considered, but one must emphasize Talbi's originality within this context of 'precursors and influences'. His thought, whatever external inspiration may have touched it, is a highly original and profound attempt to combine tradition with modernity.

Notes

1　Talbi has been equally eminent in both of his chosen fields.
2　By 'modernist' I mean that thought whose obvious objective is somehow to 'combine' modernity with traditional views, whatever the specific doctrine.
3　This fourfold division is my own. I believe it is consonant with the general structure of Talbi's thought. For a study of Talbi's thought concerning interreligious relations and dialogue, see: Nettler 1998.
4　As we shall see, for Talbi these truths are intuited by human beings through some natural, inborn faculty.
5　This is one of Talbi's main arguments against 'political Islam'.
6　Talbi never really explains his method of reading and understanding the traditional historiographical sources, nor does he allude to the vigorous debate among Western scholars on this issue.
7　For a survey of the meanings of this term in earlier Islamic thought, see 'Fitra' in the Encyclopaedia of Islam, new edition; also Izutsu 1964: 112.

8 In holding this conception, Talbi evinces a principle which has been prominent among Muslim 'modernist' thinkers.

9 In adopting such a thoroughgoing position against those who exclude the views of others, Talbi does not address the axiomatic quality of his own position of unboundaried toleration. Does his stance, then, in its own way, constitute an implicit exclusion of views which reject his position? This in no way invalidates Talbi's argument, but it does leave an important unresolved (unresolvable?) issue.

10 Talbi goes much farther here in his use of this term than the meanings usually associated with it in Islamic law. He seems to mean a sort of free marketplace of ideas.

11 In all such instances, the empirical detail and the large principle are for Talbi part of the same fabric.

12 In attributing an Islamic value such as *shura* to a non-Islamic—or a pre-Islamic—society in his ethical universalization, Talbi, of course, transcends the bounds of most traditional Islamic thinking on the subject.

13 But this ethos is, for Talbi, again, universal.

14 For Talbi, it seems, religious thought follows general cultural and social trends rather than leads.

15 This anti-authoritarian and individualistic conception of religion puts Talbi squarely in the camp of those modernizers who would see the traditional communal Islamic context as now being redundant.

16 For Talbi the mentality behind the early strife is the same as that which causes problems in modern times.

7

Can Modern Rationality Shape a New Religiosity?
Mohamed Abed Jabri and the Paradox of Islam and Modernity

ABDOU FILALI-ANSARI

Mohamed Abed Jabri is renowned as a philosopher whose main work, *A Critique of Arab Reason* (Jabri 1984—90),[1] has had a profound impact and created a large debate within the Arab world. This book has now become one of the 'classics' of conte mporary Arab thought. Jabri's field of interest, until recently, was not religion as such, since he is neither a theologian (*'alim*), nor a liberal Muslim whose aim would be to offer critical or alternative views to the prevailing orthodoxy, nor even a modern specialist in religion. But Jabri did write on ideas which certain authors had related to religion, insofar as these ideas were part of Arab intellectual history, and had contributed to its basic methods and world views. In this, Jabri acted as a philosopher and a historian of ideas attracted by the epistemological foundations of systems of thought, rather than as a thinker interested in the content or the impact these systems may have had.

During the early nineties, Jabri shifted his basic direction and published numerous articles—mostly in popular daily newspapers—on some of the most intensely debated issues related to religion. These articles were assembled into two books, tackling the highly sensitive themes of *Democracy and Human Rights* (Jabri 1994), and *Religion, State and the Implementation of Religious Law* (Jabri 1996).

These articles are, in style and format, short essays written especially for the larger public—who are not assumed to have any prior philosophical or theological knowledge. They are clear attempts to address some of the basic issues keenly debated by contemporary

156

Muslims, and to solve some of the 'aporias' of current Islamic thinking, by finding consensual or definitive answers through rational inquiry and scientific investigation. These issues revolve, to a large extent, around the relation between religion and reason, raising questions about whether and to what extent reason can help to resolve religious dilemmas and shape new religious concepts acceptable to contemporary Muslims. Jabri's writings stand apart from the abundant literature dedicated to these questions in recent years by the absence of any apologetic or polemic tone, the first all too typical of Islamist literature, and the second of secularist or modernist writings.

The convergence of Islamic and universal ethics

As a starting point of his reflections on this issue in *Democracy and Human Rights*, Jabri formulates the basic question that, in his opinion, Muslims must now answer. How can Muslims accommodate the concepts and attitudes introduced within the context of democracy and human rights to their particular conceptual world? How can a 'turn' be created within Muslim consciousness which would enable it to accept democracy and lead to a commitment by Muslims to its enactment?

We should observe that until now the answers given to these questions were offered mainly by two opposed elites, the modernists and the traditionalists, each of them proposing an alternative by which they expressed their own interests through a language and a system of concepts of their own. Beyond these elites, the larger part of society was a kind of 'silent majority', alternately attracted to the one or the other of these two currents of thought. No attempt had been made to give the word to the masses. In fact, democracy seemed to be feared by both elites.

Looking more closely at the question, and taking into account the 'model' to which our thinkers refer when they write about democracy, one finds that this concept is defined, as are other *nahda* concepts in our modern and contemporary thought, through two completely different systems of reference, neither of which is relevant to the present Arab situation: the cultural heritage system and the *nahda* system. The first one links democracy to the Arab-Islamic view of *shura*; the other derives the elements of its definition from the final stages of the three centuries old struggle for democracy in Europe (Jabri 1994: 39–40).

For a short time, the modernists' answers were supported by reformist traditional elites, when Muhammad 'Abduh attempted to
identify the rationality of Islamic principles with modern rationality,
democracy with *shura*, and so on. However, this orientation did not
prevail after 'Abduh: the 'reformists' of the second generation (Rashid
Rida and his followers) stepped back and returned to concepts which
stressed the 'peculiarities' of the 'Islamic model' and its opposition to
'Western' values and concepts.

More recently, deep and rapid changes have altered the conditions
of life in the Muslim world. These changes have imposed democracy
as the only acceptable form of legitimacy and enabled the silent majority to express its views. The alternatives—the traditional (religious
systems of government) and some modernist ones ('revolutionary' systems of government)—express the interests of limited segments within
modern societies, even in the Third World. Although the conditions
which initially made possible the birth of democracy do not probably
exist within these countries, democracy has become an aspiration and
a mode of legitimization deeply entrenched in modern consciousness.

At this point, Jabri mobilizes his philosophic resources to defend a
position which has been sharply attacked in recent decades. The attitude of Muhammad 'Abduh—the conception of modernity as an
implementation of Islamic principles—has been extensively criticized
by modernist thinkers such as Abdullah Laroui (see, e.g., Laroui 1967,
and 1974) and Aziz Al-Azmeh (see, e.g., Al-Azmeh 1993), who hold
it responsible for the ambiguities and confusions which favoured the
ideal of a restoration of the 'glorious' past as the only way to achieve
progress under present conditions. However, Jabri does not acknowledge the idea of a complete separation between traditional and modern
values and moral ideals.

While Jabri declares his firm adherence to the idea of a deep convergence between Islamic principles and the ethical foundations of
democracy and human rights, he also stresses the importance of the
historic turn which led to the birth of modernity. Two steps are needed
in order to arrive at a solution of the paradox that seems to arise when
these two ideas are put side by side, and it is also necessary to give a
clear delineation of the convergence and the turn which generate this
paradox. First, it needs to be asserted that modern concepts are not
the direct outcome of traditional Western concepts, that they owe

nothing to the traditional Western world view and cannot, in this sense, be considered as 'Western'. They must be recognized as the result of a deep reaction against such Western traditions and everything that contributed to the peculiarities of Western societies. Secondly, within the Islamic framework, the principle of *shura*, the basic principle of social and political life, expresses an ideal of social consensus which is in no way linked to any particular political system, not those traditional Muslim societies have implemented, nor even those traditional thinkers have conceived and linked to what they considered to be the ideal caliphate. *Shura* thus preserves its value and 'appeal' to modern Muslim consciousness as an ethical principle which should prevail in all conditions, taking different forms in different historical contexts.

Indeed, *shura* is linked to the conceptual environment which prevailed in classical and medieval Muslim societies. It refers to the idea of the just despot who agrees to act ethically and to consult his subjects (or at least a limited circle of advisers, who may be the 'ulama' or the notables of the community). Democracy, on the other hand, is altogether different. It did not emerge within the Islamic context and has no foundational element within it. It was born in the European environment, where the opposition between feudal masters, the church, and structures of cultural power engendered a kind of stalemate which led to the emergence of democracy. It is, at the same time, by Islamic standards, a virtue, insofar as it stresses the attitude of consultation and understanding between the members of the Muslim community. *Shura* can, therefore, be mobilized and referred to as a means for the legitimization of democracy, as a principle which points in the same direction as the new aspirations of humanity for political systems which provide the greatest opportunities for freedom and equality.

> Within the Arab-Islamic context, in both the past and the present, the state has had one particular feature: it rejects the idea of an 'associate' (*sharik*) to the man in power; while democracy is in its essence nothing but association (*shirk*) in political power. Believing in the oneness of God is a founding principle in our religious creed, and we should adhere firmly to it. However we should [also] believe that everything below God is multiple and is founded on the principle of multiplicity, especially human governance (*hakimiyya*), for which any trait of unity should be strictly denied (Jabri 1994: 57).

Some basic theological observations are presented in order to support this approach. At the level of the basic perspective, Jabri is convinced that freedom of faith and equal rights for women are among the aims (*maqasid*) of Islamic law. Historical conditions have given these principles a content which is below that of modern aspirations. The rules of the *shari'a* against apostasy and concerning the status of women are examples which illustrate how traditional Islamic societies failed to reach the ideals which contemporary Muslims expect and hope from Islam. It is therefore incumbent to examine the aims and objectives of the law in order to define new rules which would better express the aspirations of Muslims and be closer to the spirit of the law.

> Jurists have distinguished between rites (*'ibadat*)—which should not be taken as subjects for rational examination (*ijtihad*) because they are not amenable to rational justification, such as breaking the fast at sunset in Ramadan for example—and transactions (*mu'amalat*)—which are properly subjects of rational examination because of their link to the objectives (*maqasid*) of the religious law (*shari'a*), and to the conditions of revelation (*asbab an-nuzul*), which are taken to be their causes.[2] On whether it is possible to link religious commandments to objectives rather than to causes, I do not think that we should impose on ourselves a strict and absolute implementation of the rule adopted by jurists (*fuqaha*) which declares that 'commandments evolve following their causes rather than the effects sought by their implementation', because this rule has been reached through mere rational examination and nothing else.
>
> The causes (*'ilal*) of the commandments are not given by source texts, but are instead inferred by jurists through rational inquiry, and built, as they readily admit, on conjecture and probability rather than certainty and absoluteness. The most reasonable position in our view is to refer detailed religious commandments, when their objectives diverge, back to the general principles (*kulliyyat*) of the *shari'a*, because these general principles of the law are the equivalent of the explicit verses in matters pertaining to the creed. Since we have to refer the ambiguous (*mutashabih*) back to the explicit (*muhkam*), why should we not consider contradictions that arise between certain specific commandments and newly emerging objectives as kinds of ambiguity (*mutashabih*) which are resolved by reference to explicit (*muhkam*), basic and general principles? (Jabri 1994: 186–7)

This solution has a striking resemblance to the proposal of many contemporary Muslim thinkers for the reform of Islam. The programme on which all thinkers seem to converge, despite the important disparities between their initial premises, consists in pushing aside everything that tradition has accumulated on top of the basic principles of faith, and going back to the core of the creed and the perspective it was intended to create among believers.

The reign of religion and the government of politics

The opening remarks of Jabri's second book, *Religion and State, and the Implementation of the Religious Law*, emphasize the necessity of adopting what he calls an 'open reference'. This reference is twofold: it takes a particular historical episode as a paradigm of Islamic politics and attempts to employ the paradigm following a methodology respectful of the rules of modern rationality.

As for this last point, Jabri observes that the debate among Muslims nowadays is so confused because most of the leading voices do not distinguish between facts, which can be the object of knowledge, and the evaluations made of these facts, which are often built on the basis of different prejudices or preferences. No clear conception is made of what a scientific approach can be—i.e. an approach which limits itself to the fact—and how different it can be from the ideological approach. Even the amassing of facts and the ways they are described are too often informed by predominating ideological choices, and so do not lead to the establishing of a common ground for fruitful debate. In other words, Jabri insists that a scientific approach, a strict respect for facts and rational approaches, must be the starting point of any debate about contentious questions.

As for the main issue challenging the minds of Muslims today, the principle available starting point, or reference, is the experience of the early Muslim community, the polity or regime created immediately after the death of the Prophet and subsequently called the Righteous Caliphate (*khilafa rashida*).

> The original point of reference in Arab-Islamic history, which supersedes (precedes?) all other points of reference, is the practice ('*amal*) of the Companions (*sahaba*) of the Prophet during the period of the Righteous Caliphate. Since the Qur'an and hadith do not legislate in matters of authority and politics, and do not evoke the relationship between religion and state as clearly and precisely as they do for other questions like mar-

riage and inheritance, the main point of reference, if not the only one, in the question of the relationship between religion and state is therefore the practice of the Companions (Jabri 1996: 9).

One may wonder about the choice of an episode of Islamic history as a ground for theorising about such a basic issue, and even ask whether the step proposed by Jabri is a way of restoring the paradigm of an ideal Islamic model of the state and, with it, the conviction that such a model exists and has been implemented in history? Would it not be a return to the deep frustration which shaped the Muslims' predominating feeling and conception of their history, i.e., the conviction that they were prevented from fully implementing the constitution offered to them by their religion, and that this failure was the origin of all their misfortunes and sufferings? Would it not be a return to the fundamentalist approach, for which the time has come to restore such a 'true' Islamic state?

Apprehensions of this sort are rapidly put aside when one considers the way Jabri handles this 'ultimate' point of reference. The practice of the early Muslims is held in such a regard because it was the first attempt by living Islam within profane history after the end of revelation. Hence, the first distinction that should be drawn is that the political practice linked to Islam is part of the historic life of the community, not of its religious dogmas. It is a recognizable fact that no provision, no commandment, has been given to Muslims from sacred sources concerning the creation of a state or the form such a state should have. It was the Muslims who felt at a particular moment of history that, in order to enact Islamic precepts, they had to create a state.

The absence of explicit and clear texts in the Qur'an and sunna which regulate political power and the state does not mean that Islam is universally unconcerned by the question of power. In fact, the historical practice of the community (*umma*) runs contrary [to such a conclusion]; the predication of the Prophet evolved during his lifetime into the creation of a state; Muslims maintained that state, in a way or another, [since they considered it] as a necessary means for maintaining the religion and defending the domain occupied by the community. On the other hand, the Qur'an and *sunna* offer what may be considered as foundations for an ethics of political power in Islam, by way of apologetics for consultation (*shura*), the call for the implementation of justice, the care for the poor, for the deprived and all those in their situation (Jabri 1996: 3).

So in order to be understood, this historic turn should be situated in its context. In contrast to the conditions within which Judaism and Christianity were born, there was no state in Arab society when Islam appeared first. The original Muslim community was not born within an existing polity, nor was it obliged to engage in a direct confrontation with a state or its representatives, as were the Jewish and Christian communities—either in their beginning or throughout history. Hence, early Muslims adopted Islam not only as an attitude toward God, but also as a way of organizing their collective life, as a founding principle for new relationships among themselves and as a means of founding a new political entity. All that can be said is that Islam, while making no provision or regulation for the creation and management of a polity, gave birth to a process which led to the creation of a state. Further events made of this turn the essential event in their history, the deepest concern in the consciousness of Muslims, and the main process which shaped their world view. It has therefore had a profound influence on the way Muslims conceive of their religion and their history.

How all this happened is of the greatest importance today. The early Muslims reacted to the death of the Prophet as if it created an 'institutional void' (Jabri 1996: 15), and their first reaction was to appoint someone who could exert the same authority as he had, and accomplish more or less the same function. In so doing, they opted, without giving any thought to the consequences of their choice, for a system where an individual held all power and was entrusted with the organization and the control of the political power thus created, without any kind of institutional provision for the coherence and continuity of his actions. They thought in terms of persons (hence the question which dominated their debates: who should be appointed as a *khalifa?*), not in terms of institutions and organizations (hence the absent question: how should the community be organized and managed?). The theories of the caliphate which were elaborated decades afterwards were, in fact, efforts to express in theoretical form what had been implemented in earlier spontaneous actions, to justify the status quo, rather than efforts to think what the community should adopt for its organization in the light of the sacred texts and their teachings. Political *fiqh* has, therefore, been an attempt to legitimize a particular historical experience. It has involved the elevation of the past of the community to the level of a norm.

This, in turn, engendered a response which had the most devastating effects on the evolution of the community. Thus, the first and founding political experience of the Muslims has had three main consequences, which have continued to influence and shape their handling of social and political issues.

First, whenever there is a question about the political direction of the community, the law has not been derived directly from the sacred texts or from what may be considered as the spirit or the moral of these texts, but rather from the actual practice of the dominant few, however remote this may have been from the religious principles. In this sense, it may be said that *facts define the law*, instead of facts being submitted to the law.

Second, the early practice of the Muslims came to define a certain pattern, according to which no institutional provisions were adopted, but rather trust was given—in fact often merely conceded—to individuals. The rule that can be deduced from this is that in Muslim societies *persons have always tended to prevail over institutions*.

Third, the far reaching consequence of these attitudes, which have dominated the religious and social life of Muslims and deeply permeated their consciousness, is that *no 'viable' link has been made between ethical principles and the actual organization of the community*.

This latest feature manifests itself across the whole Muslim tradition. It points to the major contradiction, tragically felt by the community, of the fundamental opposition between the actual history of the Muslims—dominated by violence and the politics of coercion— and the religious consciousness which was constantly and firmly attached to ethical principles. The fact that these principles found no way into everyday practice has had the deepest influence on the feelings and behaviour of Muslims.

Should we therefore admit that it is time to opt for secularism, to admit that state and religion should be separated, and abandon any hope of implementing a religiously permeated system of government and social order? No, says Jabri:

> The question of secularism (*'ilmaniya*) in the Arab world is a false problem, in the sense that it expresses actual needs by reference to categories which do not correspond to them: the need for independence within a single national identity, the need for a democracy which protects the rights of minorities, and the need for the rational practice of political action. All

are in fact objective needs; they are even reasonable and necessary claims within the Arab world. However, they loose their justification and necessity when they are expressed through ambiguous slogans like that of secularism (Jabri 1996: 113).

Secularism is not convenient to Muslim societies, says Jabri, because it is based on the separation of church and state. Such a separation was indeed necessary at some time within the Christian milieu. Since there is no church in Islam, there is no need for such a separation. Muslim societies require that Islam be maintained and implemented as an ethical reference and as a *shari'a*, a divinely inspired law, as a ground and principle for social and political life, within the scope of an updated knowledge of the past.

The kind of secularism Jabri seems to have in view here is similar to what is called in French 'laïcité', which has been translated as *'ilmaniya*, a far more systematic and hostile attitude towards religion than is commonly understood in the English-speaking world by secularism. He shares the hostility aroused by the rigid style in which secularism, as a concept, has been translated and received in the Islamic world—*la-diniyya* and *'ilmaniya*—and the idea that these translations convey of an exit from, or denial of, religion. He also seems to be profoundly convinced that the defence of secularism by Arab intellectuals (who were mostly Christian) represents a kind of deviation, and a transfer of the specific problems of Islamic societies into alien settings.

This being said, Jabri immediately insists that, if the separation of religion and state is to be discarded, there is another separation which should be seriously taken into consideration. It is the separation between political practice and religious concepts. The argument for this is that religion aims at uniting men, while politics necessarily introduces divisions among them. Politics, being essentially the management of material interests, leads unavoidably to opposition and conflict among men. It should, therefore, be practised with reference to rational rules, or submitted to 'profane' rationality. Religion, as a system which aims at providing men with beliefs and principles which transcend their material interests, and at unifying them in ethically based attitudes, should be kept entirely apart from politics. In no way should we Muslims, as Jabri says in his other writings, 'practice politics within religion' (Jabri 1984, 90: vol. 3), or defend our political ideas and interests through concepts and representations extracted from religion.

Jabri suggests the adoption of an intermediate formula through which Islam would be freed from the expressions in which it was bound through history, and which would provide ethical foundations to the state and the society, while rules and practices would be submitted to rational considerations and to what human experience has shown to be the best solutions. These conclusions, despite Jabri's proclaimed opposition to secularism, are very close to the conceptions defended by 'Ali 'Abd al-Raziq in the famous essay of 1925, 'Islam and the Foundations of Political Power'. They respect the feeling which spread in the Islamic world toward 'Western' models and concepts such as secularism, and at the same time call for attitudes and behaviour which, while leading to these secular results, claim origins within traditional conceptions.

Is this a way, as many critics of Jabri have alleged, to reconcile what are, strictly speaking, irreconcilable views? What is proposed seems to be a secularized political practice within a system supported by, or attached to, religious norms. Religion, as with some European monarchies, reigns but does not govern. It does not provide the *modus operandi* of political practice, yet it provides the basis for a social and political consensus.

Religion, reform and modern knowledge

The previously mentioned first episode in the history of the Islamic community is not the only period to which Jabri gives his attention, for he also sketches a broad picture of the basic evolution experienced by Muslims since the advent of modernity. He attempts to isolate some basic and influential facts, and he notes, along with other observers of Islam, that popular religiosity—based on the cult of saints, myth, and celebrations—has nearly disappeared, while the religiosity of the urban elites—based on strict monotheism, doctrine, and formal rites—has survived and gained force. The most dramatic consequence of this evolution is, from this point of view, the birth of a new religious figure, the Salafi; a kind of militant who engages to restore the dignity and the strength of the community and combat internal decadence and external aggression. Everything in the Salafi's attitude makes of him a kind of modern 'saviour': he is altogether opposed to colonialism and maraboutism, he is a reliable ally to nationalism, and he is attached to progress and tradition. Finally, he emphasizes self-assertion and self-confidence.

These heroic virtues obscure ambiguities, which lead to some far-reaching consequences. The Salafi types of reaction were, in medieval history, an effective form of conservatism—enabling Muslim societies to recover their equilibrium in some circumstances, and to produce reactions useful in resisting new menaces and confronting external attacks and internal degradation. But nowadays it is clear that this kind of conservatism provides no solutions to the problems faced by the community and individual believers; it has, rather, become particularly harmful. Its main deficiency is that it prevents a realistic evaluation of the present conditions within which Muslims live. The influence exerted by Salafi doctrines has led to the rehabilitation of the fusion, which was made within traditional societies, of Islamic ethical principles and the doctrinal legal systems elaborated by jurists and theologians.

Such Salafi conservatism is no longer sufficient under present conditions. Within the world system which now encompasses the whole of humanity, where rationality and critical attitudes are implemented in all human activities and applied to all aspects of life, Salafism is no longer adequate to confront the challenges which all human societies have to face. It was possibly the most convenient reaction in a time when faith and the preparation for eternal life dominated all the endeavours and actions of men, when science and technology played no role in human concepts and life. Salafism and its outcome, the *sahwa*, are now predominantly emotional attitudes based on feeling and affective reactions; in no way do they move towards a more realistic and effective way of handling religious and political issues.

Against Salafism, Jabri proposes the historical experience of the community. What is needed, in his view, is a reorientation of certain concepts which have become deeply entrenched in the common consciousness of Muslims towards the adoption of new attitudes vis-à-vis Islamic history; or, in other terms, the very reconstruction of the historical consciousness of the community. Fundamentalism—or extremism, as he prefers to call it—has gained such a large influence in some strata of Muslim societies because Salafism did not succeed in renovating Islamic thought. Salafism is not the direct ancestor of fundamentalism, as is claimed by some observers, but is, through its failure, the progenitor of contemporary extremism. The tone of apology and the appeal to emotion, rather than rational attitudes, are directly responsible for the backwardness and closure of the predominant concepts within the community. Fundamentalism will recede only if moderate Salafi theologians indulge in the reconstruction of the *shari'a*, following modern rules and concepts.

In fact, the renewal which is needed today is not, in Jabri's opinion, that to which people refer frequently, which deals with 'consequences' and leaves 'foundations' as they were. The foundations themselves need to be 're-founded'. In order to give a precise illustration of what he means by this expression, Jabri turns his attention to the widely debated notion of *ijtihad*. He emphasizes the asymmetry between this notion and the other sources of Islamic law. While these latter (Qur'an and *hadith*) are sacred texts, *ijtihad* refers to a mobilization of the rational capacities of the human mind. In the classical period, this mobilization operated as an intensive usage of analogy (*qiyas*), a process linking a particular case to another particular case. An impressive accumulation of cases and deductions was made by Muslim scholars throughout the first centuries, to the point of literally exhausting the possibilities given by this approach. This is the real cause for what was called the 'closure of the door of *ijtihad*': all the possible combinations that were potentially available within this type of reasoning came, in fact, to be systematically explored. The exercise—concentrating mainly on particular problems, hypothetical cases, and questions of terminology—was pursued to its ultimate end, and the circle was completed.

Nowadays Muslims need something else. Shatibi, the Andalusian theologian of the eleventh century, was already aware that *ijtihad* was at a dead end. He expressed this through his call for a reformulation of the foundations (*ta'sil al-usul*). If *maslaha* (the common good or common interest) is the ultimate criterion for legislation, then the sacred texts should be read in a totally different way. The new *ijtihad* it requires would attain its objectives if it were open to actual life, as it is experienced by contemporary Muslims. In these conditions, it can depart from the methods and concepts of the traditional schools. Instead of being imprisoned in the meanings of words, and by allowing language to be an active partner in legal thinking instead of attempting to understand the literal sense of each precept and thereby 'decoding' the intentions of the Legislator in each commandment separately, *ijtihad* would adopt a single principle as the ground for all precepts and commandments and would, therefore, be based on what really transcends time and space: the common good of all men. This is the real link with the basic feature of the *shari'a*: the fact that it is founded on ethical principles and not on arbitrary usages, as is customary law. This new *ijtihad* would, at the same time, avoid ambiguity and conjecture, and build systems suitable to the conditions of modern man.

Conclusion

The original feature of the approach proposed by Jabri is that it represents a typical case of what may be considered as an invasion of the theological field by 'secular' intellectuals. Since the advent of modernity in Muslim societies, the corps of *'ulama'* and *fuqaha*, which used to play a key role in the maintenance of religious concepts and the performance of social control, has lost much of its influence and power. Society has been more efficiently controlled by the modern state than it had been by traditional rulers. The role of the traditional theologians and jurists has been consequently reduced to a mere symbolic legitimating stance. They acquired, therefore, a kind of timidity, a strict conservatism, and a sort of refusal to seriously confront the aporias of contemporary Islam. The boldest approaches are, therefore, attempted by non-theologians: political activists on one side and secular intellectuals on the other. The first group formulate in religious concepts tenets of their political and social resentment; the latter mobilize universal rationality and tools of modern historical criticism in order to attain views of religion that would be compatible with modern conceptions.

Jabri is in line with the secular intellectuals, especially when insisting on the necessity—and the possibility—of attaining a reasonable certainty and consensus on highly controversial religious issues related to politics and its control by religion. He even goes further in this direction when he formulates a sharper critique of traditional theology than do most others, insisting that this theology stresses the *duties* of the Muslim and neglects his rights. The absence of rules for the public sphere has created a deep asymmetry in the whole system of Islamic law, and made it a means of submission to the ruler rather than for the control of political power. While questions of personal status were treated with great attention and in great detail, the rights of people were largely neglected.

The *shari'a* is more of a reference system for law than a complete and closed system of commandments. Its basic tenets are transparent to reason. Its aim is to discard and to replace systems based on traditions and social usages in favour of rules based on ethical principles which are entirely accessible to reason. The attempts to assimilate the *shari'a* to a specific corpus of rules, which is what the traditional *'ulama'* did, neglected the basic inspiration of the *shari'a* and left Muslims dangerously confused.

In thus arguing, Jabri recognizes that he is no longer adhering to a scientific attitude, but rather expressing revolutionary truths, i.e., considerations and concepts intended to stimulate the present debate. The scientific approach is useful when there is a need to discard views aroused by passion, and to prepare the terrain for fresh evolution. But at another level, the intellectual has to propose bold formulae in order to realize real advances in the collective consciousness.

Jabri underscores the fact that the religious consciousness of Muslims is profoundly influenced, and to a great extent shaped, by the history of their community—and especially certain key periods. Even the sacred texts are integrated in a vast synthesis where overall conceptions of the world and man, social norms and the self-consciousness of the community, its frustrations and aspirations, are held together. This world view is organized within, and deeply permeated by, a specific consciousness of history. These views still seem to be intact, and have not been altered by the recent transformations undergone by the community. This is the origin of the main confusions which have dominated the views and conceptions of contemporary Muslims. A revision of these views and concepts must first be made, in order to allow the evolution of the two last centuries to be fully absorbed and taken into account. The Salafi intellectuals were not able to transform this historical consciousness, and, therefore, could not perform the transition to a religiosity adapted to societies which had undergone the process of modernity.

Hence the way to a true Islamic reform, which requires a sharp distinction between religious norms and historical forms, rules, and the traditions in which they were embodied, and implies a renewal of the historical knowledge Muslims have of their past. In other words, reform is neither to be expected nor attempted within theology and through the initiative of theologians, but rather from a new knowledge of the past built on modern (and rational) principles. Religious awareness is maintained and transmitted in a complex of historical representations. Therefore it is the task of modern intellectuals, who act on these representations, to provide, build, and disseminate new concepts which would make possible a real reform. It is the reform of a traditional *'ilm*, or rather its replacement by a more workable and modern knowledge, which will provide the necessary preconditions for a real renewal in the Muslim world view.

Instead of wondering what should be kept from tradition and what taken from modernity, we should be aware that we do not have to make choices between elements or components, but rather that we must change our approach and criteria.

Notes

1 A disciple and friend of Muhammad 'Abduh, editor of the review *al-Manar*, and author of *al-Khilafa aw al-imama al-'uzma* (The Caliphate or the Great Imamate), Cairo (1924).
2 The two terms *'ibadat* and *mu'amalat* signify the main divisions of Islamic law according to the *fiqh* texts. *'Ibadat*, usually translated as 'worship' or 'rites', signifies those areas of law which deal with man's duties vis-à-vis God, and *mu'amalat*, sometimes translated as 'transactions', signifies those areas concerning inter-human relations. [eds]

8

Islam, Europe, the West
Meanings-at-Stake and the Will-to-Power

MOHAMMED ARKOUN

This contribution offers an example of the strategic intervention of critical thought in the historical development of Mediterranean societies, torn as they are between religious monotheism on the one hand—in its three ritual and doctrinal forms, Judaism, Christianity, and Islam—and, on the other, a tradition of philosophical thought deriving mainly from classical Greece, but found throughout the Near East since the conquests of Alexander. The strategy here is to seek to identify the times and places of manifestation, deployment and rupture in the long history of human reason's engagement with the never-ending quest for a universally applicable meaning that will be lasting, transcendent, and able to act as a foundation for political, ethical, legal, and spiritual legitimacy. The intention to study the whole Mediterranean area may seem excessively ambitious to those who specialize in reconstructing fragmentary branches of knowledge and limited portions of history. The violent confrontations which have occurred between representatives of 'Islam' and 'the West' since the nineteenth century—and particularly in the last twenty years—have, however, made it necessary to call on general practitioners (to use a medical metaphor) rather than specialists. Programmes of research and teaching, at all levels and in all countries historically and politically connected with the Mediterranean, must now include the following:

i) A critical re-reading of the history of thought, freed from the basically ideological oppositions between theology and philosophy, and from definitions concerning substance, essence, and the transcendent which have been imposed by the three religions which view the truth as something sacred, and in particular the Christian view of revealed Truth as developed from Jewish tradition and Greek *logos*.

ii) History seen as a cultural anthropology of the past, enabling us to overcome the exclusion of Islamic thought from European thought, which has, since the sixteenth century, been associated with the will to extend European hegemony under the beneficial guise of modernity.

iii) A new evaluation of the meanings that are at stake, both on the side of the revealed religions and on that of the philosophical tradition inextricably linked with the supremacy of the democratic secularized state.

iv) A critical re-reading of modernity as a philosophical process for which a back-dated justification is constantly being sought and given in order to maintain the legitimacy of hegemonic trends in what Braudel calls material civilization, which is, in turn, imposed by physical and/ or symbolic violence on societies which have taken no part in its production. From this standpoint, present-day fundamentalism—rejected in the name of 'Western values'—appears as a defensive reaction against aggressive forms of modernity.

v) The historical, cultural, and spiritual reintegration of the Mediterranean would appear to be a philosophical prerequisite, both for the redefinition of European identity as the European Union takes shape, and for what I have called the 'critique of Islamic reason', an inevitable project which has already begun.

vi) All these tasks are urgent because they bear upon a new geopolitical order and new historical solidarities which will form within the matrix of the future historical environment of the European Union in about the year 2010. Of course, it will be impossible to ignore the universalizable gains in scientific, technological, and philosophical thought which have been made in Europe since the sixteenth century; but it is the methods and ways by which modernity is transferred to other societies which need to be changed, a modernity which has not been subjected to the necessary philosophical and critical control in the places where it has emerged and developed. Accordingly, the critique of Islamic, Christian, Jewish, Buddhist, Hindu, Marxist, liberal, etc. reason will take the form of an effort to identify the unthought and unthinkable, not with reference to a modernity which is conceptually one with the recurrent aspirations of European-Western hegemony, but by making the epistemological resolution to move towards an intellectual outlook based on the principles of overcoming, surpassing, and removing all constructions, all affirmations of identity, all truths deriving from or spread by violence. The utopian nature of this outlook does not signify a permanent retreat from the constraints of history, of language, of the individual and collective unconscious, of socio-politics, and of economics; this utopia means a constant mobility of thought, necessary if we are to keep the same critical eye on all sites, modalities, frameworks, and tools of a production of meaning which is in a constant state of change.

An urgent need can be felt at the present moment for reflection, with all the resources of the social sciences, on the objective historical content, geopolitical weight, paradigmatic values, and horizons of hope implied by the three words: Islam, Europe, the West. Since these three spheres of production of contemporary history have been subjected to unchecked ideological interpretation, a great deal of explanation, critical evaluation, and fresh analysis is necessary, especially with regard to the way Muslims and Occidentals see each other. As a teacher and researcher in the field of Islamic thought, I have always been concerned with the need for intellectual and cultural mediation, and by the constant confusion caused by political tensions. This has led me to publish three books in the format of questions and answers: *L'Islam, religion et société* (Arkoun 1982b), with the Italian journalist Mario Arosio; *Ouvertures sur l'Islam* (Arkoun 1992a); *Islam & de democratie* (Arkoun 1994). The questions addressed to me from different European contexts have spurred me on in differentiating the concepts of Europe and of the West, starting from two fundamental concepts which confront critical thinking about current realities: the history of what I call 'Islam-as-fact' and 'the societies of the Scripture-book'; and the meanings-at-stake which are connected with the will-to-power in Europe—Europe properly so-called, and Europe as belonging to what it calls the West, so as to marginalize the Mediterranean world and accentuate the ancient break between its south-east and north-west.

This means that the old debate begun by the Belgian historian Pirenne in his posthumous *Mahomet et Charlemagne* (Pirenne 1937), on the rupture engendered by a hegemonic Islam within the area unified by the *pax romana* and by Christendom, should be brought up to date and enriched by a new questioning of cultural history, or, more particularly, of the cognitive status and the psycho-socio-political functions of religion-as-fact. The reader will see that this preoccupation is present in all my responses; it even brings me to reject the immediately applicable formulaic definition the Western politician or citizen requires when faced by the 'strange' behaviour and beliefs of a growing number of Muslims.

The publisher of the Dutch book chose the title because European societies are above all preoccupied by the difficulties of integrating Muslim immigrants, without taking any account of the historical, legal, and cultural obligations of a law-ruled state and a civil society. For the Arabic Muslim audience, the confrontation between Islam and democracy has given rise to a populist and apologetic literature which has become so widely spread, and already so deeply rooted in the politico-religious imagination, that I feel it better to re-focus attention on the revision and restoration of perspectives which are ignored in most of what is written about the tensions, oppositions, and open conflicts between Islam, Europe, the West. I fear, though, that the Arabic Muslim reader will find it difficult to share an attitude which prefers the identification and critical analysis of the concepts at stake to the ancient notion of 'just war' (*jihad*), which has been currently resuscitated in an Islam which feels dominated, threatened, and distorted by a systematically hostile West. The historical contradictions have been badly thought out, and badly translated into experience, under pressure from a modernity which has been produced without the participation of any society touched by Islam-as-fact. Material modernity is a matter of consumption, sometimes over-consumption, in the wealthiest classes, those which thereby most resemble comparable classes in the West, not the popular strata which militant Islam defends. Intellectual modernity, however, has always been limited in its diffusion and its productivity by the requirements of an ideology of combat, both in the phase of secular nationalist movements and in present-day fundamentalism. The conflict between Islam—or Christianity, Judaism, Buddhism, and so on—and democracy inevitably produces anachronisms which are fruitful from the point of view of an ideology of combat, or of religious apologetics, but which are entirely unacceptable to critical historical and anthropological thinking.

I wish, therefore, to re-examine the two great axes of research, debate, and reflection already mentioned, so as to deepen the analysis of these themes and create a new space for communication and historical

action. There is no danger of exhausting the material; one is re-writing
the entire history of Mediterranean thought. I have dealt with several
aspects of this re-writing already in my works; what I would like to do
here is draw attention to the ideas of displacement (*déplacement*) and
going beyond (*dépassement*)[1] in relation to conceptual structures, cat-
egorizations, delimitations, and eliminations inherited from both
Islamic and European-Western traditions. What is undeniable is that
the rationality for which the social sciences are the vehicle is less widely
spread in so-called Muslim societies than in Western ones, where it
has always both accompanied and guided industrial, urban, political,
legal, and institutional development. To identify these functional differences, to evaluate their structural effect on the historical evolution
of the two worlds, means freeing ourselves from false explanations
which pit an anti-scientific, anti-philosophic, anti-secular Islam against
a West seen as the promoter of these values.

Islam-as-fact, and societies of the Scripture-book

The concept of Islam-as-fact helps us out of the confusions which have
accumulated around the word 'Islam', especially since states, as well as
movements of rebellion, that have proclaimed themselves to be Islamic,
have striven by ruthless over-imitation to acquire legitimacy. This process began with the first great 'dissension' (*fitna*), and has recurred ever
since in the most diverse historical and social contexts. 'Islam-as-fact'
refers to the state appropriation of religion, already apparent with the
Umayyads, richly augmented both culturally and intellectually under
the 'Abbasids, taken up again by the Ottomans, and finally seen in the
modern states with their growing determination to promote populist
religion at the expense of the great theoretical and doctrinal confrontations (*munazarat*) of classical times. The administrators of the sacred
(*'ulama'*) were subordinated to state power, and religious confraternities
sprang up wherever the central power was weak; these are the two
main characteristics of Islam-as-fact from at least the thirteenth century onwards.

This is why I have long insisted on the need to differentiate the
Qur'an-as-fact from Islam-as-fact. The first stands for the historical
emergence of an new phenomenon, circumscribed by time and space,
which cannot however be limited to the body of texts dating from its

official establishment—this requires a certain strategy of analysis and epistemological precautions (outlined in Arkoun 1991); while the second does not derive completely from the first, as the traditional view would have it, indifferent as it is to historical criticism and anxious, above all, to educate. The study of the relationship between the two demands a kind of historical, sociological, and linguistic research virtually neglected until now. Which is why millions of believers can still state today, with all the vehemence of a faith that cares nothing for the workings of historical time, that the norms of the *corpus juris* derive in an orderly and complete fashion from the Word of God as given in the Qur'an, and thus merit the name of Divine Law (*shari'a*). This most important point has been the subject of well known investigations into the abundant *usul al-fiqh* literature, but the political urgency which it derives from present-day demands for the restoration of the *shari'a* necessitates new critical work on legal reason in Islam.

Modern Islamic discourse has accentuated the doctrinal rigidity of representations of Islam 'applicable to all times and in all places' and reduced them to the socially-controlled performance of identificatory rites. Unfortunately, contemporary Islamic and political studies have added their scientific weight to the corroboration of this static and ahistorical perspective. Thus in the popular expression 'Islam and the West' there is the unproblematized presentation of a static, dogmatic, essentialist, transcendentalized religious world, following the portrayal by believers who require that their 'difference' should be respected, and who thus make it impossible for themselves to measure the distance that separates them from a dynamic, modern, secularized West, open to all innovations because it comprises agents who are more free, or totally detached, from traditional beliefs—although these agents too are sheltered from any scientific criticism. Believers consolidate their position by contemplating the mocking opposition—never thoroughly analysed—between the high and living spirituality of the 'East' and the immoral materialism of the 'West'. Thus two mutually exclusive imaginary worlds are constructed out of the postulates of a hegemonic reason, proud of its technological, economic and political successes, to such an extent that it can abolish the ancient prerogatives and authority of religion, assigning it merely rudimentary and residual functions. This is the same debate that opposed Christian reason to Enlightenment reason in the eighteenth century and recurs today in explosive sociopolitical contexts, disguised as fundamentalism, integralism, and militant radicalism making use of a religious vocabulary and justification.

Not that this contributes towards a critical understanding of religion-as-fact; there is no advance beyond outward manifestations and the (often discrediting) evaluations made by all those who have adopted the religion of secularism. This formulation is not polemic; it refers to conflicts in the management of private space—abandoned to religion—and public space—the exclusive business of the secular state. In France, the Ministry of the Interior is in charge of religious affairs; if religion overflows into the public space it is a matter for the police. In Belgium, the responsibility belongs to the Ministry of Justice. Compromises of greater or lesser depth, depending on the country, have replaced the sharp conflicts of the eighteenth and nineteenth centuries; the protection of goods and people has been transferred to the state; social security and the welfare state—as in Sweden, where it has become the main foundation of legitimacy—have deprived religion of essential functions it had exercised for centuries: hope in the afterlife; the source and guarantee of moral values which uphold social cohesion, providing the basis for vital solidarities; the regulation of transactions, and the invocation of legitimacy. Because Third World states did not make these substitutions when traditional codes collapsed, Islamic movements were immediately successful in restoring by, and for, religion its functions of refuge, protection, landmark and stepping-stone. The modernity of a party state like that of Boumédiène or Nasser has produced a great number of losers, marginal figures who are in revolt or excluded from society; only promises of justice, brotherhood, protection, dignity, spiritual advancement, and moral purification can quieten them and mobilize them anew.

So does this mean that religion exists solely to comfort those human beings who are doomed by their fellow humans to misery, distress, and oppression—moral, intellectual, and material? Is this comfort merely a dangerous illusion, a vain hope, a belief in a hallucination, an outdated mythology that confines its victims to irremediable mental and existential backwardness?

This explanation appears directly, or by implication, in all the sociological and political literature dealing with Islam. Sometimes we are reminded that there is another Islam, that of the 'High Tradition', as Olivier Carré calls it, with its majestic intellectual and cultural achievements. Thus, almost mechanically, the negative judgements which have been made upon the ideological excesses of militant Islam are refuted; in their place appear the splendours of a learned, open, tolerant Islam, associated with a brilliant civilization in its moment of greatness. These splendours are not usually considered in a chronological context, because the historical continuity or possible resurrection of this expansive and creative moment is being invoked. We are not told that the moment occurred in the Middle Ages, and that it has now been surpassed by the progress of knowledge and the alterations in *mentalité* brought about by modernity. The diffusion and assimilation of modernity have been slowed down, hindered, and in some countries brought to a standstill by an obstinate policy of constructing national identity by a process of traditionalization—the return to a fragmented, stereotyped, ritualist Islamic tradition—strongly mythologized, of course, since the historical reconstruction of the tradition is more objective and critical, and more extensive, in the works of Orientalists than in the work of Muslim researchers.

Already, in the seventies, Laroui had pointed out the importance of this 'traditionalizing' process in society, especially in Morocco; and the 'Islamic Revolution' in Iran extended the phenomenon to all societies experiencing Islam-as-fact. The process is a historical avatar of the transformation of Islam into a state religion, which, as has already been pointed out, began on a large scale under the Umayyads. It would be interesting to compare the way the developing tradition was integrated into society, before its official formulation in the third/ninth century, with the actions of modern states in charge of very different societies from Indonesia to Morocco, from central Asia to South Africa—the ways they have treated an Islam already subjected to many centuries of transformation and change. This is where the idea of Islam-as-fact assumes its full operative value: the appeal to an abstract Islam, a purely ideological construction, stripped of the historical and theological fullness of its Tradition (see Arkoun 1993), has above all served to distort the borrowings it has been forced to make from an explicitly rejected modernity, the product of an imperialist West, by the nationalist discourse of the recovery of personal identity. Islam-as-fact is always there, incontrovertibly; the colonialist experience has changed it into a power to select from, and eventually completely reject, modernity. Even the

most positive historical contributions of modernity, its ability to integrate religion-as-fact into an extended strategy that produces and
controls meaning, have been distorted to the point where the
transcultural processes and the most firmly established values of Islam
have become destabilized and disintegrated.

Thus we must concentrate on the interactions between Islam-as-
fact and modernity, not so much in order once again to go over
confrontations, rivalries, and mutual exclusions, as to better understand how Christendom and Islam—since these two religions have
accompanied rival imperial processes with hegemonic intentions
throughout their history—and modernity—as an alternative model
for the historical formation of a society—have continuously fought
with each other since the sixteenth century, and, in a sense (see Arkoun
1982a), within the Islamic context already in the 4th/10th century. A
systematic, comparative analysis of the meaning and immediate consequences—and the more remote ones too—of the most influential
confrontations which have taken place in what I call the societies of
the Scripture-book, would surely advance our interpretation of the
issues of meaning and will-to-power in these societies.

I shall not repeat here what I have already written on this complex
and essential, yet still inadequately studied, notion (see Arkoun 1992b).
I intend to transfer my analysis from the theological and often polemic
area of what the Qur'an calls the People of the Book (ahl al-kitab) to
the wider, more inclusive, and specific area of historical and anthropological knowledge, and to impose a linguistic and anthropological
examination of Revelation as it is understood by the three so-called
'revealed' religions—with their different attitudes towards the concept
of the Scripture-book as material container of God's Word—subject
to all the random modifications of written transmission and of textual
interpretation. Catholic theology, in particular, opposes the notion of
a religion of the Book, because God's Word is incarnate in the Person
of Christ and is transmitted by it. The idea of societies of the Scripture-book takes no stance on the initial pillar and transmitter of God's
Word, but recalls us to the common historical datum, which cannot
be denied, that in order to develop their theories of Revelation, the
three communities have to pass through book with a small letter—the
material object and mediator—in order to reach the Scripture-Book
with a capital B—which theological speculation has surrounded with

an over-determined aura of holiness. Le Goff says of the Bible in the Middle Ages what could also be said of the Qur'an:

> To speak of medieval culture is to speak first of all of the reference Book, in religion and out of it, in fidelity and rebellion, conformity and nonconformity. Whatever their level of culture or learning, mediaeval men and women found the foundations of knowledge and truth in the Bible. (Le Goff 1990: 48)

If the Middle Ages end in Europe in 1800, they rise again (with devastating fidelity) in the Islamic context, just as Europe and the West are talking about post-modernity, super-modernity, questioning received views—all the most productive characteristics of the Enlightenment. The Book, *al-Kitab*, obsesses all thinkers, recurs in all conversations, dominates all arguments, nourishes all kinds of hope, justifies the worst excesses and the most astonishing sacrifices; it is inseparable from the dislocated individual who is striving to reconstruct himself, from a disintegrating society which longs for unification, from an accelerated history which cruelly disappoints the recurrent hopes of believers. Yet the Book is now submerged, not only by books which owe nothing to it and which tend towards its elimination, but by an increasing flood of images and information which is modifying the conditions of the production and reception of meaning—a much more radical modification in the case where a civilization of the book remains firmly based on Holy Scripture.

The concept of societies of the Scripture-book also allows the re-establishment of a functional continuity, with ideological effects, between religious and modern, secular ways of producing, expanding, and controlling meaning in society: in both cases there is conflict 'between the oral and the written'[2]—not between two stages of a linear progression, but two between linguistic and anthropological frameworks for the articulation and cultural realization of meaning. Thus religions of the Scripture-book have struggled against paganism and its accompanying cultures; secular modernity has opposed dialects, local customs, superstitions, magic, all 'popular' manifestations associated with orality—the totality of procedures suitable for the articulation of meaning in oral culture—and its procedures, which are opposed to nation construction. In the Third World, brutality and cultural destruction have accompanied rapid social change and strategies of

national unification which have been taken over from the colonial powers. These upheavals have entailed the most serious confusions between
religion and modernity; their shared ideological function has been implemented without any critical evaluation of the different origins,
functions, and aims of the two models of historical action. The benefits of nation-building in Europe, like the advances in civilization
brought about by the religions of the Scripture-book, have caused recent nationalist movements to forget the price paid throughout history
by peoples and cultures who were, but did not necessarily deserve to
be, marginalized or eliminated. This is why both religion-as-fact and
modernity require the critical re-examination of the meanings-at-stake
for them both, and of the will-to-power which transforms the quest
for meaning into a constant expansion of the systems of domination.

Meanings-at-stake and the will-to-power

'Meaning' is a difficult word: it is used throughout society, by all groups
in search of an identity, by all schools of thought competing to demar-
cate and impose the true meaning which will derive authentically from
the basic Source and lead to the ultimate Signified. This was the method
of classical theology and metaphysics; today all claims to meaning are
turned back upon ideology, which in turn stands for the arbitrary wish
to extend the 'values' of one group, or even of one leader, to ever vaster
social groupings. The expression 'the search for meaning' is itself sus-
pect, merely standing for a more or less disguised attempt to re-establish
theological and metaphysical systems as legitimating a will-to-power.

Hence I choose the more open expression 'meaning-at-stake'. The
stake is the amount wagered by each speaker in the great world-game
of Becoming, and like any game it is a series of chance events which
each player tries to master by incorporating into successive strategies.
In the case of meaning, the game endlessly repeats itself and becomes
ever more complicated in time and space. The players are called 'social
actors' by sociologists, and the game metaphor is thus enriched by that
of the theatre, play-acting—'stage-power' as Balandier calls it. For each
social actor Foucault's 'will to know' mingles with the aim of power.
Lévi-Strauss adds another metaphor to corroborate the others on the
production of meaning, that of *bricolage*, applied to the questions of *la
pensée sauvage* and then extended by sociologists such as Bourricaud to

ideological *bricolage*; this overcomes both political and religious reasoning, and frequently philosophical and religious reasoning too. In the long run instrumental reasoning, which cares only for immediate efficacity and is not concerned with the fragility of its results, confines critical reasoning to the examination of established facts, and discourages any anticipatory effort concerning the drift of meaning.

Thanks to linguists and literary critics, one may distinguish now between the immanent meaning of a discourse and the effects produced in its hearers. The study of the conditions of reception, especially in the case of religious statements which affect all sociocultural categories, is as necessary as (and frequently more enlightening than) the study of linguistic tools and procedures which articulate meaning. During reception, individual and collective imaginal entities are constructed which, in their turn, influence perception, judgement, and behaviour. Thus the effects of meanings, which are presented as true meaning, join the ideologies which mobilize in the service of the will-to-power. All revolutions are founded on this conjuncture, which is the immediate aim of all prophets, mahdis, imams, saints, liberating heroes, and leaders, whose ability to produce effects of meaning depends on both personal charisma and historical context.

One can see the relevance of this analysis for understanding the functioning of the great foundational texts in societies of the Scripture-book, including, of course, the texts of secular religions such as communism and socialism. Social agents transform these texts into pre-texts for the operation of sacredness, mythology, and ideology— disguised as appeals to truth, transcendental justice, brotherhood and so forth. The example of the Qur'an in the societies which use it is here the most striking, but one must remember that the history of every society is interwoven with similar occurrences.

It might be objected that this theory (of a meaning which is constantly back-influenced by the effects of meaning conveyed and activated by an indefinite series of social actors) cannot apply to foundational texts whose immanent meaning remains the same throughout history, in all sociocultural contexts, and resists all forms of projection and manipulation. Here we return to Plato's Ideas, to eternal reason and its product, Eternal Wisdom,[3] with their epistemological continuations in Enlightenment reasoning. The theologies of revelation in the three monotheist religions have made considerable use of Platonism and

Aristotelianism in order to construct the idea of a Source-Meaning from which all human legitimacies and truths flow. Theologies, like classical metaphysics, further state that this Source-Meaning has been once and for all enclosed in the foundation-texts, and that it can be correctly grasped, transmitted and applied—in ethical-legal norms and the ritual practices codified by the doctors of the Law. One cannot overcome this opposition solely by the force of argument; there is a psycho-linguistic separation, emphasized in the case of religious reasoning by *in-corporation*, which implants within the individual by ritual repetition the beliefs and non-beliefs which define each religion. Argument remains speculative until it produces political, legal, economical, social, or ritual results—one thinks of the ritual of the Republic, the conduct of trades unions, political parties, the bureaucracy, and so on—and these results in turn make possible the sociocultural expansion of a new 'attitude of reason'. All revolutions, including those introduced by the founders of 'revealed' religions, make use of this paradigm of change, yet are unable to establish irreversible situations which would make resurgence and restoration impossible—note, for example, the French Revolution, which intended to be radical; and the Arabic socialist revolution, which unintentionally produced the Islamic Revolution.

Thus one has all the more reason to talk of meanings-at-stake and the will-to-power in all types of society: all social actors—collectively and/or singly—obey effects of meaning, and produce them, in their attempts to over-imitate the transcendent, intangible, founding Source-Meaning. These reach their height when Islam—emphasising the tension between militant Muslims' will-to-power and the West's view of it as diabolical—is promoted to the status of a world-wide 'threat'. Thus after a slow and complicated journey we reach the original question: how can we create a positive use of the three terms— Islam, Europe, the West—which will bring hopes for the future emancipation of mankind? At present they are more marked than ever by the struggles for hegemony which are disguised, as they were in the Middle Ages, by meanings-at-stake of an apparently transcendental nature.

Once again, we need historical details. It is the historians who have diverted the word 'West' from a geographical label to a cultural and ideological one. Within Christendom, especially since the great schism of 1054, discussions of orthodoxy have led to the distinction between

Eastern Orthodox and Western Catholic. East and West were engaged with even greater ideological intensity by both theologians and historians when Islam, after its first century of conquests (632–732) and later under the Ottoman empire, began to reinforce the Crusades of the Christian (and later secular) West against the heterodox, obscurantist, idle dreamers of the East. The eighteenth century made use of the East (and of Islam) in its campaign against dogmatism, intolerance, and obscurantism (represented by the Church), and in the nineteenth-century romanticism added its touches of picturesqueness and poetic escapism, to the extent of inventing the belly-dance and then exporting it to its supposedly original homeland.[4]

The meaning of the West in world politics took on a new dimension when the United States imposed its presence on Europe even during the wars, when the whole Mediterranean area was inexorably—though doubtless not irremediably—demoted to the status of a satellite region, a process we shall not consider in detail here, save to say that the violent communist interregnum caused Western Europe to emphasise its Western-ness as against Eastern Europe, this time fallen away into a new—and this time purely ideological—divide. The old religious schism between Orthodoxy and Catholicism, with its underlying opposition of East and West, has risen again, especially on Yugoslav territory. One wonders how the West would have handled the conflict if the Bosnians had inflicted on Belgrade the martyrdom which the Serbs had inflicted on Sarajevo. In this tragic conflict is concentrated every meaning-at-stake and every power-strategy which, since the Middle Ages, and despite the shift from theological to secular politics, has continued to mobilize agents and legitimate 'righteous wars' in this ideologically continuous but geopolitically divided area of Islam, Europe, the West.

The most recent enlargement of the West as a space for the deployment of the will to rule—of politically united but economically competing powers—occurred when Japan was added to the Group of Seven as a result of its technological, economic, and monetary strength. The primacy—and not merely the priority—of power-strategies over meanings-at-stake becomes here so obvious that it shows through all international camouflage: humanitarian action is advertised as after-sales service by weapon-dealers; the defence of human rights fails to disguise the old slogan of 'our mission to civilize'; an appeal to democracy accompanies undeniable assistance rendered to governments which deny the most basic of human freedoms. An immense and painful semantic disorder is created, fostered, and increased by the conjugated efforts of states, chancelleries, bureaucracies disseminating information, banking systems, and even armies (in that they obey the politicians).

These are serious, and seriously biased, propositions; they will tend to strengthen militant Islam's radically negative and polemical image of the West and also discourage those who, in this West, seek to correct the excesses of equally negative and polemical anti-Islamic writing and thought. I repeat that my criticisms do not propose the arbitrary disqualification of an adversary to the point of denying his objective position in the history of civilization and the responsibilities which have been his since the eighteenth century, responsibilities in the genesis of human progress, and responsibilities too for ecological, political, social, cultural, and semantic disorders. Likewise my criticisms of Islamic reasoning show that I have taken my stand in that area of historical and philosophical confrontation which lies between meanings-at-stake and will-to-power, two linked and recurrent constants in human affairs.

If the European Union had not become a political and economic reality—soon to be likewise a monetary one—there would be no need to draw a distinction between this West and Europe. Fortunately, the way Europe is built has forced Europeans to concern themselves with questions of identity, although discussions are inspired more by nationalist ideologies—or resistances—than by the need to open a new space for thought and historical action; these must be able to cope with the difficulties inherited from intra-European wars, from colonial expansion, from membership in a West whose ideological divagations need the restraint and control which only the European Union can guarantee.

Seen politically and historically in its world-wide context, and from the viewpoint of Islam, this role of Europe must entail restoration of the Mediterranean area to the universe of meanings and values which first shaped European identity. I say 'area' in order to open up fully all possibilities of redistribution in the matter of ownership, allegiance, values, and historical development. In this time of ideological violence, real or imagined fears, and the cultivation of ignorance, it seems unrealistic to talk of the political, economical, and especially cultural and historical reconstitution of the Mediterranean. We must also mention the priority which the European Union gives to the reintegration of Eastern Europe, with its natural connections with the liberal Christian Western world. This orientation makes clearer the distrust which is felt towards the South-East Mediterranean; an exception is made for Greece on account of the 'Greek miracle'—about which all European schoolchildren learn—but the history of the Ottoman empire is still relegated to Oriental Studies departments and general works on 'Islam'.

Yet nearly ten million Muslims live on European soil; the peoples of Arabia, Turkey, and Iran are re-writing their history and re-interpreting their religious thought by using the inescapable methods and epistemology of critical reason; Europe, always ahead of the rest of the world, is leaving behind the outdated intellectual frameworks of her political thought and her humanism. The theologies of the three religions cannot resist much longer the repeated contradictions of history and the increasingly radical challenges of science. All these factors suggest that we may envisage, for 2010 at the latest, an overcoming of political disagreements, of ideological schism, mutual exclusion, imaginary truths, and master-servant relationships, which have characterized the Mediterranean ever since the first clashes between, on the one hand, the rising religious symbolism of monotheism, and, on the other, the analytical strength of the Greek *logos*, the Roman imperial order, and the flexibility of the pagan pantheon.

Unfortunately, the political classes do not cultivate historical memory as critical historians endeavour to reconstruct it; they prefer to make selections from 'places of memory'[5] imposed by official historiography—images with the power to mobilize, such as noble moments and conquering heroes; these are meant to galvanize national energies and to exaggerate the qualities of each people's genius; enemies are useful for purposes of apologetics. European leaders—and, even more so, those of states/nations/parties in the South Mediterranean—still think in terms of the old procedures for mobilizing sacred national egotism, and intellectuals are abdicating their competence-as-knowledge, while politicians and experts take over all competence-as-decision. Yet it is now that we need frequent critical interventions, not only to limit ideological—even more seriously, demagogic and electoral—divagations in debate, but also to spread as widely as possible the results of new research. A great number of institutions, conferences, and publications rich in material on the Mediterranean question remain unknown even to what we call the educated public. How different was the uproar caused by the struggles for national liberation or construction in 1959–60 (although it is true that Maoism and Soviet communism were then accepted as efficacious and unavoidable roads to definitive liberation).

I pass over the question of the intellectual's status in those Arabic, Turkish, and Iranian societies which are directly concerned with the expansion of a politico-cultural vision to respond to the expectations and explicit demands made by some considerable sectors of the European Union. An unfortunate prejudice survives from the period of independence, when, in the euphoria of ill-used victories, many valuable intellectuals joined what quickly became a bureaucratic *nomenklatura*. Algerian intellectuals are paying a high price for their solidarity with a party-state which aspires to popular democracy; some accepted this as a deliberate calculation, and others through political naïvity and lack of information. This tragic experience may help to create throughout the South-East Mediterranean that critical engagement which is still needed for a radical re-reading of these people's historical destiny; it must overcome all errors, dogmatisms, artificial values, destructive confrontations, and all the exaggerated exclusions which have stifled and delayed until now the appearance of an indestructible hope.

Notes

1   For an elaboration of these notions, see Arkoun 1995.

2   As in the title to the anthropologist Jack Goody's *The Interface Between the Oral and the Written*, Cambridge: Cambridge University Press (1987).

3   A notion to be found throughout medieval thought, with its theory of Agent Intellect and acquired intellect, which guarantees the continuance and ontological foundation of Truth. See Arkoun 1982a.

4   Oleg Graber showed how art criticism is inseparable from the history of 'Islamic' art as seen by nineteenth-century Orientalists in his lecture *'Penser l'art islamique'* at the Institut du Monde Arabe in Paris in 1995.

5   *Lieux de mémoire* is the title of an important collected volume edited by Pierre Nora, 7 vols, Paris: Gallimard (1984–92).

9

Divine Attributes in the Qur'an
Some Poetic Aspects

NASR HAMID ABU ZAID

This essay is primarily intended to present some aspects of Qur'anic poetic language, especially concerning the expression of God's Names and Attributes. Some modifications have been necessary, however, to indicate the later impact of such linguistic exposition on Islamic thought. Since it has not only been the literary nature of the Qur'anic text which is questioned in recent Islamic discourse, but its very textuality as such, the question has to be dealt with.

Oral before written

The word *Qur'an* means, as its linguistic root *qara'* suggests, either 'to recite' or 'to collect'. Here I favour the first meaning, for reasons which should be explained. The first reason depends on the fact that the Qur'an was originally transmitted by God to the Prophet Muhammad in oral form. It is explained everywhere in Islamic literature that the Holy Spirit recited it to the Prophet in the process of revelation, and the Prophet used to recite it afterwards to his companions. It was then committed to some sort of written form. The second reason is the fact that, in spite of being committed to writing, the Qur'an was never dealt with as a written text in the daily life of the early Muslim community. It had, in fact, to wait until the print age to be considered as such. Even now, although the Qur'an has become a printed text, what is important for a Muslim is committing it to heart, and the ability to recite it according to the classical principles of recitation, *tajwid*. Lastly, the aesthetic characteristics of the Qur'anic language exert a strong influence on Muslim daily life. One of its major aesthetic effects is that which is generated by its poetic language when recited privately or collectively.

That is why the recitation of the Qur'an is a very important practice in the community as well as in the life of the individual. On almost every occasion, a part of the Qur'an is recited: at marriages, funerals, and the inauguration of festivals or celebrations, not to mention in rituals, regular prayers and other religious occasions (see Graham 1993, especially pt 3).

But this supremacy of the oral character of the Qur'an should not lead us to neglect the impact of its written form. If its recitation has developed specific musical features, its written form has developed two kinds of visual art, that is, calligraphy and book decoration. The art of calligraphy related to the Qur'an consists in transforming the written text into visual tableaux. Letters and words are only elements in forming the whole piece of art, they are no longer meant solely to be read. In calligraphy, the readability of the written text of the Qur'an is of secondary importance. According to the theory which suggests that the Qur'an represents the eternal exact utterance of God—*kalimu allahi l-azali'l-qadim*—the Qur'an is believed to have had a previous existence in Heaven where it was, and still is, recorded on the Well-Preserved Holy Tablet. It is written there in magnificent Arabic letters, each of which is as great as a mountain, specifically Mount Qaf, which is supposed to surround and encompass the whole planet Earth (see Zarkashi 1972: vol. I, p. 229). It is appropriate to suggest that the art of calligraphy related to the Qur'an has some sort of connection to this very interesting imaginative perception of the text. Its aim, one may suppose, is to capture the metaphysical image of the text in order to represent it in the form of visual art .

Book decoration, on the other hand, is an art developed by Muslims through their efforts to invent 'markers' or 'indicators' in order to help make the written text easy to recite consistently. First of all, diacritical points had to be added to differentiate similar written forms of Arabic letters. Secondly, signs had to be inserted to indicate 'short vowels' within and at the end of the word. Thirdly, the verses (*ayat*) of each chapter had to be numbered, and the beginning and the end of each sura indicated. Various coloured artistic motifs were employed which were, and still are, highly esteemed. The making of the binding and the cover of the manuscript was considered a sacred craft to be performed only by those who were well trained and had extensive experience.

Why is it felt necessary to raise the question of the textuality of the Qur'an, even though the issue seems so obvious and self-evident? The issue is taken for granted in Western Qur'anic scholarship (see Wild 1996).[1] It has also been recognized implicitly in classical Qur'anic studies, and explicitly in modern Islamic thought. But, recently, some Muslim scholars seem to have found using the word 'text' to refer to the Qur'an unacceptable. In response to my book about the Qur'an, *The Conception of the Text* (Abu Zaid 1990), a professor at the Azhar university, the leading Islamic institution in the Sunni world, protested against the use of the word 'text' in reference to the Qur'an. His argument was that: 'In all the history of Islam, no-one has used in reference to the Qur'an words other than those God himself used in the Qur'an. None of the *'ulama'* has ever dealt with the Qur'an as a text, may God forgive this, because it is an orientalist European (not Islamic or Arabic) way of dealing with the Qur'an' (Abu Musa nd.: 19). That is why the textuality of the Qur'an is to be defended. Before explaining some of the most general features of its textuality, the reasons behind such reluctance need to be analysed. Two factors at least are to be introduced. The first is the fact that the Arabic word for 'text' in modern usage, *nass*, has a different meaning in classical usage. Because the modern meaning has no connection with the old one, confusion is to be expected. The second factor is the resurrection of an old debate concerning the nature of the Qur'an.

Semantic confusion

In classical Arabic the verb *nassa* means 'to raise', as in the example *'nassata'l-naqatu jidha* ('The she-camel raised her neck'). From this original meaning developed the connotations of physical obviousness and clarity, as in the example *'minassat al-'arus'* ('the bridal throne')—the connotations of the word *'minassa'* in modern Arabic are nearly the same. Another development took place in classical Arabic when the connotations of the word moved from the semantic field of physical things to the field of ideas. Besides referring to the movement of raising, or to a high position or a 'raised platform', the meaning of the verb *nassa* extended to cover 'to fix, lay down, appoint, stipulate, provide, specify, determine, and define'. For example, in *'ilm al-hadith* (the science of the Prophet's traditions) the expression *'nassa al-hadith'* means that the narrator provided all the names of those who were in the chain of transmission, *isnad*, of what he reported.[2]

In the field of the Qur'anic Sciences, *'ulum al-Qur'an*, and jurisprudence, *usul al-fiqh*, the word *na* became a semantic term referring to any very clear and obvious statement of the Qur'an which needs no explanation. Deriving from the Qur'anic text's declaration that it includes both clear verses—*ayatun muhkamatun*—which are the backbone of the Book and ambiguous verses—*ayatun mutashabihatun*—which should be interpreted in accordance with the clear ones (Qur'an III:7), clarity and ambiguity were, in their turn, subdivided. So four semantic levels came to be considered. The first and the most clear is *al-nass*; the second is called *al-zahir* (the 'apparent'), because there are two possibilities for its meaning of which the 'apparent' is more appropriate. The third level is *al-mu'awwal* (the 'metaphorical'), for which the hidden meaning is the more appropriate than the apparent. The fourth and the last level is *al-mujmal* (the 'ambiguous') (see Suyuti 1952: vol. 2, pp. 31–2).

As the word *'nass'* now has the same meaning as the English word 'text', confusion is created unless a definition is given. If, for example, the principle is agreed that there should be no intellectual speculation, *ijtihad*, where there is a *nass*, it should be understood that the word *nass* here refers to the classical semantic term only. So there is a semantic manipulation of religious terminology when the word is used in modern Islamic discourse to imply that it means the whole text of the Qur'an (see Abu Zaid 1995b: 117–26). The creation of such a confusion, such semantic manipulation, is essential for some groups in order that they may attain their political objectives, groups who uphold the Islamic prohibition because it closes off the whole text of the Qur'an for any but their own interpretation, which in itself is nothing but the classical orthodox literal one. This point will become clearer in the analysis of the second factor.

The Word of God

This emphasis on the infallibility of the holy text in modern Islamic thought is nothing but the logical conclusion of the notion that the text is the exact verbal utterance of the Divine Absolute Reality. But while this notion was an extremist doctrine in Christianity, 'where theology worked on the basis of four Gospels' (van Ess 1996: 192), it has been an essential doctrine in Islamic theology since the third/ninth century. The intellectual battle between Muslim theologians concerning the nature of the Qur'an during the second/eighth century was politically resolved in favour of 'orthodoxy' against 'heterodoxy'. That issue has at least four aspects: two theories concerning the invention of language, the relationship between language and reality; and two concepts concerning the relationship between the signifier and the signified. Accordingly, there are two theories about the Qur'an: *makhluq muhdath*, i.e. *muhdath* as message, and *makhluq* as divine action, or *qadim azali* as one of God's attributes.

The Mu'tazilite theory of the relation between man, language, and holy text was the most rationalistic one; it concentrated on man as the addressee of the text and the one to whom its teachings were directed. Language is a human invention, in that it reflects social convention regarding the relationship between the sound and the meaning. On the other hand, language does not refer directly to reality; instead, reality is conceived, conceptualized, and then symbolized through a system of sounds. This is verified by the fact that there are words in every language without any referent; words like 'phoenix' or "*anqa*", in English and Arabic respectively, do not refer to any existent reality. The Mu'tazilites therefore drew from the Qur'anic text on the assumption that it was a created action and not the eternal verbal utterance of God. In other words, the relation between the signifier and the signified exists only by human convention; there is nothing divine in this relationship. They endeavoured to build a bridge between the divine word and human reason. This is why they maintained that the divine word was a fact which adjusted itself to human language in order to ensure well-being for mankind. They insisted that language was the product of man and that the divine word respected the rules and forms of human language.

The anti-Mu'tazilite trend of thought held another notion about language in general, and about God's speech in particular. Language, according to this notion, is not a human invention; it is a divine gift to man. Therefore, if the referent does not exist in the real, 'seen' world, it must have existence in the unseen reality. Qur'anic verses were quoted which, taken literally, support these assumptions about the divinity of language (e.g. II:31)—the Mu'tazilites gave a metaphorical interpretation for these verses (see Abu Zaid 1996b: 70–82). The relation between the signifier and the signified is, therefore, according to this position, made by God himself; it is a divine relation. It was thus concluded that God's speech was not a created action but rather one of His eternal attributes.

The Qur'an is God's speech; on this there has been no disagreement among Muslims throughout the centuries. However, the discussion which centred upon the question whether the Qur'an is eternal, or temporal and created, led to fierce dispute and even to the persecution of adherents of one or the other of the two positions. The time of that great persecution, called the Mihna, or inquisition, lasted from 218/833 till 243/ 848. The hero of that period was Ahmad b. Hanbal (164/780–241/855) who firmly objected to the temporality of the Qur'an.

It is worth noting that the choice between the two answers, eternity or createdness of the Qur'an, had great implications for the believer thinking about God and the world. The belief that the Qur'an is eternal implies, for instance, that God preordained any event described in it, and leads to the belief in God's absolute preordination; whoever denies predestination must believe the Qur'an to be created. To mention another example, someone who advocates the doctrine of God's absolute unity and unicity (a central Islamic belief) and wishes to take this in the strictest sense, is forced to deny an uncreated Qur'an existing together with God in all eternity. With respect to the point being made in this essay, the notion of an eternal Qur'an leads automatically to strict adherence to the literal meaning of the text (Peters 1976: 3).

General textual features

If the textuality of the Qur'an is to be asserted, it should be asserted by the Qur'an itself, as any text explicitly or implicitly exposes its own nature. God chose the Prophet Muhammad to be His Messenger, *rasul Allah*, to convey His Message, which is Islam. This message is essentially expressed in the Qur'an, which was not sent down simply as a book, but was revealed orally in portions to the Prophet. This process of revealing (*wahy*) is nothing but an act of communication which naturally includes a speaker, which is God in this case, a recipient, which is the Prophet Muhammad, a code of communication, which is Arabic, and a channel which is the Holy Spirit. It is clearly indicated in the

Qur'an that there are only three possible types of verbal communication from God to man: by *wahy*, or from behind a veil *(min wara'i hijabin)*,
or by sending a messenger *(rasul)* to reveal with His permission what
He will (XLII:50–1). As the word *'wahy'* is semantically equivalent to
God's speech—*kalam Allah*—in the Qur'an, and as the Qur'an is a
message, it should not offend Muslims to deal with it as a text.

The fact that the structure of the Qur'an, that is to say the arrange-
ment of its suras and verses *(tartib al-suwar wa-'l-ayat fi'l-mushaf)*, is not
the same as its chronological order of revelation *(tartib al-nuzul)* might
be taken as a second support for the Qur'an's textuality. The question
is not who arranged it, but rather why, and according to which norms
or values? The question has nothing to do with the authenticity of the
Qur'an as the wholly divine revelation from God; it has to do with
exploring the wisdom of God *(al-hikma al-ilahiyya)*, which stands behind the structure of the Qur'an. If the serial nature *(tanjim)* of its
revelation reflects the historicity of the message of Islam, its structure
should reflect a rather different aspect, which, I suggest, is its textuality.
Solid evidence for my suggestion is to be found in one of the sciences
of the Qur'an *('ulum al-Qur'an)* which deals with the correlation between verses and suras *('ilm al-munasaba bayn al-ayat wa-'l-suwar)* and
provides the exegete or the reader with an active interaction with the
text, since in these correlations there inhere possibilities that may be
discovered in the process of reading. The uncovering of the correlations between the verses and the suras does not entail the fixing of
closed or permanent relations within the text, but is rather an expression of the recipient's response to the text which could well vary from
one reader to another.

Another feature of its textuality is the Qur'anic declaration that it
includes clear verses *(ayatun muhkamatun)*, which are the backbone of
the Book, and ambiguous verses *(ayatun mutashabihatun)*, which should
be interpreted in accordance with the clear ones (III:7). There is no
consensus among Muslims scholars on the verses that comprise each
type, but there is agreement that the Text is a measure unto itself and,
hence, that the meaning of a verse should be determined in the light of
intra-Qur'anic evidence. Once again the interactive reader/text relationship is activated. The reader should thus not only identify the
'ambiguous' verses, but also decide the 'clear' verses to be the 'key' that
explains and clarifies them. The Mu'tazilites, for example, used the

concept of 'metaphor' (*majaz*), as used in human verbal communication, to interpret the ambiguous verses of the Qur'an. Because what was considered 'clear' by the Mutazilites was considered by their opponents to be 'ambiguous' and vice versa, *ta'wil* was considered to be the other, inseparable side of *tanzil*.

Just as clarity/ambiguity is a fundamental characteristic of textuality, so also is explanation and/or interpretation. In early Muslim history, as early as the era of the third caliph 'Ali b. Abi Talib, there existed an awareness of the inseparable relation of *ta'wil* and *tanzil*. When Mu'awiya's supporters lifted copies of the Qur'an (*masaluf*) in the battle of Siffin, asking for the Qur'an to be the arbitrator in order to save Muslim blood, 'Ali is reported to have said that the Qur'an does not speak by itself but through man. It is also reported that he added: 'During the Prophet's time we fought them [the Banu Umayy] about its revelation, and now we fight them about its interpretation (*harabnahum 'ala tanzilihi wa-'l-yawm nuharibu-hum 'ala ta'wilihi*)' (Tabari, 1961: vol. 5, pp. 48–9).

Historical context

Any text is a historical phenomenon, and has a specific context. This principle is applicable to the Qur'an insofar as it is a text, and also to its interpretation as a historical phenomenon. Accordingly, the context in which the Qur'an has been studied within various schools of interpretation should be investigated. So far, the explicit point has been made that the historicity of the Qur'an as a text does not, and should not, mean that it is a human text. As the Qur'an is the revelation and/or the manifestation of God's words in a specific time and place, it should follow that what was revealed in Arabic in the seventh century AD to Muhammad is a historical text. This historical text is the subject of understanding and interpretation, whereas God's words exist in a sphere beyond any human knowledge. Therefore, a socio-historical analysis is needed for its understanding, and a modern linguistic methodology should be applied in interpretation. Up to now, only the philological approach has been acceptable, and the socio-historical analysis has been absolutely rejected, not only in the domain of textual interpretation, but also in the domain of scholarship on Islamic thought. The notion that religious texts, though divine and revealed by God,

are historically determined and culturally constructed is not only rejected but also condemned as 'atheism'. This is due to the fact that the
notion of the Qur'an as the 'eternal', exact utterance of God, which is
part of a specific classical theological school of thought, has become
the accepted dogma in Sunni Islam. Scholars only know that there
was another school of theology that claimed that the Qur'an was 'created' and that it was impossible for it to be eternal; but very few Muslim
scholars accept the notion of non-eternity. As so often in the history
of Islam, these theological positions were directly associated with socio-
political positions. Nevertheless, in modern Islamic discourse these
positions are examined, analysed, and evaluated in terms of 'right and
wrong', 'true and false'.

To present this issue in a greatly simplified way: If the Qur'an is
not eternal, it is then created in a certain context, and the message it
contains has to be understood in that context. This view leaves room
for the reinterpretation of religious law, because God's word has to be
understood according to the spirit, not according to the letter. The
final consequence is that public authorities and/or society are entitled
to the prime role in the interpretation and application of the law. If, on
the other hand, God's word is eternal, uncreated, and immutable, the
idea of reinterpretation within new situations becomes anathema; there
is no difference between the letter and the spirit of the divine law, and
only theologians are entitled to the prime role in its maintenance and
guardianship. In this sense, an Islamic authority akin to the Christian
Church is needed, and this is virtually what has happened in the socio-
political and cultural history of Islam since the ninth century AD, when
the notion of the 'eternity' of the Qur'an, with all its implications, was
declared by the political authorities as the 'true faith'.

Just to illustrate the importance and complexity of this problematic of the divine text in modern Islamic thought, I quote the famous
Egyptian intellectual reformist of the nineteenth century Muhammed
'Abduh. In his treatise *Risalat al-tawhid*, the first modern treatise on
Islamic theology, 'Abduh decided to select from classical theological
discourse what he considered 'best' and 'most useful' for modern Muslims. He therefore combined together dogmas from different
theological schools and presented them as a synthesis. In the first edition of the book, 'Abduh adopted the notion of the Qur'an as 'created',
but retreated in the second edition to the opposite notion ('Abduh

1977: 13, 52). Was this from fear of provoking the influential majority of the scholars of al-Azhar? Or was it 'Abduh's conviction that changed? Nothing can be certain about this.

Islam is a 'message' revealed from God to man through the Prophet Mohammed, who is the Messenger of God, and who is himself human. The Qur'an is very clear about this. A message represents a communicative link between a sender and a receiver through a code or a linguistic system. Because the sender in the case of the Qur'an cannot be the object of scientific study, it is natural that the scientific introduction to the analysis of the Qur'anic text should be through its contextual reality and culture. Reality is the socio-political condition which embraced the actions of those who were addressed by the text, and which embraced the first receiver of the text, who was the Prophet and Messenger of God. Culture, on the other hand, is the world of concepts which are embodied in the language, the same language in which the Qur'an is also embodied. In this sense, to begin with the contextual cultural reality in analysing the Qur'anic text is, in fact, to start with empirical facts. Through the analysis of such facts a scientific understanding of the Qur'an may be accomplished. It should be very obvious, clearly understandable and beyond dispute that, in this sense, the Qur'an is a cultural product. However, the matter is more complicated because being a cultural product is only one side of the text, the side of its emergence as a text. The other side of it is that the Qur'an has become a producer of a new culture. In other words, the Qur'an first emerged as a text from within a specific socio-cultural reality embodied in a particular linguistic system, Arabic; subsequently a new culture gradually emerged out of the Qur'an. The fact that the Qur'anic text was understood and taken to heart has had irreversible consequences for its culture.

Textual peculiarities: meaning and significance

Speaking about the Qur'an as a message entails the fact that, although embodied in the Arabic linguistic system, the Qur'anic text has its own peculiarities. As a unique text, it employed special linguistic encoding dynamics in order to convey its specific message. These peculiarities were acknowledged by the Arabs and were admired even by some of those who fought against its message. From these peculiarities, and the challenge imposed on the Arabs by the Qur'an itself to try to produce a text like the shortest chapter in the Qur'an, emerged the notion of the absolute 'inimitability' (i'jaz) of the Qur'an.

It will always be necessary, however, to analyse and interpret the Qur'an and the authentic Traditions of the Prophet within the contextual background in which they were originated. In other words, the message of Islam could not have had any effect if the people who first received it could not have understood it; they must have understood it within their socio-cultural context, and by their understanding and application of it, their society changed. But the understanding of the first Muslim generation and the generations which followed should not, by any means, be considered final or absolute. The specific linguistic encoding dynamics of the Qur'anic text always allow an endless process of decoding. In this process the contextual socio-cultural meaning should not be ignored or simplified, because this 'meaning' is vital for indicating the direction of the 'new' message of the text. Having this direction facilitates moving from the 'meaning' to its 'significance' in the present socio-cultural context. It also enables the interpreter correctly and efficiently to extract the 'historical' and 'temporal', which carry no significance in the present context. As interpretation is the other inseparable side of the text, the Qur'an, being decoded in the light of its historical, cultural, and linguistic context, has to be recoded into the code of the cultural and linguistic context of the interpreter. In other words, the deep structure of the Qur'an must be reconstructed from the surface structure. Subsequently, the deep structure must be rewritten as another surface structure, which is that of today.

This entails an interpretive diversity, because the endless process of interpretation and re-interpretation cannot but alter with time. This is necessary, because otherwise the message would degenerate and the Qur'an would always be, as it is now, subject to political and pragmatic manipulation. Since the message of Islam is believed to be valid for all humankind, regardless of time and space, diversity of interpretation is inevitable. But being aware of the difference between the original contextual 'meaning', which is almost fixed because of its historicity, and the 'significance', which is changeable—in addition to the awareness of the necessity that the significance is to be firmly related and rationally connected to the meaning—will produce a more valid interpretation. It is only valid, however, as long as it does not violate the above-mentioned methodological rules in order to jump to some 'desired' ideological conclusions. If the text is historical though originally divine, its interpretation is absolutely human.

Textual inimitability

From the very beginning of its revelation, the Qur'an had captured the Arab imagination by its unique linguistic features. The Arabs tried their best to explain its effect on them in terms of the types of text they already knew; these explanations were mentioned but refuted in the Qur'an itself. When the Arabs explained the nature of the Qur'an as 'poetry' and accused the prophet of composing it, the answer given to such an explanation and accusation was: 'We have not taught him poetry; it is not seemly for him (XXXVI:69).'³ When they said that Muhammad was nothing but a soothsayer, the Qur'an replied: 'By thy Lord's blessing thou art not a soothsayer neither possessed (LII:29).' In the context of that debate the nonbelievers claimed that the Qur'an was nothing but some stories forged by Muhammad, and falsely claimed by him to have been revealed to him by God. Since for them it was nothing but a forged text, the nonbelieving Arabs thought it was easy for them to fabricate a text like the Qur'an. Facing such a challenge, the Qur'an made its own counter-challenge, asking them to bring forth 'ten forged chapters like it (II:13)'. When the nonbelievers failed to respond to this strong challenge, the Qur'an, pretending to make it easier for them, decreased the challenge from ten chapters to only one (X:38). The last step was to indicate the absolute failure of the Arabs to challenge the authenticity of the Qur'an:

> And if you are in doubt concerning that We have sent down on Our servant (Muammad) then bring a chapter like it, and call your witnesses, apart from God, if you are truthful. And if you do not—and you will not—then fear the Fire, whose fuel is men and idols, prepared for unbelievers (II:23–4).

The fact that the Arabs failed to respond to this challenge affirmed the Muslim belief about the nature of the Qur'an, including its supremacy as a text. It is entirely incomparable with any human text—whether in the past, present, or future. Many stories are preserved in Islamic literature which tell even of the unbelievers being fascinated by the overwhelming poetic effect of the Qur'anic language, an effect incomparable to that of poetry itself.

Relevant to these stories is the report mentioned about one of the scribes of the revelation, who was so transported by what was being dictated to him by the Prophet that he reached the point of spiritual unity with the text. Being able to anticipate the final wording of the verse under dictation, he thought he had attained the state of prophethood. The story is as follows: the Prophet Mohammed was dictating verses 12–14 of sura XXIII to one of his scribes, verses which explain the process of man's creation in sequential sentences, the first of which leads to the second, the second to the third, and so on. The sentences are arranged in this order:

1   We created man of an extraction of clay,
2   then We set him, a drop, in a receptacle secure,
3   then We created of the drop a clot,
4   then We created of the clot a tissue,
5   then We created of the tissue bones,
6   then We garmented the bones in flesh;
7   thereafter We produced him as another creature.

When the Prophet finished the last sentence, the man was so deeply impressed that he exclaimed: 'So blessed be God, the fairest of creators', a sentence which fits the Arabic rhyming pattern of the verse and closes it. The Prophet was highly surprised, the story tells, because what the man said was exactly the last sentence revealed to him.

Although the hero of the story thought he could produce something like the Qur'an, and accordingly claimed that the Qur'an had been invented by Muhammad (see Tabari 1958: vol.1, p. 45, and vol. 11, pp. 533–5),[4] there is a deeper significance to be found beyond the surface of the story. It indicates the aesthetic dimensions which always affect those who encounter the Qur'an. The language of the text was able to capture a man's imagination, and inspire him to anticipate what comes after, because of its poetic structure.

The rhyming pattern of the verses according to the last word in every sentence is in the following order:

1	clay (*ṭīnin*)	A
2	secure (*makin*)	A
3	clot (*'alaqatan*)	B
4	issue (*muḍghatan*)	B
5	bones (*'iẓamānan*)	C
6	flesh (*laḥman*)	C
7	another creature (*ākhar*)	D

Then the last sentence pronounced by the scribe comes to close the rhyming pattern:

8	creators (*khāliqīn*)	A

In addition to this rhyming pattern, there is an internal rhyme produced by the verb form used, i.e. the first person plural, which ends with the suffix *nā* in Arabic, and appears as 'we' in English translation. There is, lastly, the sentence pattern repeated seven times, creating a specific second internal rhyming pattern whose components are subject, verb, first object, and second object. These seven sentences are connected to each other by the particle 'then'—in Arabic *thumma* and *fa*—a syntactical pattern which produces a visual effect corresponding to the making of man. This linguistic exposition and the various gradual stages of the creation of man can be compared with the process of creating a piece of art.

In both cases a beautiful production is made out of clay, so to speak, gradually, step by step. But in the case of God, the creation is no artificial thing; it is, in fact, the living human being. It is, therefore, the duty of this creature, man, to glorify his Creator, 'the fairest of creators'. That was exactly the simultaneous reaction produced in the man in this story, and it is the way the Qur'an declares it should be.

The notion of the supremacy (*i'jaz*) of the Qur'an, or rather of its incomparability, was developed later and explained in terms of the text's rhetorical characteristics. Since the challenge made by the Qur'an against its enemies was met with no substantial response, it was proven that, in spite of their eloquence, even the Arabs failed to bring forth the like of the smallest chapter of the Qur'an. They produced poetry and prose but they could not produce anything like the Qur'an. Even the so-called false prophets who emerged after Muammad's death produced nothing but simple and naive imitation of either soothsaying or the rhyming patterns of the Qur'an.

Many theories were introduced in Islamic theology to explain those features which constitute the incomparability of the text, but all of them agreed on one essential point: it is the very nature of the speaker himself, God, which makes it impossible to speak of any kind of similarity or comparability between the Qur'an and any other text. But the fact remains that this notion situtates the Qur'an within the overall cultural and literary context of pre-Islamic Arabia. For the Qur'an to relate to its audience and influence them, it had to be similar to the literary conventions to which the Arabs were used, while, for it to claim i'jaz, it had to be different. Even the famous literary critic 'Abd al-Qahir al-Jurjani, who introduced the theory of *nazm* (syntax) in his *Dala'il al-i'jaz* (Proofs of Incomparability), affirmed this basic point, although his theory is based on the assumption that human texts, namely poetry, should be thoroughly investigated in order to uncover the laws of *nazm* and to uncover, accordingly, the features of the Qur'an's supremacy (see Jurjani 1989: 8–9).[5]

This notion of the nature of the speaker as the essential reason behind the supremacy of the text paved the way to the establishing of another notion, this time concerning the nature of language itself. According to this notion, language is not a human invention but a gift given from God. It was not difficult to support such a notion by quoting the Qur'an itself, where it is mentioned that God taught Adam *all the names* (II:31). Explaining the teaching of names as teaching language made language a divine code of communication given to man as a blessing from God. Any comparison between God's speech and man's speech definitely implies involvement in heresy. It has recently been very dangerous to open a new discussion concerning this understanding of the 'incomparability' issue, even in the way al-Jurjani did.

Poetic aspects of the text

The linguistic exposition of the Divine Attributes in the Qur'an can be approached through two passages of the text, each of which deals with one aspect of the divine reality, namely God's nature and His attributes. As for the first aspect, the Qur'an tells the Muslims that

God is the light of the heavens and the earth; the likeness of His light is as a niche wherein is a lamp, the lamp in a glass, the glass as it were a glittering star, kindled from a Blessed Tree, an olive that is neither of the East nor of the West whose oil wel l nigh would shine, even if no fire touched it; light upon light; God guides to His light whom He will. And God strikes similitudes for men, and God has knowledge of everything (XXIV:35).

We are here in the 'similitude' mode of expression, where the nature of God is compared to the nature of light. But this light of God is not the ordinary light we know and enjoy in our daily life, it is an extraordinary kind of light which can only be perceived through another 'similitude'. The similitude is expressed in an extraordinary linguistic way in order to convey the extraordinary nature of God's light. It is compared directly to a niche (*mishkat*), but, since that niche contains a lamp (*misbah*), which is contained in a glass (*zujaja*), in itself extremely radiant [like a glittering star, *ka'annaha kawkabun durriyyun*], it is understood that God's light is compared only indirectly to the light which comes out of such a lamp.

Instead of directly explaining the purity of the oil used in lightning that lamp, the Qur'an uses an indirect and extraordinary mode of expression, which relates the lightening of the lamp to the olive-tree not to the oil of the tree: *yuqadu min shajaratin mubarakatin*. It is a way to specify the tree which is not an ordinary olive-tree either; it is a Blessed Tree which exists nowhere in the universe known to us, neither in the East nor in the West: *la sharqiyyatin wa-la gharbiyyatin*. Such a Tree would produce an extraordinary kind of oil which shines by itself: *yakadu zaituha yudi'u wa-law lam tamsashu nar, nurun 'ala nur*. Although this indirect mode of expression is made in order to specify the Tree, the phrase ends with 'light'—which is the focal subject of the verse.

The notion of the whole universe as light emanating from the light of God had developed out of this verse of the Qur'an. Although the poetic nature of the linguistic structure of the verse is obvious, the literal understanding prevails. This might be explained by the fact that this kind of highly complicated similitude, which contains so many sub-similitudes in addition to the indirect mode of expression, was not known to the Arabs. The opening statement of the verse, *God is the light of the heavens and the earth* (*Allahu nuru'l-samawati wa'-l-ard*) made it easily possible to interpret most of the essential words of the whole verse as expressions of certain aspects of existence. Words and phrases such as lamp, niche, glittering star, blessed tree, oil, and fire have been taken to demonstrate the different and gradual degrees of the divine manifestation of God's light.

The last part of the statement concludes its description of the nature of God as *light upon light* (*nurun 'ala nur*) and promises the true believer that he will be guided to His light, *yahdi 'llahu li-nuri-hi man yashaa*. It was reasonable, therefore, not only to speak about the whole universe as a reflection of God's light, but to speak also about the believer's knowledge of God as an illumination revealed to his heart by the light of God. It was thus theologically and philosophically explained that God's light had two correlated ontological and epistemological aspects. If existence was defined as God's light, nonexistence should be defined as the absence of light, i.e. darkness. The same categorization was applied to epistemology, knowledge as light and ignorance as darkness.

The well known and celebrated Muslim thinker of the twelfth century AD, Abu Hamid al-Ghazali, devoted a treatise to explain in detail the whole conception of the Divine Light with reference to the abovementioned Qur'anic verse. Entitled *Mishkat al-anwar* (The Niche of Lights), the book explains the different grades of manifestation emanating from the original source of light, God, on both the ontological and the epistemological levels. Starting with some semantic justifications concerning the 'real' and 'true' meaning of the word 'light' al-Ghazali asserts that language expresses 'truthfully'—*haqiqatan*—the metaphysical world, while it expresses 'metaphorically'—*majazan*—our witnessed world. This notion is essential to al-Ghazali's treatise because it enables him to turn the similitude in the Qur'anic verse upside-down. It is not meant to explain what cannot be explained otherwise, but it is rather meant to uncover the hidden reality of things which would not be perceived otherwise. Since God's light is the only one reality which is manifested from the top to the bottom, it was easy for al-Ghazali to conclude his treatise by labelling the whole universe as 'nonexistence' when compared to the unique Real Existence of God (see Ghazali 1924: 45–65).

This conclusion paved the way for the great thirteenth-century Andalusian Muslim mystic Muhyi al-Din Ibn al-'Arabi to develop an Islamic pantheistic system of thought, according to which the existence of the world is an imaginative one. He differentiates three grades of manifestation, namely the state of absolute unity, *al-wujud al-mutlaq al-haqq*; Godhood, *al-uluha*, which contains God's names and attributes; and lastly the universe, or the world of multiplicity (see Yahya 1969: 238). These different grades of manifestation do not reflect any kind of multiplicity within the state of absolute unity, nor do they have any sequential order. They are all connected with each other in an inward-outward relation: the first is the inward Divine Reality, the outward of which is Godhood. As the second manifestation, Godhood is in its turn the inward reality, the outward of which is this world of multiplicity.

This pantheistic system of Ibn al-'Arabi includes an essential idea concerning the Reality of Muhammad as an inward hidden reality which is manifested in all the prophets from Adam, until it reaches its final and complete manifestation in the historical Muhammad of Mecca. This Reality of Muhammad is the epistemological parallel to Godhood, which is the ontological agent between Pure Absoluteness and the world of multiplicity (see Abu Zaid 1996: 57–67). Becoming so entirely equivalent to God, the personality of the historical Muhammad started to be the light from which the whole of creation emanated. In Islamic folk belief, Muhammad, as he is the first created (although he is the last-appointed prophet) is the light of God's throne. This notion finds its expression now in folk songs, proverbs, proper names, and legends.

God's Names

Coming to the second aspect of the linguistic exposition of the Divine Attributes, below is the passage (three verses of the Qur'an) dealing mainly with His Names and Attributes.

> He is God;
> there is no god but He.
> He is the knower of the Unseen and the Visible;
> He is the All-merciful, the All-compassionate.
> He is God;
> there is no god but He.
> He is the King, the All-holy, the All-peaceable,
> the All-faithful, the All-preserver,
> the All-mighty, the All-compeller, the All-sublime.

Glory be to God, above those [partners] they associate [with Him]
He is God, the Creator, the Maker, the Shaper.
To Him belong the Names Most Beautiful.
All that is in the heavens and the earth magnifies Him;
He is the All-mighty, the All-wise. (LIX:22–4)

Here we have one proper name and fifteen attributes, all to be
counted among 'The Most Beautiful Names of God'—*asma' allahi al-
husna*. It was later that other names and attributes, mentioned in other
parts of the Qur'an, were added to this list, until 'The Most Beautiful
Names of God' reached the number of ninety-nine. This was mainly
the achievement of the Sufis. Supposing that there is a secret name,
i.e. the Supreme Name revealed only to the chosen believers, namely
the prophets and the Sufi saints, the count of God's Names reaches
the round number of one hundred. Except for the proper name God,
or Allah, all the other names of God are manifested in the universe.
The universe, according to Ibn al-'Arabi, is nothing but the outward
aspect of God's attributes, which are in themselves nothing but the
outward manifestation of the hidden reality of the Absolute Divinity.

These Most Beautiful Names of God were divided into two categories: the Names of Beauty (*asma' al-jamal*), and of Might (*asma'
al-jalal*), each of which reflects certain ontological and epistemological
aspects of the Divine Reality. As the contemplation of God's Names is
considered a very important major part of the mystical spiritual discipline, which aims at the attainment of direct and true knowledge of
that Divine Reality, the newcomer to the Sufi path should start by
contemplating the Names of Might because they are associated with
the experience of fear (*khawf*) related to the beginning of the Sufi spiritual journey. As spiritual experience develops, contemplation moves
from the Names of Might to the Names of Beauty, where the Sufi
enjoys contentment (*rida*) instead of fear. Moving up from one state to
another, the Sufi attains higher and higher levels of Divine knowledge
until he gradually reaches the ultimate goal of his experience.

Such experience is in fact a journey through the Names of God by
which the Sufi attains the Attribute of God related to each one. When
he finally attains all the Attributes of 'The Most Beautiful Names' he
becomes annihilated in the Divinity, where there is neither duality of
knower and known, nor any multiplicity of names and attributes. The

only reality remaining is the Absolute Divinity, which is referred to in the Qur'an by the proper name 'Allah'. In later Sufi orders the practice of *dhikr*, the collective pronunciation of God's Names in semi-dancing circles, reaches its final stage with the repeated recitation of the name 'Allah'. The end of the whole performance is reached by a fast repetition of only the first and the last letters of the word 'ah' indicating the state of annihilation.

Since the name *Allah* is the focal name which includes all God's other Names and Attributes, it became, and it still is, subject to many theosophical interpretations. A great portion of Sufi literature is dedicated to the explanation of the multiple signification of each letter of the name *Allah*. The great Sufi Ibn al-'Arabi deals repeatedly with this topic in all of his books. In calligraphy, the name *Allah* is presented either individually, or in the centre of the other Names, in a great variety of artistic representations. Some representations are in the form of a circle; others are in the form of a square or triangle. Each representational form is an artistic expression of a specific Sufi explanation of the Divine Reality. The form of the circle, for example, is a visual mode of expressing Ibn al-'Arabi's theory concerning the relationship between God's Names. While 'Allah' occupies the centre of the circle which represents the the universe, the other Names of God, being countless, are represented as lines extending from the centre to every point of the circle (see Abu Zaid 1996: 233–54).

The Most Beautiful Names of God have been recently produced on widely distributed gramophone records. They are not the work of any individual singer, but, like folksongs, are performed by whomsoever has a beautiful and strong singing voice. In this respect, the musical representation of God's Names is very much like their representation in calligraphy: both of them are practised freely and individually. It might also be emphasized that both of them reflect, in different ways, various theological and mystical beliefs as referred to above. In the musical version the singer usually brings together God's Names and Muhammad's Light; he starts with the Names and ends with the Light of Muhammad, reflecting, so to speak, the process of manifestation explained by Ibn al-'Arabi and others.

It is perhaps obvious by now how the Qur'anic language captured the imagination of the Muslims and the Arabs from the very moment of its revelation, and how it affected almost every field of knowledge:

theology, philosophy, mysticism, linguistics, literature, literary criticism, and the visual and other arts. The linguistic structure employed in the exposition of God represents only an example (a very representative one however) that illustrates the very specific nature of the Qur'anic *parole* in its relation to the Arabic *langue*. It seems that *parole* in this specific case dominates *langue* by transforming the original signs of its system to act as semiotic signs within its own system. In other words, the Qur'anic language comes to dominate the Arabic language by transferring its linguistic signs to the sphere of semiotics, where they refer only to one absolute reality which is God.

The function of such a transformation is to evade the seen reality in order to establish the unseen Divine Reality of God; that is why everything in the whole of seen reality, from the top to the bottom, is, according to the Qur'an, nothing but a 'sign' which refers to God. Not only are natural phenomena, both animate and inanimate, semiotic signs, but human history, which is presented in the Qur'an as an expression of the everlasting struggle between truth and non-truth, is also referred to as a series of signs. The Arabic word for 'sign' is *'aya'*. The Qur'an itself is divided into chapters, suras, everyone of which is divided into verses, *ayat*. This comprehensive employment of the word *'aya'* in the Qur'an constitues solid evidence for this explanation.[6]

The fact that Muslims nowadays are so determined not to accept anything which lacks a reference in the Qur'an testifies to the validity of the explanation given here. Even the facts of science reached by biological experiment, or by the deployment of highly advanced apparatus in the natural and physical sciences, are unacceptable unless some Qur'anic verses are presented to justify them. There are now many academic institutions in many Muslim countries which are concerned mainly with so-called 'scientific' interpretation of the Qur'an, *al-tafsir al-'ilmi li-'l Qur'an* or *al-i'jaz al-'ilmi li-'l Qur'an*. Unlike their ancestors centuries ago, contemporary Muslims are unaware that there are at least two books to be thoroughly read in order to comprehend the true message of God presented in the Qur'an: the book of nature and the book of man. In other words, the true message of the Qur'an cannot be reached by ignoring reality or evading human experience attained through history; it is only attainable, and consequently its artistic language is more enjoyable, through a profound knowledge and deep understanding of reality.

Notes

1 Ironically, the field of rhetoric *(bayan)* in Arabic literature is intimately connected to the study of the Qur'an as a text. It is, in fact, one of the Qur'anic sciences *('ulam al-Qur'an)*. Mohammad 'Imara (1996: 6–7) also expresses his surprise at, and, therefore, implies his rejection of, calling the Qur'an a text.

2 See *Lisan al-'arab*, qv, and Hans Wehr's *Dictionary of Modern Written Arabic*, qv.

3 The translation of the Qur'an follows Arberry 1964 throughout.

4 The scribe's name was 'Abdullah b. Sa'd b. Abu Sar; for his biography, see Ibn Sa'd 1991: vol. 7, p. 744.

5 See Jurjani 1989: 8–9.

6 For a comprehensive study of this topic, see Schimmel 1994. An elaborated analysis is presented in Abu Zaid 1995: 213–85.

Bibliography

Abaza, Mona (1995), 'An Arab Origin Mosque in Singapore: functions and networks', Research Working Paper Series no. 3, Centre of Religious Cultures and Social Change, Deakin University, Geelong, Victoria, Australia.

Abd Allah, Umar F. (1983), *The Islamic Struggle in Syria*, Berkeley: Mizan Press.

'Abduh, Muhammad (1977), *Risālat al-tawḥīd*, ed. Mahmud Abu Rayyah, Cairo: Dar al-Ma'arif.

—(1987), *al-Islām wa-'l-muslimūn*, ed.Tahir al-Tanahi, Cairo: Dar al-Hilal.

Abrahamian, Ervand (1989), *Radical Islam: the Iranian Mojahedin*, London: Tauris.

Abrams, M. H. (1980), *Natural Supernaturalism: tradition and revolution in romantic literature*, New York: W. H. Norton.

Abu Musa, Muammad (n.d.), *al-Tawīr al-bayānī: dirāsa taḥlīliyya li-masā'il al-bayān* , Cairo: Wahba Library.

Abu-Zahra, Nadia (1983), 'A Comment on Some Kuwaiti and Egyptian Arabic Anthropological Writings on Kuwait', Review Article, IJMES, 15, 398–410.

—(1988), 'The Rain Rituals as Rites of Spiritual Passage', IJMES, 20, 507–29.

—(1991), 'The Comparative Study of Muslim Societies and Islamic Rituals', *Arab Historical Review for Ottoman Studies*, 3, Zaghouan, Tunisia.

—(1997), *The Pure and Powerful*, Reading: Ithaca Press.

Abu Zaid, Nasr Hamid (1990), *Mafhūm al-naṣṣ: dirāsa fi 'ulūm al-Qur'ān*, Cairo: al-Haya al-Misriyya al-Amma li-'l-Kitab.

—(1995a), *al-Naṣṣ, al-sulṭa, al-ḥaqīqa*, Casablanca.

—(1995b), *Naqd al-khiṭāb al-dīnī*, 3rd ed., Cairo: Madbuli.

— (1996a), *Falsafat al-ta'wīl: dirāsa fi ta'wīl al-Qur'ān 'ind Muḥyi al-Dīn Ibn 'Arabī*, 3rd ed., Beirut: al-Markaz al-Thaqafi al-'Arabi.

—(1996b), *al-Ittijāh al-'aqlī fi'l-tafsīr*, 4th ed., Beirut.

Adorno, Theodor W. and Max Horkheimer (1979), *Dialectic of Enlightenment*, transl. John Cumming, London: Verso.

Ahmad, Aziz (1967), *Islamic Modernism in India and Pakistan 1857–1964*, London: Oxford University Press.

Ahmed, Akbar A. (1992), *Postmodernism and Islam: predicament and promise*, London: Routledge.

Ali, [Syed] Ameer (1922), *The Spirit of Islam: a history of the evolution and ideals of Islam*, London: Christophers.

'Ali, Haidar Ibrahim, ed. (1992), *al-Ustādh Maḥmūd Muḥammad Ṭaha: rā'id al-tajdīd al-dīnī fi'l-Sūdān*, Casablanca: Sudanese Studies Centre.

Ali, Imran (1988), *Punjab under Imperialism 1885–1947*, Princeton: Princeton University Press.

'Ali, Sa'id Isma'il (1986), *Dawr al-Azhar fi'l-siyāsa al-Miṣriyya*, Cairo: Dar al-Hilal.

Amin, Husayn Ahmad (1987), *Dalīl al-muslim al-ḥāzin ilā muqtaḍā al-sulūk fi 'l-qarn al-'ishrīn*, 3rd edition, Cairo: Maktabat Madbuli.

—(1987), *Ḥawla al-da'wa ilā taṭbīq al-sharī'a al-Islāmiyya*, Cairo: Maktabat Madbuli.

—(1988), *al-Islām fi 'ālam mutaghayyir wa-maqalāt Islāmiyya ukhrā*, Cairo: Matba'at Atlas.

Arberry, Arthur J. (1964), *The Koran Interpreted*, Oxford: Oxford University Press.

—(1976), *The Koran Interpreted*, 7th ed., New York: Macmillan.

Arkoun, Mohammed (1982a), *Humanisme arabe au IVe/Xe siècle*, 2nd ed., Paris: J. Vrin.

—(1982b), *L'Islam, religion et société*, Paris: Éditions du Cerf.

—(1991), *Lectures du Coran*, 2nd ed., Tunis.

—(1992a), *Ouvertures sur l'Islam*, Paris: J. Grancher.

—(1992b), 'Le concept de sociétés du Livre-livre', in *Interpréter: hommage à Claude Geffré*, Paris: Éditions de Cerf, pp. 211–26.

—(1993), 'L'Islam actuel devant sa tradition', in idem., *Penser l'Islam aujourd'hui*, Algiers: ENAL.

—(1994), *Islam & de democratie*, Amsterdam: Uitgeverij Contact.

—(1995), 'Transgression, déplacement, dépasser', *Arabica* 42 (1995) pp. 28–70.

Al-Azmeh, Aziz (1993), *Islams and Modernities*, London: Verso.

—(1996), *Islams and Modernities*, 2nd ed., London: Verso.

Baig, Sajjad Mirza (c. 1940), *Tashīl al-balāghat*, Delhi: Baig Sufi.

Baljon, J. M. S. (1949), *The Reform and Religious Ideas of Sir Sayyid Ahmad Khan*, Leiden: E. J. Brill.

Batatu, Hanna (1982), 'Syria's Muslim Brethren', *MERIP Reports*, 12/9: 12–20.

Bayly, Christopher (1994), 'Returning the British to South Asian History: the limits of colonial hegemony', *South Asia*, 2, 1–25.

Binswanger, Karl (1981), 'Politischer ,Islamischer Fundamentalismus': das Beispiel der Syrischen Muslimbrüderschaft', *Orient* 22/4: 644–53.

Boroujerdi, Mehrzad (1994), 'The Encounter of Poet-Revolutionary Thought in Iran with Hegel, Heidegger, and Popper', ch. 4 in Serif Mardin (ed.), *Cultural Traditions in the Middle East*, Leiden: E. J. Brill, pp. 236–59. [See also Boroujerdi (1996).]

—(1996), *Iranian Intellectuals and the West: the tormented triumph of nativism*, Syracuse, New York: Syracuse University Press. [Ch. 7, 'Debates in the Postrevolutionary Era', has appeared in another version: Boroujerdi 1994.]

Brass, Paul (1974), *Language, Religion, and Politics in North India*, Cambridge: Cambridge University Press.

Brown, Judith M. (1994), *Modern India: the origins of an Asian democracy*, Oxford: Oxford University Press.

al-Buti, Muhammad Sa'id Ramadan (1958), *Mamū Zayn: qiṣṣat ḥubb fī 'l-arḍ wa aynha'a fī'l-l samā'*, n. p. repr. Damascus: Dar al-Fikr, 1997.

— (1965), *Ḍawābiṭ al-maslaḥa fī'l-sharī'a al-islāmiyya*, n. p.

— (1968a), *Fiqh as-sīra al-nabawiyya ma' mūjaz li-ta'rīkh al-khulafā' ar-rāshida*, n. p.

— (1968b), *Kubrā al-yaqīniyyāt al-kawniyya: wujūd al-khāliq wa wazīfatal-makhlūq*, n. p.

— (1969), *al-Lā-madhhabiyya, akhṭar bid'a tuhaddid al-sharī'a al-islāmiyya*, n. p.

— (1970), *Muḥāḍarāt fī'l-fiqh al-muqārin*, Beirut: Dar al-Fikr al-Hadith.

—(1971), *Bāṭin al-ithm: al-khaṭar al-akbar fī ḥayāt al-muslimīn*, Damascus: Maktabat al-Farabi.

— (1972a), *Min al-fikr wa-'l-qalb: fuṣūl an-naqd fī 'l-'ulūm wa-'l-ijtimā' wa-'l-adab*, n. p.

— (1972b), *Manhaj tarbawī farīd fī'l-Qur'ān*, Damascus: Maktabat al-Farabi.

— (1973a), *al-Islām wa-mushkilāt al-shabāb*, n. p.

— (1973b), *al-Insān wa 'adālat Allāh fī'l-arḍ*, Damascus: Maktabat al-Farabi.

— (1973c), *Min asrār al-manhaj al-rabbānī*, Damascus: Maktabat al-Farabi.

— (1975a), *Min rawā'i' al-Qur'ān: ta'ammulāt 'ilmiyya wa-adabiyya fī kitāb Allāh 'azza wa jall*, 2nd ed., n. p.

— (1975b), *Ilā kull fatāt tu'min bi-'llāh*, Damascus: Maktabat al-Farabi.

— (1976a), *Man huwa sayyid al-qadr fī ḥayāt al-insān?*, 2nd ed., n. p.

— (1976b), *Mas'ala taḥdīd al-nasl wiqāyatan wa 'ilājan*, n. p.

— (1977), *Man al-mas'ūl 'an takhalluf al-muslimīn*, Damascus: Maktabat al-Farabi.

— (1978), *Naqd awhām al-mādiyya al-jadaliyya al-diyālaktīkiyya*, n. p.

— (1980), *Manhaj al-'awda ila 'l-Islām: rasm li-minhāj wa ḥall li-mushkilāt*, n. p.

— (1988), *as-Salafiyya: marḥala zamaniyya mubāraka lā madhhab islāmī*, Damascus: Dar al-Fikr.
— (1990a), *Tajribat al-tarbiyya al-islāmiyya fī mizān al-baḥth*, n. p.
— (1990b), *Hādhihī mushkilāti-hum*, Beirut: Dar al-Fikr al-Mu'asir.
— (1990c), *Ḥiwār ḥawla mushkilāt ḥadāriyya*, n. p.
— (1992), *Manhaj al-ḥaḍāra al-insāniyya fi'l-Qur'ān*, n. p.
— (1993), *al-Jihād fi 'l-Islām: kayf nafhamu-h wa-kayf numārisu-h?*, Beirut: Dar al-Fikr al-Mu'asir.
— (1994a), *Qaḍāyā fiqhiyya mu'āṣira*, n. p.
— (1994b), *al-Dīn wa-'l-falsafa*, n. p.
— (1994c), *... wa hādhihī mushkilātu-nā*, n. p.
— (1994d), *Zawābi' wa-aṣdā' warā' kitāb al-jihād fi 'l-Islām*, n. p.
— (1995), *Hādhā wālidī: al-qiṣṣa al-kāmila li-ḥayāt al-Shaykh Mullā Ramaḍān al-Būṭī min wilādati-h ilā wafāti-h*, Beirut: Dar al-Fikr al-Mu'asir.
— (n.d.), *Hākadhā fa-'l-nadw ila'l-Islām*, Damascus: Maktabat al-Farabi.
Chehabi, H. E. (1990), *Iranian Politics and Religious Modernism: the Liberation Movement of Iran under the Shah and Khomeini*, London: I. B. Tauris.
Chiriyankandath, James (1996), 'Hindu Nationalism and Regional Political Culture in India', *Nationalism and Ethnic Politics*, 2, 44–66.
Christian, William A., Jr. (1982): 'Provoked Religious Weeping in Early Modern Spain', in J. Davis (ed.), *Religious Organization and Religious Experience*, London: Academic Press.
Commins, David (1990), *Islamic Reform: politics and social change in late Ottoman Syria*, New York: Oxford University Press.
Corbett, Greville (1991), *Gender*, Cambridge: Cambridge University Press.
Crecelius, Daniel (1978) 'Nonideological Responses of the Egyptian 'Ulama to Modernization', in Nikki Keddie (ed.), *Scholars, Saints, and Sufis: Muslim religious institutions since 1500*, Berkeley: Univ. of California Press.
Dabashi, Hamid (1993), *Theology of Discontent: the ideological foundations of the Islamic Revolution in Iran*, New York: New York University Press.
Dennis, Barbara, and David Skilton, eds. (1987), *Reform and Intellectual Debate in Victorian England*, London: Croom Helm.
Dessouki, Ali E. Hillal (1987), art. 'Islamic Modernism', *The Encyclopedia of Religion*, New York: Macmillans, vol. 10, pp. 14–17.
Doi, 'Abdur I. Rahman (1984), *Shari'ah: the Islamic law*, London: Ta Ha Publishers.
Dols, Michael W. (1992), *Majnun: the madman in medieval Islamic society*, ed. Diana E. Immisch, Oxford: Clarendon Press.
Duran, Khalid (1985), 'The Centrifugal Forces of Religion in Sudanese Politics', *Orient*, 26/iv, 572–600.
—(1992), 'An Alternative to Islamism: the evolutionary thought of Mahmud

Taha', *Cross Currents*, 42/iv, 453–67.

van Ess, J. (1996), 'Verbal Inspiration? Language and revelation in classical Islamic theology', in Wild (1996).

Fayyad, Nabil (1995), *Yawm inḥadara al-jamal min as-saqīfa*, 3rd ed., Beirut: Exact.

Foucault, Michel (1989), *Madness and Civilization: a history of insanity in the age of reason*, transl. Richard Howard, London: Routledge.

Freitag, Sandra B. (1989), *Collective Action and Community: public arenas and the emergence of communalism in north India*, Berkeley: University of California Press.

al-Ghazali, Abu Hamid (1924), *The Niche for Lights*, transl. W. H. T. Gairdner, London: Royal Asiatic Society.

Giddens, Anthony (1991), *The Consequences of Modernity*, Cambridge: Polity Press.

Gilsenan, Michael (1982), *Recognizing Islam: religion and society in the modern Middle East*, London: Longman.

Le Goff, J. (1990), *Le moyen âge s'achève en 1800*, Paris.

Graham, William A. (1993), *Beyond the Written Word: oral aspects of scripture in the history of religion*, Cambridge Mass.: Harvard University Press.

von Grunebaum, G. E. (1962), *Modern Islam: the search for cultural identity*, Berkeley: University of California Press.

Gunayna, Ne'mat Allah (1988),*Tanzīm al-jihād: hal huwa al-badīl al-Islāmī fī Miṣr?*, pref. Sa'd al-Din Ibrahim, Cairo: Dar al-Huriyya.

Habermas, Jürgen (1986), *Knowledge and Human Interests*, Cambridge: Polity Press.

Haddad, Yvonne Yazbéck (1982), *Contemporary Islam and the Challenge of History*, Albany: State University of New York Press.

Hale, Sondra (1996), *Gender Politics in Sudan: Islamism, socialism, and the state*, Boulder, Col.: Westview Press.

Hali, Altaf Husain (1879), *Musaddas-e madd o jazr-e islām*, Lahore: Ferozsons.

—(1890), *Majmū'a-e naẓm-e Ḥālī*, Delhi: Matba'-e Murtazavi.

—(1893; 1953), *Muqaddama shi'r o shā'irī*, ed. Vahid Quraishi, Lahore: Maktaba-e Jadid.

—(1964), *Nuqūsh: āp bītī nambar*, ed. Muhammad Tufail, Lahore: Idara-e Furogh-e Urdu.

Hassan, Ibrahim (1980), 'La Syrie de la guerre civile', *Peuples Méditerranéens*, 12: 91–108.

Haq, Abdul (1950), *Chand ham-'aṣr*, Karachi: Anjuman-e Taraqqi-e Urdu.

ter Haar, J. G. J. (1990), 'Murtaḍā Muṭahharī (1919–1979): an introduction to his life and thought', *Persica*, 14, 1–20.

Hardy, Peter (1972), *The Muslims of British India*, Cambridge: Cambridge

University Press.

Hasan, Mushirul (1997), *Legacy of a Divided Nation: India's Muslims since Independence*, London: C. Hurst & Co.

Hijazi, Maskin Ali (1988), *Pākistān o Hindūstān men Muslim ṣaḥāfat kī mukhtaṣar-tarīn tārīkh*, Lahore: Sang-e Meel.

Hinnebusch, Ramond A. (1982), 'The Islamic Movement in Syria', in Ali E. Dessouki ed., *Islamic Resurgence in the Arab World*, New York: Praeger.

Hoodhboy, Pervez (1991), *Islam and Science: religious orthodoxy and the battle for rationality*, London: Zed Books.

Houot, Sandra (1996), 'Le rôle de la fatwa chez le Sayh syrien Sa'id Ramadan al-Buti, ou le glissement de la dimension légale à la dimension éthique, au détour du corps', unpubl. paper at the EURAMES conference.

Hourani, Albert (1983), *Arabic Thought in the Liberal Age 1798–1939*, Cambridge: Cambridge University Press.

Hourani, George (1971), *Islamic Rationalism: the ethics of 'Abd al-Jabbar*, Oxford: Oxford University Press.

—(1985), *Reason and Tradition in Islamic Ethics*, Cambridge: Cambridge University Press.

Hudson, Michael C. (1983), 'The Islamic Factor in Syrian and Iraqi Politics' in James Piscatori (ed.), *Islam in the Political Process*, Cambridge: Cambridge University Press.

Ibn Sa'd (1991), *al-Ṭabaqāt al-kubrā*, eds Ahmad Shams al-Din et al., Beirut: Dar al-Kutub al-'Ilmiyya.

'Imara, Muhammad (1996), *al-Tafsīr al-markistī li-'l-Islām (The Marxist explanation of Islam)*, Cairo: Dar al Shuruq.

Iqbal, Mohammad (1982), *The Reconstruction of Religious Thought in Islam*, Lahore: Sh. Muhammad Ashraf.

Izutsu, Toshihiko (1964), *God and Man in the Koran: semantics of the Koranic Weltanschaung*, Minatoku, Tokyo: Keio Institute of Cultural and Linguistic Studies.

Jabri, Muhamed Abed (1984–90), *Naqd al-'aql al-'arabī* (A critique of Arab reason), vol. 1: *'Takwīn al-'aql al-'arabī'* (1984); vol 2: *'Binyat al-'aql al-'arabī'* (1986); vol 3: *'al-'Aql al-siyāsī al-'arabī: muḥaddidātu-h wa-tajaliyyātu-h'* (1990), Casablanca & Beyrouth.

—(1994), *al-Dimuqratiyya wa-ḥuqūq al-insān*, Beyrouth.

—(1996), *al-Dīn wa-l-dawla wa-taṭbīq al-sharī'a*, Beyrouth.

al-Jurjani (1989), *Dalā'il al-i'jāz*, ed. Mahmud Muhammad Shakir, 2nd ed., Cairo.

Kamali, M. Hashem (1991), *Principles of Islamic Jurisprudence*, Cambridge: Islamic Texts Society.

Keddie, Nikki (1968), *An Islamic Response to Imperialism: political and religious writings of Sayyid Jamal al-Din 'al-Afghani'*, Berkeley: University of California Press.

Kelidar, A. R. (1974), 'Religion and State in Syria', *Asian Affairs*, 61/1: 16–22.

Khan, Sayyid Ahmad (1913), *Taḥrīr fī uṣūl al-tafsīr*, Lahore: Naval Kishore Press.

—(1984), *Maqālāt-e Sir Sayyid*, 16 vols, Lahore: Majlis-e Taraqqi-e Adab.

Khatemi, Mohamed (1997), 'Our Culture Belongs to a Bygone Era', *Islam* 21, 3 (July 1997).

Khayati, Mustapha (1991) 'Introduction à la pensée de Mahmud Muhammad Taha, réformiste et martyr', in Hervé Bleuchot, Christian Delmet, and Derek Hopwood (eds), *Sudan: history, identity, ideology*, Reading: Ithaca, pp. 287–98.

Khory, Kavita R. (1995) 'National Integration and the Politics of Identity in Pakistan', *Nationalism and Ethnic Politics*, 1, 23–43.

Laroui, Abdullah (1967), *L'idéologie arabe contemporaine*, Paris: Maspero.

—(1974), *La crise des intellectuels arabes: traditionalisme ou historicisme?*, Paris: Maspero.

Lelyveld, David (1978), *Aligah's First Generation: Muslim solidarity in British India*, Princeton: Princeton University Press.

Lyotard, Jean-Francois (1986), *The Postmodern Condition: a report on knowledge*, transl. Geoff Bennington and Brian Massumi, Manchester: Manchester University Press.

Majeed, Javed (1993), 'Putting God in His Place: Bradley, McTaggart, and Muhammad Iqbal', *Journal of Islamic Studies*, 4/ii, 208–36.

Mardin, Şerif (1982), 'Bediüzzaman Said Nursi (1873–1960): the shaping of a vocation', in John Davis (ed.), *Religious Organization and Religious Experience*, London: Academic Press.

Markaz al-Dirasat al-Siyasiyya wa-'l-Istratijiyya bi-'l-Ahram (1995), *Taqrīr al-ḥāla al-dīniyya fī Miṣr*, 3rd edition, Qalyub, Egypt: al-Ahram.

Mayer, Thomas (1983), 'The Islamic Opposition in Syria, 1961–1982', *Orient*, 24/4: 589–609.

McGann, Jerome (1983), *The Romantic Ideology: a critical investigation*, Chicago: The University of Chicago Press.

Miller, Judith (1997), *God has Ninety Nine Names: reporting from a militant Middle East*, New York: Simon and Schuster.

Minault, Gail (1986), *Voices of Silence: English translations of Khwaja Altaf Husain Hali's Majalis un-Nissa and Chup ki Dad*, Delhi: Chanakya Publications.

Moaddel, Mansur (1993), *Class, Politics, and Ideology in the Iranian Revolution*, New York: Columbia University Press.

Munson, Henry, Jr. (1988), *Islam and Revolution in the Middle East*, New Haven:

Yale University Press.

an-Na'im, Abdullahi A. (1986), 'The Islamic Law of Apostasy and its Modern Applicability: a case from the Sudan', *Religion*, 16, 197–224.

Naim, C. M. (1975) 'The Theme of Homosexual (Pederastic) Love in Premodern Urdu Poetry', in ed. M. U. Memon (ed.) *Studies in the Urdu Ghazal and Prose Fiction*, Madison: University of Wisconsin.

Nawfal, 'Abd al-Razzaq (1966), *Allāh wa-'l-'ilm'l-ḥādith*, Cairo: Maktabat Sayigh.

Nettler, Ronald L. (1998), 'Mohamed Talbi: "For a dialogue between all religions"', in Ronald L. Nettler and Suha Taji-Farouki (eds), *Studies in Muslim–Jewish Relations, 4: Muslim-Jewish Encounters: intellectual traditions and modern politics*, Reading: Harwood Academic Publishers, pp. 171–99.

Nisbet, Robert (1980), *History of the Idea of Progress*, New York: Basic Books.

Oevermann, Annette (1993), *Die 'Republikanischen Brüder' im Sudan. Eine islamishe Reformbewegung im zwanzigsten Jahrhundert*, Frankfurt am Main: Peter Lang.

Page, David (1981), *Prelude to Partition: All-Indian Muslim politics, 1921–1932*, Delhi: Oxford University Press.

Pandey, Gyan (1990), *The Construction of Communalism in Colonial North India*, Delhi: Oxford University Press.

Peters, J. R. T. M. (1976), *God's Created Speech: a study in the speculative theology of ...'Abd al-Jabbār*, Leiden: E. J. Brill.

Pirenne, H. (1937), *Mahomet et Charlemagne*, 3rd ed., Paris.

Platts, John T. (1983), *A Dictionary of Urdu, Classical Hindi, and English*, Lahore: Sang-e Meel.

Pritchett, Francis (1994), *Nets of Awareness: Urdu poetry and its critics*, Berkeley: University of California Press.

Rahman, Fazlur (1982), *Islam and Modernity*, Chicago: The University of Chicago Press.

Rahnema, Ali (1994), 'Ali Shariati: teacher, preacher, rebel', ch. 9 in Ali Rahnema (ed.) *Pioneers of Islamic Revival*, London: Zed Books.

Rajaee, Farhang (1993), 'Islam and Modernity: the reconstruction of an alternative Shi'ite Islamic worldview in Iran', in Martin E. Marty and R Scott Appleby (eds), *Fundamentalism and Society: reclaiming the sciences, the family, and education*, Chicago: The University of Chicago Press.

Reissner, Johannes (1980), *Ideologie und Politik der Muslimbrüder Syriens*, Freiburg: Klaus Schwarz Verlag.

Robinson, Francis (1974), *Separatism among Indian Muslims: the politics of the United Provinces' Muslims, 1860–1923*, Cambridge: Cambridge University Press.

—(1993), 'Technology and Religious Change: Islam and the impact of printing', *Modern Asian Studies*, 27/i, 229–51.

Rogalski, Jürgen (1996), 'Mahmud Muhammad Taha—zur Erinnerung an das Schiksal eines Mystikers und Intellektuellen im Sudan', *Asien Afrika Lateinamerika*, 24, 47–61.

Sadig, Haydar Badawi (1988), 'The Republican Brothers: a religio-political movement in the Sudan', unpubl. MSc diss., University of Khartoum.

Safi, Louay M. (1994), *The Challenge of Modernity: the quest for authenticity in the Arab world*, Lanham, New York: University Press of America.

Schaikh, Farzana (ed.) (1992), *Islam and Islamic Groups*, London: Longman.

Schimmel, Annemarie (1975), *Classical Urdu Literature from the Beginning to Iqbal*, Wiesbaden: Otto Harrassowitz.

—(1994), *Deciphering the Signs of God: a phenomenological approach to Islam*, Edinburgh: Edinburgh University Press.

Schirazi, Asghar (1997), *The Constitution of Iran: politics and state in the Islamic Republic*, transl. John O'Kane, London: I. B. Tauris.

Shackle, C, and J. Majeed (1997), *Hali's Musaddas: the Flow and Ebb of Islam*, Delhi: Oxford University Press.

Shahin, Emad Eldin (1995), 'Rashid Rida, Muhammad', *The Oxford Encyclopedia of the Modern Islamic World*, vol. III, New York: Oxford University Press.

Shepard, William. E. (1996), 'Muhammad Sa'id al-'Ashmawi and the application of the *shari'a* in Egypt', *IJMES*, 28/i, 39–58.

Smith, William Cantwell (1957), *Islam in Modern History*, Princeton N.J: Princeton University Press.

—(1985), *Modern Islam in India: a social analysis*, New Delhi: Usha Publications.

—(1993), *What is Scripture? A comparative approach*, London: SCM Press.

Suroush, 'Abd al-Karim (1977a), *Naqdī va dar-āmadī bar taḍādd-i diyāliktikī*, Tehran.

—(1977b), *Nihād-i nā-ārām-i jahān*, Solon, Ohio.

—(1979), *Dānish va arzish: pizhuhishī dar irtibāṭ-i 'ilm va akhlāq*, Tehran: Intisharat-i Yaran.

—(1987), *'Ilm chī-st, falsafe chī-st*, 10th ed., Tehran: Mu'assasa-yi Farhangi-yi Sirat.

—(1990), *Qabḍ-u-basṭ-e ti'ūrīk-e sharī'at*, 1st ed., Tehran: Mu'assasa-yi Farhangi-ye Sirat.

—(1992), *Awṣāf-e pārsāyān; sharḥ-e khuṭbe-ye Imām 'Alī 'alay-hi 'l-salām dar bārih-yi muttaqīn*, Tehran: Mu'assasih-yi Farhangi-yi Sirat.

—(1994a), *Qiṣṣe-yi arbāb-e ma'rifat*, Tehran: Mu'assasih-yi Farhangi-yi Sirat.

—(1994b), *Ḥikmat va ma'ishat: sharḥ-e nāme-ye Imām 'Alī be Imām Ḥasan 'alay-huma 'l-salām*, vol. 1, Tehran: Mu'assase-ye Farhangi-yi Sirat.

—(1996), *Mathnavī-ye maʿnawī, bar asās-e nuskhe-ye Qūnawī*, ed. with intro. by ʿAbd al-Karim Surush, Tehran: Shirkat-e Intisharat-e ʿIlmi va Farhangi.

Sperl, Stefan, and Christopher Shackle (1996), *Qasida Poetry in Islamic Asia and Africa*, 2 vols, Leiden: E. J. Brill.

Steele, Laurel (1981), 'Hali and His Muqaddamah: the creation of a literary attitude in nineteenth-century India', *Annual of Urdu Studies*, 1, 1–45.

Stowasser, Barbara Freyer (1994), *Women in the Qurʾan, Traditions and Intepretation*, New York, Oxford University Press.

al-Suyuti, ʿAbd al-Rahman Jalal al-Din (1952), *al-Itqān fī ʿulūm al-Qurʾān*, Cairo: al-Bab al-Halabi.

Tabari, Abu Jaʿfar Muhammad ibn Jarir (1961),*Taʾrīkh al-rusul wa-ʾl-muluk* , ed. Muhammad Abu ʾl-Fadl Ibrahim, 4th ed., Cairo: Dar al-Maʿarif.

—(1958–),*Jāmiʿ al-bayān ʿan taʾwīl āy al-Qurʾān*, ed. Mamud Muammad Shakir, Cairo: Dar al-Maʿarif.

Taha, Mahmud Muhammad (1966), *Risālat al-ṣalāt*, Omdurman.

—(1971), *al-Qurʾān wa-Muṣṭafā Maḥmūd wa-ʾl-fahm ʾl-ʿaṣrī*, Omdurman.

—(1986/1407), *al-Risāla al-thāniyya min al-Islām*, 6th ed., Omdurman. [For Engl. transl. see Taha (1987).]

—(1987), *The Second Message of Islam*, transl. Abdullahi A. an-Naʾim, New York: Syracuse University Press. [Engl. transl. of Taha (1986).]

Talbi, Mohamed (1992), *ʿIyāl Allāh: afkār jadīda fī ʿalaqa al-muslim bi-nafsihi wa-bi-ʾl-ākharīn*, Tunis: Ceres Editions.

—(1996), *Ummat al-wasaṭ*, Tunis: Ceres Editions.

El-Tayeb, El-Tayeb H. M. (1995), 'The Second Message of Islam: a critical study of the Islamic reformist thinking of Mahmud Muhammad Taha (1909–85)', unpubl. PhD diss., University of Manchester.

Tibi, Bassam (1981), *Die Krise des modernen Islams: Eine vorindustrielle Kultur im wissenschaftlich-technischen Zeitalter*, Munich: C. H. Beck'sche Verlagsbuchhandlung. [For Engl. transl. see Tibi (1988).]

—(1988), *The Crisis of Modern Islam: a preindustrial culture in the scientific-technological age*, transl. Judith von Sivers, Salt Lake City: University of Utah Press. [Engl. transl. of Tibi (1981).]

Troll, C. W. (1978/9), *Sayyid Ahmad Khan: a reinterpretation of Muslim theology*, Karachi: Oxford University Press.

Turner, B. S. (1994), *Orientalism, Postmodernism and Globalism*, London: Routledge.

Vatikiotis, P. J. (1991), *The History of Modern Egypt from Muhammad Ali to Mubarak*, 4th edition, Baltimore: The John Hopkins Unversity Press.

Warburg, Gabriel (1978), *Islam, Nationalism, and Communism in a Traditional Society: the case of Sudan*, London: Frank Cass.

Washbrook, David (1981), 'Law, State and Agrarian Society in Colonial

India', *Modern Asian Studies*, 15/iii, 649–721.

—(1982), 'Ethnicity and Racialism in Colonial Indian Society', in Robert Ross (ed.), *Racism and Colonialism*, The Hague: Leiden University Press.

Watt, W. Montgomery (1988), *Islamic Fundamentalism and Modernity*, London: Routledge.

Whitcombe, Elizabeth (1972), *Agrarian Conditions in Northern India: the United Provinces under British Rule 1860–1900*, Berkeley: University of California Press.

Wild, Stefan (1996), *The Qur'an as Text*, Leiden: E. J. Brill.

Woodsworth, Nicholas (1995) 'A Fundamental Battle for Hearts and Minds', *The Financial Times*, 27 May 1995.

Wörtz, Eckart (n. d.), 'Traditionelles islamisches Selbstbild und Moderne. Grundzüge einer aktuellen Diskussion in Syrien', unpubl. MA diss., Friedrich Alexander Universität, Erlangen.

Yahya, 'Uthman (1969), 'Nuṣūṣ ta'rīkhiyya khāṣṣa bi-naōariyyāt al-tawḥīd fi'l-fikr al-Islāmī', in Ibrahim Madkur (ed.), *al-Kitāb al-tidhkarī li-Muḥyi al-Dīn Ibn 'Arabī*, Cairo: al-Haya al-Misriyya al-'Amma li-'l-Kitab.

al-Zarkashi, Badr al-Din Muhammad b. 'Abd Allah (1972), *al-Burhān fī 'ulūm al-Qur'ān*, 3rd ed., Beirut: Dar al-Ma'rifa li-'l-Taba'a wa-'l-Nashr.

Index

223